My Li...

IRA

The Border Campaign

MICHAEL RYAN

Edited by Pádraig Yeates

MERCIER PRESS

MERCIER PRESS

Cork

www.mercierpress.ie

© Text: Michael Ryan, 2018

© Introduction and Epilogue: Pádraig Yeates, 2018

ISBN: 978 1 78117 518 7

A CIP record for this title is available from the British Library

Printed and bound in the EU.

DEDICATION

To my mother, who was always involved in fighting for the rights of her community and neighbours, and quietly supported me through all the tough times; to my father, who always felt passionately about social issues and suffered greatly; to Anjo, my wife of thirty-eight years, who supported me through good times and bad, and continues to care for me; and to all the brave men and women who took great risks and made great sacrifices in the cause of freedom.

CONTENTS

ACKNOWLEDGEMENTS

This book is based on my own recollections of a period now long past and of experiences I shared with many people, some of whom are no longer with us. They include friends and comrades such as Nicky Boggan, the Collins family in Navan, Cathal Goulding, John Hobden, Tomás Mac Giolla, Proinsias McAirt, Jack McCabe, Dan Moore, Charlie Murphy, Tommy Nixon, Ruairí Ó Brádaigh, Eamonn Ó Murchú, Redmond O'Sullivan, Seamus Ó Tuathail, Tommy Smith, Leo Steenson, Pádraig Ó Snodaigh, the lads in Knockatallon, north Monaghan, Sean Keane of Milwaukee, the Prendiville family in San Francisco, Seamus Collins and the late, great Dick Walsh of *The Irish Times*. I also wish to express my gratitude to my other friends around the country whose names are too numerous to mention and still support our struggle for a better Ireland. I would like to thank Brian Hanley and Scott Millar for their research and work on *The Lost Revolution*, which helped revive my own memories; Pádraig Yeates, long-time friend and comrade, without whom this book would not have been 'sorted'; and the Mercier team for advice and help in preparing it for publication.

INTRODUCTION

Pádraig Yeates

This is a memoir of growing up in Dublin in the 1940s and 1950s, and of the author's subsequent involvement in the IRA border campaign of 1956 to 1962. It is a tale of times past and things that happened rather than an explanation of why they happened. It is a testament, not an apologia. The author has recalled people and events as honestly as recollection allows because they are important to him and to a dwindling band of comrades who participated in that campaign. They also had a bearing on subsequent events, especially in the North of Ireland, a few years later.

Mick Ryan grew up in East Wall, Dublin, a working-class community permeated by the history of Ireland's struggle for independence. As a boy his father had been one of the many civilians injured in the Easter Rising and his first teacher at St Laurence O'Toole's National School, otherwise known as 'Larrier's', was Frank Cahill, a member of the Irish Citizen Army and 1916 veteran. According to the author, Cahill was one of only two teachers he encountered there 'who had a natural sense of culture, or the gentleness that comes from a strong and generous spirit'. This is one of many pen portraits of contemporaries provided by the author that are, largely, sympathetic and judicious.

What makes this book of particular interest to students of modern Ireland, the Republican movement and the still largely neglected history of the 1950s and early 1960s, is that the author was one of a handful of IRA volunteers to serve in the border campaign from beginning to end, his service only broken by two relatively brief periods of imprisonment. It is a story of suffering, hardship, frustration and constant disappointment that will leave some readers wondering why anyone would become involved in such a patently hopeless cause and, even more so, why these volunteers persisted when defeat loomed from an early stage.

But the author and his comrades were different from the vast majority of their contemporaries. They regarded the objectives of 1916 not as pious aspirations but as a bequest from previous generations of revolutionaries that provided them with the opportunity to give meaning to their own lives. Mick Ryan had 'a deep sense of regret' that he had not been born early enough to participate in the Easter Rising and the subsequent struggle for independence. For him and his comrades to give up would have been a form of self-betrayal akin to the loss of a vocation among his more religiously inclined contemporaries. Even many who lost faith in the successful outcome of the border campaign still believed in what, to them, was the self-evident justice of their cause.

His story also provides glimpses of a society on the brink of change, albeit one that was still weighed down by poverty, superstition and social deference. Life in East Wall was hard, yet it was harder on the border, where the homes of many of the movement's supporters were still lit by oil lamps, water was drawn from a well, and the farmer's dole, poitín making and smuggling bridged the gap between living in poverty and not living at all. They felt no affinity to the 'Free State' and their hopes of a better life rested with the yet-to-be-realised Irish Republic. As Mick Ryan remarks, the nature of that republic was rarely discussed. That they believed it would be better than what they had was essentially an act of faith.

Note on IRA structures: An army convention was a meeting of the supreme governing body of the IRA, composed of delegates representing its constituent units, where policy was determined and an Army Executive of twelve members was elected. The Executive appointed an Army Council of seven, usually, but not exclusively, drawn from within its own ranks. The Army Council was charged with implementing the policy of the organisation between conventions. It was appointed in this way to protect the identities and positions held by members of the Army Council. The Army Executive retained a power of oversight. It could convene another army convention when it deemed it necessary.

Catholics and Protestants: In this book Catholics and Protestants are regarded as largely synonymous with nationalists and unionists respectively in the 1950s and 1960s. While there were many exceptions to this general rule, most Catholics living in the areas where Mick Ryan operated were deeply alienated from the unionist-controlled government in Stormont. Whether or not they shared the author's republican outlook, they were sympathetic to his cause, as this narrative clearly shows.

1

A DUBLIN CHILDHOOD, 1936–50

My mother was a native of Oldcastle, Co. Meath, but it was a place I seldom visited in my youth. It was Killary in Co. Meath, the birthplace of my maternal great-grandmother, and Collon in Co. Louth, the home of my maternal grandfather, where my siblings and I spent almost every summer holiday.

My father was Dublin-born and proud of it. His father and mother came from Golden, near Cashel, Co. Tipperary. They eloped in 1898 and settled in Dublin. My grandfather joined the tram company of William Martin Murphy, the notorious Dublin employer who locked out the workers in the infamous 1913 Dublin Lockout. My grandfather was one of the few inspectors who joined the subsequent strike. As a result, he lost his job and was thrown out of the company house in Dock Street, where he had lived from the time he became an inspector. The hardship endured by my father's family because of the strike left its mark and he was never to forget it. My father had an abiding hatred for Murphy, as did thousands of Dubliners who had suffered terrible deprivation in the Lockout. He was only twelve when the Irish Volunteers and the Citizen Army made their brave revolt against British rule in 1916, but he became one of the casualties nevertheless when he was wounded in the lower left leg by a bullet or piece of shrapnel. The wound never healed properly. It caused him pain and gave him a limp for the rest of his life.

At sixteen he began work, selling coal door-to-door from a handcart. He later bought his own horse and cart and expanded his round, so that by 1932, at the age of twenty-eight, he was making a good weekly income and was able to marry my mother, who was eighteen at the time. He bought his house outright for £300. However, he was something of an enigma, on the one hand capable of deep sensitivity and sympathy, while on the other sometimes very cruel in his treatment of my mother. He became addicted to drink and would get fiercely angry when drunk, invariably taking it out on her. He would also have bouts of insane jealousy and accuse her of all kinds of infidelity.

I was born in 1936 and my memory of childhood was one of constant fear as well as deprivation. There was a permanent shortage of money to buy food, clothes and other essentials. Things were in short supply generally in the war years because of rationing. Together with my father's abuse of drink, it made life seem almost intolerably sad for me, my five sisters – Eithne, Monica, Gertie, Gretta and Minnie – and my younger brother, Nicholas.

Coal shortages after the outbreak of war saw my father emigrate to England to find work. He earned good money, sending back enough for my mother to make ends meet. My memory of these years is vague, but I was certainly conscious of the war because of the blackouts, the shortage of food, clothes and money. There was the anxious wait for letters from my father and relatives in England, so we would know they were all right. More immediate news was hard to come by because very few people on our road had a radio. On the day of a big match in Croke Park, if the weather was fine, people with radios would put them in their front parlour and open the window so that neighbours could gather round to hear the commentary. We would generally go to our Aunt Molly McLean's to hear the match or a play, and my uncle, John Geraghty, used to call regularly and tell us of the latest broadcast from Berlin by 'Lord Haw-Haw' (the nickname for pro-German broadcaster William Joyce, who was hanged by the British after the war). There was always an air of seriousness when there was talk of the latest developments because so many families had relatives in England or in the British forces.

There always seemed to be a wan twilight in the houses at the time, probably because of the blackouts and fuel shortages. Our cooking was done on a Stanley range in the kitchen, and Mother did wonders with our rations. Our diet was supplemented by the odd sack of spuds, a chicken or a few eggs that came from our grandfather in Collon. And every summer from when I was seven until I was fourteen I went to his house for a few weeks. The food, the freedom and security, along with the happy family atmosphere, made it seem like a paradise compared with home.

After my father's return from England once the war finished, he began selling turf. It was mainly winter work, as most people who bought from the 'bellman' (so called from the bell that hung from his horse's collar to announce his arrival) couldn't afford a fire from May to October, and carried out in appalling conditions of snow, rain and sleet. From 1947 his limp began to give him trouble and he decided to invest in a motor truck that a 'friend' said he could buy for £100. The idea was that the truck could be used for other business when the winter fuel season ended. He had to borrow the £100 from a loan company in Castle Street at exorbitant interest, mortgaging our house as collateral. The truck never went right; it was old and in bad repair. He did get a few weeks' work hauling oranges from the docks when the first big shipment arrived after the war. Then the truck just stopped. It took years to pay off the debt. I cried a lot in those days and was increasingly angry at my father's behaviour and the wrong he had done to our family.

The worst aspect of his drunkenness and his treatment of us over the years was the fact that all the neighbours knew what was going on. For me this was a terrible source of shame and embarrassment, affecting almost everything I did or thought. Our poverty also meant that neither my sisters nor I could consider staying on in school. Even before we left, we supplemented his meagre social welfare payments (he had never paid social insurance contributions) by making a small handcart and buying loads of short pieces of wood from a local timber merchant. We chopped them into thin sticks at home and tied them into bundles for kindling. The load would cost about a shilling and we would get perhaps 120 to 140 bundles out of the load, which we would then load into our boxcar and sell door-to-door. We would all take a hand in the chopping and tying, but my sister Gretta and I usually did the selling. We sold some to local people, but our main sales were on the Howth Road and in Marino, which were well-to-do areas by our standards and where, I suspect, people bought from us as much out of sympathy as for the firewood.

It was hard work, but we had no other way of making money until we left school. It was always a thrill when the last bundle was sold and we could head home on a Friday or Saturday night, cold but with twelve or fifteen shillings to give to Father, who handled the money; he would then hand some part of it over to Mother. So, indirectly, he felt he contributed.

I don't wish to give the impression that my father was intrinsically cruel. He had a hard life, the final blow of which came in 1948 when he developed gangrene and had to have his leg amputated. He spent almost a year in hospital and in a convalescent home. After that, his reduced mobility meant that he was no longer able to instil the same fear into us and I think he suffered remorse. Although he never referred to it, it came through in other ways. From the time of his operation until he died he was more like his real self – a man who was sensitive, loved music and literature, and was extraordinarily well read and informed on Irish history and international events. Needless to say, the experience of the truck, the way he was pursued by the loan company for repayments and the amputation of his leg left him bitter about life and society. It was certainly a factor in his hatred of capitalism, landlords and loan sharks, as well as his gradual conversion to socialism. He was also a romantic, and some of that he no doubt passed on to me.

**

As a child, I had a very tender conscience, the kind that leaves one in a constant state of anxiety. It made even the prospect of confession – never mind the event itself – a worrying experience. I was particularly apprehensive about my confession before being confirmed because it was a thorough investigation of one's qualifications for membership of the 'league of strong and perfect Christians'. I had had mental reservations when I took confession for my First Communion, but Confirmation was an altogether more serious matter and I was more aware of what a serious step it represented. That summer of 1947, I had helped unload thousands of oranges at Dublin port onto my father's truck to be carted to the fruit importers. The sight and smell of so many oranges was delicious and a source of wonder to me and to the rest of the children of Dublin, who had never seen an orange in the flesh. In the process, I must have eaten dozens of them and given dozens more to my pals. But they were never noticed out of all those millions. I had been to confession every month for six months previously and had managed to avoid mentioning the business of the oranges; but conscience and fear got the better of me ahead of my confession for Confirmation. I went into the confessional expecting that my regular confessor, a quiet, friendly priest, would be there, but it was the parish priest, Father Browne, a gruff, loud-voiced, thick man inclined to deafness. I was nearly last in the queue and was petrified when I discovered he was in the box. I couldn't move elsewhere, as the curtains were only partly pulled over and he could see me waiting. Showing a preference for one priest over another by leaving a queue was regarded as extremely unseemly.

So I started with a more than usually pious recitation of my sins, starting of course with the most innocuous. 'I didn't do the First Friday this month, Father.'[1] This of course wasn't

---

1   'First Friday' refers to a Catholic practice of attending mass and receiving Holy Communion on the first Friday of each month for nine months. Those who did this believed they would die in a state of grace.

a sin, but I felt it would impress him: 'I took the Lord's name in vain a few times ... I cursed a few times, Father' (you always repeated the 'Father' bit, as it helped to cement your acknowledgement of his superiority and underlined your tone of sorrow and obedience). 'How many times, my son?' he'd say, and invariably the reply would be 'Four or five times, Father', usually an uneven number, as that would look like you actually kept a count.

Then came the hard ones. 'Father, I had bad thoughts, seven times since my last confession.' This always brought the question: 'And did you encourage these thoughts, or take pleasure from them, my son?' in a tolerant manner to get you to tell the real truth. Usually I'd reply, 'I tried not to bring them on but they came into my head, Father, without me thinking of them, and I tried not to take pleasure in them.' Then, hoping I'd struck the right mood, I burst out with the big ones. 'Father, I committed a bad action on my own, and I'm heartily sorry; and, Father, I also stole some oranges,' followed in a most heartfelt whisper by, 'I'm sorry for all my sins and promise not to do them again, Father.'

I was hoping he'd deal with the impure one and let the oranges go, it being the lesser of the two, or so I thought. But no. In a voice loud enough for anyone within ten feet of the box to hear, he said, 'You stole oranges? This is terrible!' He was really angry. 'How many did you steal, boy?' At this point I was afraid that he'd ask *when* I stole them, and then

I'd really have been in the soup, because I'd stolen them six months before and had never confessed to what was clearly a really serious sin before now. 'I stole thirteen, Father,' I said in a whisper, really frightened now, especially as the real figure would have been nearer 113. Coldly and quite mercilessly he asked, 'And are you going to pay back to the merchant what you stole before you make your Confirmation?'

And all I could say was that I wouldn't be able to, that I had no money, and we'd no money at home to pay it back that soon. 'No good, no good at all,' he said with the finality of a hanging judge. 'Leave the box, young man; I cannot forgive you your sins until you pay back what you stole.' And he closed the little shutter on me, and immediately I heard the shutter on the other side being pulled back and the murmuring of the boy on the other side intoning the Confiteor.[2]

It was several seconds before I could compose myself sufficiently to leave the box. I kept thinking about how, without confession, I wouldn't be allowed to be confirmed. I walked past the others waiting outside without showing that I was nearly in tears. Those nearest heard it all and looked up in silent shock and admiration. I waited outside for my best friends to emerge and hear their advice on what I should do. Out they came, speedier than usual because of what had happened.

---

2   The Confiteor is the 'I confess' prayer with which Catholics normally begin their confession.

By this time the word had gone around the church in dramatic whispers that 'Mick was put out o' the confession box by Father Browne', and speculation was rife. I told them about the oranges and they were thrilled at this happening to one of their pals. It was a kind of notoriety. So there was much swapping of stories, none of them relevant or coming near to solving my problem, except for one lad, Christy, who said, 'Hey, Mick, why don't you go to another priest and don't tell him about the oranges. You'll get confession and then later some time you'll be able to pay yer man back for the oranges you robbed? Anyway,' said Christy, 'Browne leaves the box earlier than the rest. We'll wait until he goes and tell yeh. Then yeh can go to yer usual man.'

This was the plan agreed to. When Browne duly crossed the street to the parochial house with his slow, sanctimonious tread, I headed back into the church. But I wasn't taking any chances this time, so the tale of the oranges was not related, and out I came, relieved beyond belief, ready to become a strong and perfect Christian.

The real fear of the stigma that would have attached to my family and me if I had been refused Confirmation is hard to relay nowadays.

***

My school days were not the happiest of my life. After East

Wall Infants' National School I had graduated to St Laurence O'Toole's National School, 'Larrier's', at the tender age of eight, where the harsh and sometimes cruel actions of some teachers probably affected me even more because of the problems at home. But there were two great exceptions. One was Frank Cahill, my first teacher, who had been a member of the Irish Citizen Army, had fought in 1916 with James Connolly and had a grand attitude to children and to people generally. The other was the teacher in charge of the choir, Brother Cordiale, who was perhaps the only teacher apart from Frank Cahill who had a natural sense of culture, or the gentleness that comes from a strong and generous spirit. Both were generous with their time and had a strong sense of humanity, which they expressed in many ways.

Frank Cahill was intensely patriotic, and one of my first lessons on joining his class was to learn the Fenian song 'Deep in Canadian Woods', followed closely by 'A Nation Once Again'. They had to be sung loudly and with feeling, putting the emphasis on the right words. Frank was dead set against moneylenders, pawnbrokers – who did a great trade in those times – and the 'cheque man', who provided a form of hire pur-chase at exorbitant interest. He lumped them together as 'those cursed Jewmen', and unfortunately most of us equated the le-galised robbery that constituted moneylending in all its guises with Jews. Of course I discovered in time that a fair proportion of usurers were Catholics, Irish and, worse still, Dubliners.

Otherwise, Frank gave us a solid grounding in human values. But, alas, that first year flew, and it was not long until I joined the class of Brother Leonard, a Kerryman who had a great interest in hurling and athletics but little else. He didn't seem to understand anything at all of the complexities of young boys, their fears, shyness, or the law of uneven development. If you didn't know the answer to a question, or were hesitant in giving it, he would swish quickly past your desk and hit you on the back of your head with his closed fist, or lift you out of the seat by your ear. He practised a form of psychological warfare. With head bent downwards, as though getting inspiration from the floor, he'd ask a question slowly, and raising his head and sweeping the class with those penetrating X-ray eyes, would home in on those who didn't know the answer.

It seemed that he gloated over the ignorant rather than seeking the cause of their ignorance and doing something to correct it. He instilled such fear of not knowing answers that many who felt they did have the answers were too afraid to take the chance of being wrong. The pulling of ears or rabbit punches – quick blows to the back of the head or neck – were only a prelude to the formal punishment of four or five strokes of the leather, applied with all his force, usually so that the tip of the strap snaked an inch or two up over the palm of the hand onto the soft skin of the wrist. There is no doubt that the intention was to inflict pain. If he was in particularly bad form, which was frequently, you would be put standing against the wall at the top of the room until the next break, all of which was fairly normal for a punishment cell in a barracks but not a classroom.

We all heaved a sigh of relief when the year with Brother Leonard ended, thinking that the year with the worst master we were ever likely to encounter was over. We were soon disabused of that notion, for on returning to school after the summer holidays we discovered that our new teacher was Billy O'Neill.

'Billier', as we called him, was, if anything, worse than Leonard. He was six foot in height, weighed about sixteen stone and spoke with what he thought was a cultured Cork accent. On the first morning he made a lengthy speech about the opportunities that were opening up for lads who had the privilege of going to O'Toole's, and that he was a fair-minded man who used the leather or the wooden pointer as a last resort. Their use hurt him more than they hurt us, and one day we'd appreciate all he had tried to do for us. Then he went over our names. Were we related to someone of the same name who had been in his class the year before? O'Neill would refer to these as either a bad puppy or a hard-working, intelligent chap, neither of which was usually true. And your performance was then judged against your relatives. He'd ask what your father worked at and whether you were in the school team or the choir or whatever. A natural snob, he looked down on those whose fathers were labouring, as distinct from being a tradesman or a shopkeeper. The latter category was the most privileged in the class, closely followed by the tradesmen's sons. At the bottom of the heap were the sons of bellmen, dockers and labourers.

I found it extremely difficult to apply myself, being very shy and lacking confidence. O'Neill's tendency to ridicule did not help. He gave me the nickname 'Musical Johnny' because I was in the choir. For some reason he did not like the choirmaster and he attributed all my shortcomings to the time I spent in choir practice. I can say that one of the greatest reliefs of my life was the day I left O'Neill's class and could look forward to the following year in Brother Cordiale's class, who was also the choirmaster and a man who understood the nature of teaching and had an empathy with his pupils.

With Brother Cordiale an English lesson or Irish lesson, poetry or Irish history, were explorations of strange places for hidden treasure. I can safely say that the year spent with him was the only one I learned anything worth learning. Other than that, all my learning came from my parents, particularly my mother, who seemed to know most things. It was my mother, too, who explained why a knowledge of Irish and of Irish history was important.

Overall, I suppose school mustn't have been too bad, because I survived and I have some good memories of those years. There was the great feeling of release at Christmas and summer, and from seeing the classroom altar decorated in early May with daffodils and tulips. The scent would fill the classroom, particularly on a day when the sun was shining into the room. It wasn't just the flowers, though, but the thought of summer that flowers inevitably brought to my mind – of a quiet, friendly, happy Killary and Collon, havens of my youth, and the deeply felt religious faith I held at that time, wanting to believe in all the promises that were made on its behalf by our teachers, which were bolstered by the lectures of visiting priests and missionaries.

There was also a tremendous feeling of elation and well-being getting up early in the morning and going out into the still-dark streets to 7 a.m. mass. I remember receiving communion in the weeks of Lent and sitting among the scattering of the devout, prayerful people gathered in the seats nearest the altar, waiting for the communion; the ting-a-ling of the bells and the sleepy-eyed altar boys intoning the magic, unknowable words in rhythm with the priest in his colourful golden-threaded vestments.

Mother was pleased I went, the teacher was pleased to note that ten of his pupils went to daily mass, and I was pleased at not having to lie that I did. For years I thought the communion wafers came into the tabernacle by aid of a Godly miracle. Otherwise why was there so much secrecy surrounding the golden-clad darkness of the tabernacle, which, even when open, was blocked from your vision by the priest's raised cloaked arms? I'd be all right as long as I didn't spot a beautiful girl, and I would concentrate my thoughts on the holiness of all things, at least until I had received the communion bread.

***

I had a constant love–hate relationship with the church and religion. I wanted to believe all that was promised, even if it was only in the next life, but at times it was impossible to even think the right things, never mind act on them. Once, when I was eleven and Father had been particularly bad, I remember clearly swearing that I was leaving home. I walked up towards the old Wharf Road, intending to go to Fairview Park, thinking all kinds of thoughts, mainly of the lack of fairness in the world and the cruelty of things. And just as I was passing the old church I slowed down and spat on the footpath at the entrance gates and said grimly under my breath, 'Fuck you, God. Fuck you, fuck you. I don't believe in you', and almost cried with the frustration of knowing how bad things really were. That was the first time I really faced up to the reality of our home predicament and contrasted it with the prosperous and happy homes of my pals, all of whom were very good to me.

But it made going to my next confession very difficult. Swearing and cursing was one thing, bad thoughts were bad enough, orange-stealing worse still – but to actually curse God was the limit. In fact, the priest refused to believe me when

I told him. He said, 'Ah, my son, you only think you meant to curse God or to deny his existence. Isn't that so?' And of course by that time I had forgotten my resolve not to believe in God, the church or religion and was hugely relieved when he left me the opening. 'Now, be a good boy and say you are sorry to God. Promise him that you'll never say such terrible things again. Even if you don't believe them, they are still a sin against God. So say your Act of Contrition and say one decade of the rosary in honour of the Blessed Virgin Mary, the mother of God.'

I couldn't believe my luck. I was sure he would ask me my name and see my parents about it. So, having said my Act of Contrition, very slowly and with feeling, I left the box and made my way up towards the altar, where I said my decade of the rosary amidst thoughts of my near escape and trying to understand why he was so lenient.

It was around this time that my father had bought a horse and cart and began selling turf, as there was still no coal available because fuel shortages lasted until well after the war. The turf was stacked in 'clamps' containing thousands of tons in the Alexandra Basin, not far from our home, and in the Phoenix Park. These 'clamps' were a hundred yards long and about twenty feet high. They were far too big to allow the turf to dry; only the outside layers were dry and the rest would be damp or even sodden.

Both places were exposed, but where we collected the turf on the Alexandra Road was the colder of the two, with a biting wind that always seemed to sweep over the docks. The cart men would have to queue for hours, beginning at 6 a.m. to be near the top of the queue when the loaders arrived for work at 8 a.m. But, however early we left home, we were never first in the queue.

The Phoenix Park was different. In the park there was always the prospect of seeing the racehorses out with their riders. The thrill of seeing them was matched only by the secret hope that one day I might be a jockey myself. Then there were the squirrels, birds of all kinds and deer among the trees and little woods. The park was also a place that Father, in better days, before he was soured with Mother and with life, had brought us on summer Sundays to hear the bands playing on the bandstand in The Hollow, which most day trippers made their way to at some point. Besides the music of the band and the colours of children in their Sunday best, there was the prospect of an ice cream from the man with the big icebox on his three-wheeled bicycle. My father would often bring us over to the sky-high monument built to commemorate the battles won by the Duke of Wellington, a Dublin-born man who spent many years living in Trim, 'near where your mother was born'. We would climb the steps to the base of the 100-foot spear and try to look up the side of it, but it made me dizzy with the effort and I'd quickly abandon the attempt.

Then maybe we'd go over to the Gough statue, that magnificent memorial to General Hubert Gough on his horse.

My father would say, 'That's the finest statue of its kind in the world, and it was done by a Dublin man named Foley. That's bronze,' he'd say, and he'd walk us round the statue, examining the beautiful lines of the horse. The proud, seated figure on it and the strength and unity of horse and rider never failed to thrill me and provoke my imagination to thoughts of the battles he fought and to regret that I had never done such things.

After a few more words to some other admirer of the statue, we would start the long walk back to Parkgate Street for the bus to the North Strand and then the mile walk home, tired but thrilled with the memory of Wellington and Gough and the band, and maybe some inner feelings, vague but disturbing, that I could not understand or bring myself to understand.

Easter was another time for a trip, this time to the city centre to watch the military parade march past the General Post Office (GPO). It was always thrilling to sit on my father's shoulders watching the thousands of soldiers and the armoured cars go by. The blood would race through my veins at the sound of the pipe bands. The leaders of the state standing solemnly to attention were reminiscent to my child's mind of the soldiers of Easter 1916, when they took over the GPO on that historic Monday. I would feel a tremendous elation at the folk memories that stirred within me, and I longed to have lived in that great time and played my part alongside the heroes, Connolly, Pearse and Ceannt, or in the Fianna of the romantic Constance Markievicz.

And in years when Easter was late, the day itself would be fine, with the promise of the balmy days of June to September, which seemed to suit the implied promise of what the Easter parade commemorated. We would go home by way of Madigan's pub, where Father would buy a pint of frothy-topped Guinness for himself and a glass of lemonade for the lad. He'd have another pint and then we'd be out for the walk home by way of Marlborough Street, Abbey Street, past the old Abbey Theatre. He'd always make some remark about F. J. McCormick or some such famous name who'd be playing there in *The Plough and the Stars* or *The Righteous are Bold,* none of which meant much to my young mind, but I'd do my best to look as if I was impressed.[3]

Then we'd walk on to Beresford Place to within a few yards of the old Liberty Hall, where Father would point and say, 'That's the place where poor Jem Larkin and Connolly spoke to thousands of the strikers in 1913. Ah, Jem Larkin was a great man. You should have heard him talk to the men. He wasn't afraid of anyone – the Peelers, them dirty DMP [Dublin Metropolitan Police], or [William] Martin Murphy either ... His son isn't the man that Jem was.'[4]

Then we'd travel round by the railings on towards the

---

3   F. J. McCormick was the stage name of well-known Abbey Theatre actor Peter Christopher Judge.

4   'Peelers' is a slang term for the police. It is more commonly used in the North, and usually refers to the RIC or RUC.

Custom House. 'That's where the IRA burned all the government records in 1920, and that was a big blow to the British that time. Look, you can still see the bullet marks made by the big British guns in the Tan War.' And, right enough, there were large pockmarks that looked like they were made by bullets. And all the history of that marvellous epoch would come alive for me.

On down by the Liffey towards the gantry, over the canal bridge and the ships moored to the quays; past Campion's pub, where there were still a few stragglers making polite exchanges of 'Nice day', 'Bad day', or whatever. We would pass onto Wapping Street, a dead street, like the rest of the quays on a Sunday, deserted and depressing, with nothing but the steady thrumming of the Pigeon House pumping-station in the background.

At last we'd reach Barnabas' Church, a Protestant church, and move up Johnny Cullen's Hill. Not far to go now, and just as well, for I'd be very tired and the hill was steep enough. At the top we had a view of the many railway lines passing under the bridge, and the cranes of the docks stretching their giant arms to the sky. Down the hill now, on the home stretch, on to East Road, past Cullen's Yard and Boland's, Dinan Dowdall's, and here we were in Caledon Road, a relief but a letdown all the same. For it was as if our journey back in time had only been an illusion.

***

It seemed that we were always short of money, though the horse was well cared for and my father could always buy all the drink he wanted and buy rounds for his friends. But when he came home drunk all his worst instincts would emerge: his jealousies, suspicions and, perhaps, his frustrations with life and the restrictions fate had placed on whatever secret ambitions he had.

I often went out with him on the turf round after school on winter evenings and on Saturdays, and would call to the doors ahead of the cart and get the orders. I'd be delighted when I'd be asked to leave a bag or two, as the more orders I got the more pleased Father would be and the sooner we'd be able to fold the last empty sack and light the candle in the lamp on the outside of the cart and start home in the darkening evening.

Heading home was great when my father was in good humour and if he wasn't too drunk. On those occasions he'd let the horse go at a fast trot and he'd even let me take the reins for the straight run down the Old Wharf Road. The horse would always know he was heading back to the stables and his feed of warm bran and linseed oil. He'd soon be at the turn at Cadbury's and heading down Church Road and into the stables. We'd both unyoke the horse and I remember well the thrill the first time my father let me brush the horse down. The stable seemed snug and warm after the cold and dampness of the winter streets.

The summers were always slack, with little demand for turf, but the rounds would be done anyway. But the stops outside Gaffney's, Cole's and Murphy's became more frequent. He'd be inside for an hour sometimes, leaving me outside with the warning: 'Mind the horse and take the nosebag off when he's finished. Mind, now, d'ya hear? That's a good lad.' But after an hour or so even the horse would be fretting and lifting his head up and down, twisting around at odd times, looking at the door of the pub.

There were many summer Sundays when Father would take us all out for a jaunt into the 'country' or to the seaside. It would begin with the intention of spending the entire day around Coolock or Portmarnock; but in those days the *bona fide* law still applied: if you travelled five miles from your home you were a *bona fide* traveller and so could get a drink in any pub after hours. So Campion's pub in Balgriffin, which was just over the five miles from our home, would be the first stop. Once there my father would make his way inside and a minute or two later come out with lemonade for the kids, and then back inside for a pint or two, then on a bit further and another stop at another favourite pub, and the same ritual until eventually we'd get to the seaside, a little late but still with time to get to the strand and wolf down the tea and sandwiches, usually bread and jam and tomatoes, and then, after a couple of hours' play-acting around the beach, yoking the horse again for the long journey home.

On the way home there'd be only the one stop at Campion's for a couple of pints to kill his thirst. He'd say, 'I'll have to get a pint; me tongue feels like blottin' paper.' Then he'd emerge, thirst slaked and in good form. He'd slap the reins lightly over the horse's rump and she'd move off at a nice fast trot, sensing that we were heading home.

By now there would be others travelling home to the city centre, for at that time, the mid-to-late 1940s, the city ended at Killester, Whitehall and the little cottages of Coolock. They'd be travelling mainly in horse-drawn vehicles: ponies and traps, high gigs, fancy closed cabs, and hacks hired by a few thirsty Dubliners to travel out to the *bona fides* of Campion's on the north side or the Dead Man's at Lucan or the Strawberry Beds on the back road out of Chapelizod. There would be a few, like my family, who would have painted the cart in bright summer red, blue and yellow to make it appear less like a work cart. Then there would be the long open coaches with the seats running down both sides, which the workers of Collen Brothers, the East Wall building firm, would have for outings to Baldoyle Races or Fairyhouse. It was horses all the way, with only an odd Baby Ford or Austin Seven passing the horses out. The horse drivers – including my father – looked with derision on the cars and complained about the noise of them, the way they frightened the horses and the danger they were to everyone else on the road. All of us identified with our father in his sentimentality, whether it was against cars and for the horse, for the good old days as against the rude present, for the sailing ship as against the motor vessel, and so on.

There was many a summer Sunday when we'd go nowhere, of course. On such days, particularly if the weather was bad and if there was a particularly good film on in the Strand or the Fairview cinemas, or the last episode of the follower-upper (a weekly cinema serial) was showing, my pal Terry, whose father was a painter and handed up all his wages to his mother, would call to see if I'd go to the pictures. Then would begin the long, nervous way around my father or mother for the four pence. Most times I wouldn't get it, because it wasn't there. My father would tell me not to be filling my head with that nonsense – a walk to the park would be much better for me. It might have been, but it could never compensate for not seeing the great *Destry Rides Again* or whether Buck Jones won out against the crooks. That night my pal Terry would relate blow by blow all that happened in the film and some of his accounts were so good that years afterwards, when I saw some of the films on television, I had the distinct feeling that I had seen them before.

My father and mother at those odd times when things were good between them went to a good few pictures together. They both enjoyed the singing of Jeanette MacDonald and Nelson Eddy, and the acting of Greta Garbo, and the humour of Charlie Chaplin. And, like with many of their sentimental attachments, I in turn liked them all, developing an obsession for Greta Garbo. I first saw her beautiful haunting eyes in *Camille* when it was reissued in the Adelphi. Whenever a Garbo film was shown after that I'd go to it. Some of them weren't so good, but I couldn't bring myself to be disloyal by letting myself dwell on their faults. I loved her tragic, wistful roles and my obsession continued into Garbo's old age, when I myself was in my forties. Later in life, when I became immersed in republicanism and the mystique that surrounded Ireland's heroic past, I was to feel the same intense pathos and affection for Constance Markievicz the first time I saw that picture of her standing at the fireplace in the long room of Lissadell.

I was also affected by the strong sense of community and history in the area where I grew up. There were two dairies in East Wall, both of which kept their own cows, made their own butter and sold their milk door-to-door. Barber's was in a back lane off Church Road, and Cullen's was on the East Road at the bottom of Johnny Cullen's Hill. I preferred to go to Cullen's, because I would always be allowed into the front room to get the jug filled, and there were lots of interesting things in that room. It was always dark with the blinds drawn halfway down to keep out the sunlight and stop the milk going sour. There was a large earthenware crock into which Annie Cullen would dip the pint measure carefully and empty it into the jug, then she'd always dip it in again for another drop to make up for any spilt. Mrs Cullen would ask who you were and made you feel important. She seemed always to be clean and smelling of Lifebuoy soap. Her hair would be pinned tightly back into a bun and both she and her sister, Annie, wore old-fashioned, navy, flowered dresses that were almost a uniform.

The area generally was steeped in history. I often thought sadly of the Young Irelander John Mitchel and how he must have felt that day he passed along Seville Place on his way to the North Wall and deportation to Van Diemen's Land.[5] There were times when I could imagine him shackled hand and foot to a Peeler looking out the window of his horse-drawn cab, getting his last glimpse of Dublin's streets and its citizens.

Frank Cahill often spoke of the Invincibles and Joe Brady, one of the men hanged for assassinating the chief secretary, Frederick Cavendish, and his under secretary, Thomas Burke, in the Phoenix Park in 1882.[6] Brady had lived in a little street off Seville Place and still had relatives alive. 'Ah,' Frank would

---

5   Van Diemen's Land was the original name for modern-day Tasmania.
6   The Invincibles was a splinter group from the Fenian movement based in Dublin. It had a penchant for assassinating informers, real or imagined, as well as members of the DMP. It considered kidnapping senior Dublin Castle officials to secure the release of Fenian prisoners but is best known for the Phoenix Park murders. On 6 May 1882 members of the Invincibles assassinated Lord Frederick Cavendish, the newly appointed chief secretary for Ireland, and Thomas Burke, the under secretary, with surgical knives while the pair were walking in the Phoenix Park. Five Invincibles were subsequently executed for their part in the assassinations.

say, 'remember poor brave Joe Brady and never forget Skin the Goat [cab driver James FitzHarris], the man they couldn't get to betray his comrades, even though he was offered a fortune in gold and his passage to any part of the world.' Frank would enthral us with vivid accounts of recent history, almost making them come to life again.

When I'd hear these stories I always felt a strange mixture of sadness and elation, wishing I had lived through those exciting times and been part of such great adventures that gave life meaning. Ballybough, which was a village about a mile from my home, also had its Invincibles, and during my childhood there were characters such as Fluther Good, whom Sean O'Casey immortalised in *The Plough and the Stars*. Fluther became famous overnight. One spin-off was that he was made honorary president of East Wall Soccer Club. The trouble was that he knew nothing about soccer, his main skill being cadging pints of stout. But it didn't prevent him from attending matches in Fairview Park and shouting, 'Come on, yiz silly bastards! I taught yiz all I know and yiz still know nothin'!'

My father knew Fluther well and would usually buy him a drink. There would be Fluther standing outside the pub. As my father climbed down off the cart Fluther would be over like a shot. 'Here, Ned, I'll look after the nosebag for yeh; go on in.' My father, of course, would make his way in, leaving Fluther to take the nosebag down and fix it over the horse's eager head. Then, after a respectful few minutes my father would feel Fluther at his elbow and Fluther would declare: 'Jasus, Ned, the horse is in great order. He's a credit to you. How's business? Things are bad enough around here.' And at that point my father would call for a pint for Fluther, who would make his usual half-hearted protest and then recount his latest row with the police, removing his hat after a couple of pints to show his bumps and scars.

Ballybough was a sort of old-world village in the 1940s with tiny secret lanes, thatched cottages, odd piggeries and dairies. John Walsh's forge at the back of Poplar Row was where my father would bring the horse once a month for shoeing and the odd treatment for a bad hoof, or to get a wheel band tightened. Though Merriman, the farrier and smith, was a better wheelwright, my father preferred to go to John Walsh, as did I. There was a feeling of things old, grand and hidden in the forge: the smell of the hoof burning to prepare it for the shoe, the smoke and the magic of the farrier's touch, never hitting a nail in the wrong way. It was a great place on a cold day, with the darkness and the intermittent red glow of the coke fire blazing up when he'd bellows it, fading to a nice reddish glow in between times.

John Walsh wasn't the huge giant you expected a farrier to be but he was lithe and muscular. He wielded the hammer and tongs deftly, using just the right amount of force. He achieved a kind of rhythm when knocking the red-hot iron into the horseshoe shape by striking the anvil, or rather bouncing the hammer off it once for every two blows on the red-hot iron: ga-aang, ga-aang, ga, ga, gang, one-two-three-four, one-two-three-four, it would go. And gradually, from a flat, dead-straight length of cold iron would be shaped the U of the shoe.

He was a great man to handle a horse, no petting as such, but he'd be firm and few horses would chance to frolic about with John Walsh, though he'd talk to the horse being shod all the time. 'Come on, girl. Come over outa that. That's a girl, that's a girl. Shewo, wo. That's it, that's it. Take her, Ned, there, now,' and all the time with the horse's hoof caught between his knees and resting in the lap of his leather apron. He'd be pulling out the old nails and removing the worn shoe; then would begin paring and evening the hoof to take the new shoe, with an examination of the upper hoof and hock for any weakness or damage. Then the best moment of all, the burning of the hoof, the nailing on of the new shoe and painting the hoof black. Now the horse, which would have been getting restless by this time, would start fretting and almost dash out when we'd be ready to go.

During those years of childhood, which now seem to have been long and packed full of events, many of which were not so happy, the years with the horse seemed to extend right through, but they could only have been four years and they were difficult ones.

There were many other things happening of which I was only vaguely aware through what I heard my father and mother discuss at odd times, or by listening to my father and John Walsh. These were years when religion and puritanism were paramount, when Brinsley MacNamara's novel *The Valley of the Squinting Windows* was banned, as well as James Joyce's works and many others. The saddest censorship of all, the burning by local priests of Eric Cross's *The Tailor and Ansty* in a west Cork village, will only make people wonder today why such a harmless account of an earthy married couple could arouse such anger, spite and fear.

This was the period too when Dublin dockers refused to unload Russian timber, simply because it came from Russia. The Soviet Union was, according to our rulers, our teachers, our priests and nuns, the devil incarnate. The great American singer Paul Robeson was not allowed to perform at the Theatre Royal in Dublin, because he was a suspected communist.

At school we were always saying prayers for the missionaries in darkest Africa and China, asking God to help bring Catholicism to these primitive and savage people. Every schoolroom had its little box for the 'black babies'. There was usually a little black baby sitting on top and when a penny was placed in the box its head would nod in thanks. We were all expected to contribute and teachers kept a tally at the end of every month. I was hardly ever able to give a penny.

A tally was also kept during Lent to show how many

from each class went to mass and communion during the six weeks. A large chart of mass attendance was displayed in each classroom, just inside the door, so that all could see at a glance what the state of play was. The tally was taken every morning at the start of class, with the brother or master asking all who had attended mass and communion to raise their hands. Even those who had not attended would raise their hand on odd occasions so as not to be regarded as pagans. But the master would then ask the ones he doubted a question about which priest said mass, what colour vestments he wore, what the gospel was, or other vital data that could be known only to those who were there or had taken the precaution of asking a pal for the necessary information.

And so the years passed in 'Larrier's' until I reached my thirteenth year – the final year before I could leave school and go to work.

2

GOING TO WORK
AND JOINING THE IRA,
1950–54

My sister Eithne was the first of the family to start work. She was about thirteen and a half at the time and got a job in a sewing factory in Foley Street. It was piecework and it was a real sweatshop, but the money helped her pay her own way and contribute to the general income. I was next, in 1950, also at thirteen-and-a-half, beginning as an office boy in Palgrave Murphy, shipping owners and agents. I got the job as a great favour through the good offices of the choirmaster and the head brother of O'Toole's school, who knew someone in Palgrave's and spoke for me. I, of course, felt privileged. A job in a shipping office was regarded by most working-class people as well-paying, secure and pensionable. But not so. Firstly, the pay was very bad. I started on £1 a week – this would rise by annual increments of five shillings over the next two years if I was diligent, worked hard and showed promise. I did all three, because we couldn't afford the luxury of me leaving.

Palgrave's was run almost on Dickensian lines. The managing director was Captain Alan Gordon, British Army, retired; his wife, Audrey, was on the board of directors, as was Captain J. P. Jameson, who was related to the distillery people and was also retired from the British Army. Captain Gordon would arrive each morning at 9.05 a.m. and carry out what amounted almost to a barrack-room inspection. He would start his tour with the ground-floor staff, call to each desk to see what work you had in hand, make an appropriate comment and so on through the building; thence to his own room where he gave an audience to the directors. These directors held the traditional view of the working class as being their social inferiors who should consider themselves lucky to have a job and be grateful for whatever wage they received. I was only there a short time when I discovered the low wages they were paying to grown men and women, most of whom had gone to secondary school or even to boarding school and whose parents had spent large amounts educating them. At least I had the advantage that my education cost very little.

Shipping was booming and Palgrave's profits ran into the hundreds of thousands annually, yet office staff remained on a pittance, while dockers and seafarers were paid much better because they were organised in militant trade unions.

After I had been employed there for over four years, a colleague, Frank Higgins, and I contacted the Irish Transport and General Workers' Union (ITGWU) secretly because such behaviour had warranted instant dismissals in the past. We then approached selected members of the staff to try to reach the fifty per cent needed to start a section, as required by ITGWU rules at the time. I was only eighteen and a little worried that I might lose my job and the £2 per week I was now earning, on which my mother depended. But I overcame my fear with the help of Frank, my enthusiastic and courageous fellow-conspirator.

Most of those we approached were in favour, but terribly afraid of discovery before the section could be established. In the event, we succeeded in getting a majority to join the union. Then, with the union's help, we drafted our first demand for better wages and conditions. The directors were surprised, even a little shocked, when we presented our demands, and put off any decision until they could discuss them.

Meanwhile the firm had commissioned a new ship from a Dutch shipyard and Mrs Gordon had travelled over to launch it. We were all summoned to the boardroom a few days later, at 5.30 p.m., finishing time. Most of us expected to hear the directors' decision regarding our wage demands. Imagine our surprise when Mr Jameson announced that Mrs Gordon would tell staff 'of the delightful trip she had to Holland'. She proceeded to relate all that had happened, quite oblivious to our lack of enthusiasm. She looked on us much as she and her husband would have regarded their Indian servants during his time with the army. Her final, triumphant moment came when she produced the small silver axe with which she had cut the rope at the launching ceremony and handed it around for us to inspect. I can see still the incredulity and the embarrassment on the faces of those opposite me who were gathered around the board table. It was a relief when the tableau ended and we clapped politely before leaving the room as quickly as decency allowed.

As for our pay claim, as it happened there were more women than men in the union and, as things were in those times, women didn't expect to be paid as much. The directors divided us by offering the women something near what they had asked for and cutting our other demands drastically; but with the women being satisfied and in the majority, the package deal was accepted.

***

An arms raid on Gough Barracks, Armagh, in the summer of 1954 was the first real indication for me that the IRA was still in existence; a discovery that felt almost like an answer to a prayer.[1] Over the previous three years I had developed an intense interest in Ireland's struggle for freedom and felt

---

1   The Armagh raid took place on 12 June 1954 and almost 300 weapons were taken, including pistols, rifles, sub-machine guns and light machine guns, as well as quantities of ammunition.

a deep sense of regret that I had not been born early enough to participate.

My sense of nationalism, or patriotism, was shaped partly by my parents and then through texts like Kickham's *Sally Cavanagh* and *Knocknagow*, Michael Doheny's *The Felon's Track*, with its vivid and moving account of his time on the run after the abortive rising of 1848, William Bulfin's *Rambles in Éirinn*, Brian O'Higgins's ultra-nationalist *Wolfe Tone Annuals* and Patrick Pearse's writings and speeches. Unfortunately, James Connolly was hardly ever mentioned in the literature of the 1950s. I think the only place one could get a book by or about Connolly was the bookshop in Pearse Street run by the Communist Party, then known as the Irish Workers' League. I was aware that the shop existed for the simple reason that I had to pass it every day for two years on my way to Pearse Street Post Office, where I picked up the post for Palgrave's.

The Armagh raid was the turning point in my life. The decision to join the IRA was easy, as I was already mentally committed to a united and independent Ireland. But how to go about joining it was another matter entirely. I didn't know anyone in the IRA and, not surprisingly, it didn't advertise for recruits. It was, after all, a secret and illegal organisation. The *United Irishman,* the monthly paper published by the republican movement, solved my problem. A week or so after the Armagh raid I got my first copy from a local Fianna boy, who lived only a few doors away. I read it from cover to cover. Inside was a notice:

> Ireland unfree will never be at peace.
> Join the Republican Movement and help to free Ireland.
> Call to 94 Seán Treacy Street and join.

I decided that I would call there the following Friday after work. I entered the address in Talbot Street (which republicans at that time insisted on calling Seán Treacy Street in memory of the leading IRA member who was killed there during the War of Independence) and it was with some trepidation that I started to make my way to the top floor, where the office was. As I climbed the stairs, I began to ask myself: 'Who am I to think that I'd be good enough to join the IRA?' Outside the door I began to think that the whole thing had an air of unreality about it. The appearance wasn't what I imagined and my natural shyness took over. I made my way silently back down the stairs to the street.

On my way home, I was angry with myself for allowing my shyness to inhibit me from joining. I was determined to call back the following Friday and this time opened the door to be confronted by an empty office. I left my details on a piece of paper on the counter. After about three weeks I was sent word to attend a meeting at a house in Marino on a Friday night. So this was it, my first contact with the IRA.

There were four or five people in the parlour when I arrived. None of us spoke to each other as we waited for the proceedings to begin. The man in charge, Liam Dalton (who, a year or so later, attempted to stab to death the chief of staff of the IRA, Tony Magan, on O'Connell Bridge), waited about half an hour for another four people to arrive, but eventually started without them.

It was soon apparent that this was not an IRA, but a Sinn Féin meeting. And when, at the end of his short introduction, he began to distribute copies of the *United Irishman* for us to sell, I called him aside and told him it was the IRA I wanted to join. He wasn't too happy about this, but promised to 'try to put me in contact with the right people'. I walked back to East Wall, dejected. I went to bed and read by the light of a candle a few pages of *The Felon's Track*.

About a month later, as I walked home from work on a Friday evening, a man who lived a few streets from me, Paddy Considine, stopped me and – having established that I was the Mick Ryan who wanted to join the IRA – promised that I would be contacted in a week or so.

Shortly afterwards, in October 1954, I was admitted to the Dublin unit and began attending training camps. The very first time I did so I caught a bus from Eden Quay beside Liberty Hall out to Rathfarnham on a Friday evening after work. We marched up to the Sally Gap and spent the weekend doing weapons training and forced marches. This continued on most weekends up to the start of the border campaign. Apart from the Thompson sub-machine gun, most of the weapons were of Second World War vintage, such as the Lee-Enfield Mk IV rifle and the odd Sten gun. There were also some weapons from the War of Independence era. We slept in a disused hunting lodge that used to belong to Joe McGrath, but he had no idea we were there.[2] We would return home in a truck about 6 p.m. or 7 p.m. on a Sunday evening.

The other venue for training was behind the British Legion building in Stillorgan, which was beside the station on the old Harcourt Street train line. These sessions usually occurred on mid-week evenings. There was a strong emphasis on physical training and developing our stamina, rather than on weapons or developing our shooting skills, partly because of a shortage of arms.

Following the initial training sessions, I was appointed a member of a special intelligence section, the sole task of which was to monitor the activities of IRA dissidents led by

---

2   Joe McGrath was a 1916 veteran who was a close associate of Michael Collins in the War of Independence and subsequently Minister for Labour, Industry and Commerce in the first Free State government. He was also head of military intelligence, and suspected of involvement in the torture and execution of anti-Treaty members of the IRA. He later became one of Ireland's most successful businessmen, with a fortune founded on the Irish Hospital Sweepstakes. Many of the agents who sold tickets in Britain and North America were former IRA members, who fought on both sides in the Civil War.

Seosamh Mac Criostail, Liam Kelly and his splinter paramili-
tary group Saor Uladh, and Jack Holland, who ran a photo-
graphic business from a house in Parnell Square.[3]

We were given no special training and little or nothing
in the way of information or equipment to carry out our
task. I had never seen Mac Criostail, Kelly, Holland, or any
of the other main dissidents, but I was supplied with their
photographs, home addresses and addresses they were likely
to frequent. Another problem was that we were not familiar
with the real or imagined reasons for the split or what it was
thought they intended to do, so we were unable to assess the
significance of anything we observed. It wasn't until a year or

---

3   Seosamh Mac Criostail was a student at University College, Dublin. He
     had played a leading role in the arms raid on Gough Barracks, Armagh,
     which first alerted many to the continued existence of the IRA. He also
     participated in the unsuccessful attempt to capture arms from another
     British Army barracks in Omagh. Tensions with the IRA leadership
     arose after Mac Criostail organised the National Students Council and
     engaged in various publicity stunts, including the theft of a painting
     from the Hugh Lane collection at the National Gallery to highlight the
     disputed codicil in Lane's will gifting the collection to Ireland – this cost
     the IRA a safe house in London. He was expelled from the IRA and took
     a significant number of IRA members in Dublin with him, making the
     organisation's leadership fearful that he would launch his own campaign.
     He subsequently linked up with Liam Kelly's Saor Uladh, a paramilitary
     group based in Tyrone that was itself a splinter group of the IRA. The
     two men organised a number of joint operations before Kelly emigrated
     to the United States, handing over most of his material to the IRA. Mac
     Criostail went on to qualify as a barrister and lecturer at Rathmines
     College of Commerce. He died in 1998.

so later that I discovered the full extent of the Mac Criostail split. The leadership was anxious to play down its significance and that of the personnel involved, who included some key Dublin IRA personnel. It was even hinted that Mac Criostail and the others were frightened after their near-capture in the Omagh Barracks raid and were looking for an easy way out.

This was still the era of the bike. It was also an era of strict IRA discipline and unquestioning obedience. You did what you were told. The surveillance operation usually began at 7 p.m. each evening and lasted until midnight, or whenever the target returned home. It was a seven-day-a-week job. Typically, I would take up position on my bike within viewing distance of Mac Criostail's house, or whichever house I was allocated, at 7 p.m. on weekdays and 9 a.m. on weekends. I would note who visited the target. We had discretion as to who to follow afterwards, either the main target or his visitor.

Although we only had bikes, so had our targets, but Mac Criostail and most of his colleagues were first-class racing cyclists whose bikes were equipped with numerous gears, whereas my Hercules Kestrel's only claim to being a distant cousin of a racing bike was its dropped handlebars. In addition, Mac Criostail and his associates sometimes had the use of a car, or took to the bus. In those circumstances losing one's quarry was not unusual. On those nights all you could do was head for the target's most likely destination or meeting-place and resume the vigil there, wait till 11 p.m.

or so, note who came and went, and head home. Our targets became aware they were under IRA surveillance within a week of the operation beginning, apart altogether from the fact that they would have been on their guard against Special Branch surveillance. Strangely, though, I saw little or no Special Branch surveillance of my targets.

A plus on my side was that I was completely unknown, both to the dissidents and to the Special Branch. I was truly a secret member of the not-so-secret IRA, largely because my family had no prior involvement and I had never attended any republican events, other than the symbolic renaming of King's Bridge on the Liffey as Seán Heuston Bridge (a name that was later adopted officially). There I was just one of a hundred or so desultorily interested citizens. It was where I first saw and heard the great Tomás Mac Curtáin – son of the murdered mayor of Cork – speak.

I remained a member of the special intelligence section for about eight months, during which time the extent of the split, the identities of the main participants and with whom they were in contact was established. I think too that we contributed to the recovery of some weapons the dissidents had misappropriated.

In late 1955 another volunteer and I were assigned to attend the reburial in north Monaghan of Connie Green, a member of Saor Uladh who had died in an 'unofficial' operation against the RUC. We were to note who the main organisers, stewards and speakers were, take photographs of those on the platform and report to our officer commanding (OC) the following Tuesday. We duly travelled to Co. Monaghan that Sunday morning, armed with a Kodak Brownie box camera loaded with a roll of film and nothing else but our wits. Because this was the funeral of a member of a non-IRA group, and our leadership thought that only a few hard-core dissidents would attend, we were instructed to arrive shortly before the ceremony was due to begin so as not to draw attention to ourselves. We timed our arrival to coincide with the approximate start of the ceremony only to find the graveyard packed. It was impossible to get closer than 200 feet to the platform. We took some pictures anyway, which, not surprisingly, were worthless. We both felt like fish out of water. We'd been led to believe that this man, and the organisation to which he belonged, had no support, yet crowds of ordinary citizens had travelled from miles around to commemorate him. Virtually the only person we recognised was Liam Kelly, the head of Saor Uladh who, with his mop of prematurely grey hair, was unmistakable.

My partner and I, political innocents as we were, made our way out of the graveyard without exchanging a word. We had little to say to each other on the journey home. I think we were both perplexed at the size of the crowd in the light of what our leaders had told us, but we barely wanted to admit that to each other. We had been led to believe that the IRA was the one true Irish revolutionary army and Saor Uladh was simply a breakaway group. The idea that it could receive such support was inconceivable to the IRA leadership, and therefore to us, so we rejected the funeral attendance as an aberration. In case we were in any doubt on our return, our intelligence officer reminded us of the stipulation in the IRA constitution that 'the only organisation entitled to bear arms in defence of the republic is the IRA'.

The intelligence section remained in existence until the early summer of 1956 when, at a special parade, the adjutant-general, Charlie Murphy, informed us that it had more or less fulfilled its function and we'd be returning to the Dublin unit. He went on to say, however, that headquarters (HQ) was initiating a course of intensive training in June designed to make every volunteer physically fit and capable of engaging in military operations. He added that the course would entail training two nights a week and every weekend for the following four or five months. From now on only those who were prepared to participate in operations could remain in the army. This last point surprised me as I assumed that all volunteers were in the army to fight. He concluded by giving us two weeks to think over what he'd said and to report to our OC with our decisions.

To my amazement, out of the nine who formed our section, only four of us opted to stay on, and when it came to 10 December 1956 and mobilisation for the border campaign, only myself of the original nine who started out was ready for the 'great adventure'. The training was intensive, with the main emphasis on physical fitness and proficiency in the handling of weapons. Even then, some of us only had one actual shoot-off, and that was during a night exercise in October 1956 in the Dublin Mountains.

This was the final exercise for the Dublin Active Service Unit (ASU), as well as some volunteers from Co. Meath who were considered eligible. But the shoot occurred in darkness, so we had no way of testing our accuracy and our handling of weapons under near-combat conditions. The exercise was not the success HQ expected it would be. The director of operations and the training officer were angry and embarrassed, not alone at the obvious failure of the exercise but because present that night was Tomás Mac Curtáin and, I think, another member of the Army Council. However, the net result was that a two-night session of all present was called for the following week at our training ground in Stillorgan behind the British Legion, where we would have a final opportunity to get the drills for assault and covering parties correct. And we did. But, of course, we weren't using live ammunition.

While ASU members were 100 per cent fit and highly trained in the weaponry end of things, we were abysmally ignorant of military tactics and politics. Few if any of us understood the relationship of force to politics or the effect that particular military activities might have on the people, the state forces, the Protestant and Catholic populations in the North, or indeed the governments of either Irish state. We left all that to the leadership. As far as most volunteers were concerned, they were the leaders and we were there to be led.

3

THE BORDER CAMPAIGN, FIRST PHASE, 1956–57

On 5 December 1956 I was contacted by a Dublin IRA officer who asked me how I felt about taking part in an operation. It was a strange question, I thought, as that was the reason I was in the IRA. I'd already given a commitment to operate in the early summer, which was why I'd been included in the intensive training course. When I said I was prepared to go into action he told me to be at the Ashtown Gate of the Phoenix Park at 8 p.m. two nights later, which was a Friday; to bring all my gear, battledress (British Army khaki), boots, blanket, groundsheet, billycan and clothing repair kit (needles, thread, etc.), and to tell nobody that I was going on a job but that I'd be away for a few days. I was to make some excuse to my parents explaining my absence.

I thought I was being mobilised for a 'job'. Given the pattern of IRA operations up to that time, I assumed this would be another raid for arms, like Armagh, and I'd be back home in East Wall on Sunday, or Monday at the latest. I had no idea it was the start of a campaign that would last almost six years.

That Friday evening I told my parents, who knew by now that I was in the IRA, that I'd be away for the usual weekend training. They, of course, had maintained secrecy about my membership of the IRA and could be relied on not to tell anyone why I'd be away. I wasn't blasé about risking my life and liberty, but this was the moment I'd waited for; this was the reason I had joined the IRA. Nevertheless, I wanted to say a goodbye to my parents, just in case I was killed or captured, but as that would have given the game away I just said to my father (my mother being at work) that I'd be home on Sunday evening.

So it was with mixed emotions that I left home, with my haversack on my back, to walk to O'Connell Street and catch a bus to the Ashtown Gate. It was about 7 p.m. and dark. This wasn't the kind of departure I'd envisaged in my fantasies: a truck, or a van at least, calling to the door to pick me up; some of the other lads already inside; my mother and father waving goodbye; or some such romantic and supportive departure, even if there were no bands playing us down the road. The real thing was indeed different. It took me only three-quarters of an hour to reach the Ashtown Gate, but it was one of the longest and loneliest journeys of my life.

Early as I was, one of the other lads was already there, concealed behind some bushes. I was delighted to see him.

We said hello, but we didn't say much after that; we were too preoccupied with our reasons for being there. Three more volunteers arrived over the next half an hour or so. As each one arrived we greeted each other, but that was virtually the end of the conversation. Even if anyone had knowledge of the operation we were about to engage in, we were under strict instructions not to discuss it.

Just about the time it was due, our transport arrived. This was one of the very few occasions over the next five years on which transport, or anything else, arrived on time. We piled into the car and the driver headed off. He was friendly and chatted about everything except the IRA. About an hour later he turned into the driveway of an isolated house near Athboy, Co. Meath, and said, 'Here we are. Good luck, lads!'

It was a huge old house about a quarter of a mile from the road and a couple of miles from the nearest village. It was owned by an old republican called Charlie Prendergast; a bachelor and somewhat deaf, he was a grand and friendly man. We entered the house and saw dozens more volunteers from Dublin and elsewhere standing around. Not knowing anyone else, we automatically joined the rest of the Dublin ASU. Having listened to chat from 'those in the know', it dawned on me that we were about to participate in a 'campaign', rather than the one-off operation I'd anticipated. This was surprising news, but I soon adjusted to it. And anyway, I thought, I'll be going into action with the rest of the Dublin

ASU, in whom I had the utmost confidence, having trained with them for a solid four months. We were all 100 per cent physically and mentally fit for operations and well trained in weapons – by our standards, that is – and I had equal faith in the Dublin ASU officers.

Naturally shy, I listened rather than talked. There was plenty of tea and sandwiches, so no one was hungry. As time passed, more and more volunteers arrived, each arrival adding to the air of excitement and anticipation, and a raising of morale and confidence. There's strength in numbers, after all.

When everyone had arrived, we fell in and were given a pep talk by Charlie Murphy, the adjutant general, who also warned us not to go outside. He concluded with, 'If anyone feels he can't go ahead, for any reason, he is to inform his OC … he could return home … and there'll be no recriminations.' Then, with an instruction to sleep wherever we wanted, we were dismissed.

Pals found pals and spaces on the floor to lay our sleeping bags or blankets. Few slept, however. There was too much excitement, too much speculation about our destinations and our destiny.

Most of the next day was spent in much the same way. Eventually, about 8 p.m. on the Saturday, when everyone who was expected had arrived, a member of HQ ordered us to form ranks again and handed us over to Seán Cronin, who, I think, was director of operations at the time.

This was the decisive moment. No one stirred. He began with another pep talk about the campaign we were about to embark upon and repeated the offer to anyone who wanted to step down to do so without fear of recrimination or shame. He then dismissed us and told us to reassemble in fifteen minutes. We Dublin lads stayed in a group, more or less, as did those from other units, and speculated about where we'd be going and what we'd be doing.

After about a hundred of us reassembled in the largest room, in tight ranks from wall to wall, we were brought to attention and Cronin, after another pep talk that helped to sustain our morale, read out the areas where each column would operate, who would lead it and the names of volunteers assigned to it. He began, I think, at the Derry/Donegal end, read out the name of the OC and the names of the volunteers assigned to that column, then onto Tyrone, Fermanagh, Armagh, south Derry, south Down and so on.

As he continued I was amazed and disappointed to hear the names of most of my Dublin comrades being allocated to those units. Finally, when he came to the column for the last remaining area, north Antrim of all places, there were only three of the original twenty-odd Dublin ASU men left: Liam Nolan, Phil Donaghue and myself. He then named the rest of the column: five volunteers from the Cork ASU and two from north Antrim, one of whom was Frank McCarry. Tony Cooney of Cork would be OC, Liam Nolan of Dublin was number 2 (second in command) and McCarry was to be our guide.

I'd never met Cooney and had no idea what he was like. I knew Liam Nolan and had a great deal of confidence in him, as I had in the rest of the Dublin officers. I met Frank McCarry for the first time when we arrived in north Antrim and I never met anyone else who had such an uncanny sense of direction, or better knowledge of that vast mountainous area. As far as I know, McCarry hadn't much military training or experience, but he had courage aplenty. The remaining Dublin ASU volunteer, Phil Donaghue, was at a peak of physical fitness and an obviously courageous youth.

I soon got over my disappointment at our unit being split up, or thought I had. There was too much else to think about. I heard afterwards that the reason for the split was that some units' training wasn't up to par, so they were put with members whose training was adequate. Nevertheless, I believe this to have been one of the major weaknesses in the early, critical days of the campaign. It might not have made much difference as far as the border columns were concerned, but for the north Antrim column, operating under uniquely difficult conditions, it made an awful difference. The Cork lads with us were certainly not lacking in courage and commitment, but they weren't physically fit, and fitness was essential to survival.

Not alone that, but our gear proved completely unsuitable for the north Antrim winter weather. Like many volunteers,

I was wearing a second-hand British Army uniform with a tricolour flash. The IRA was anxious to be recognised as a legitimate army, but the khaki absorbed rain and snow like blotting paper and was impossible to dry out overnight, even if you were lucky enough to find decent shelter. Moreover, rapid movement in wet khaki was extremely difficult. The trousers would weigh as heavy as wet woollen blankets, making leg movement arduous, particularly climbing or descending hills. The same applied to our boots. Leather boots are good for service in dry climates and on paved roads but hopelessly inadequate in damp, cold conditions. As a result, we seemed to be wet and cold almost all the time.

This criticism of our clothing is with hindsight on my part, but I think they were factors that the architects of the campaign should have taken into account. These problems wouldn't have been too difficult for a week or so, but in an open-ended campaign with limited billeting arrangements, no spare boots or clothing posed serious handicaps.[1] At least I was in excellent physical shape and inured to cold weather, not alone from the previous four months' training in the Dublin Mountains, but from the winters spent selling turf, coal and kindling door-to-door as a child. Even so, winter in north Antrim would be a harrowing and debilitating experience. At

---

1   A billet is a place – usually a civilian's house – where soldiers stay temporarily.

least the shortage of food would not bother me because I was never a big eater, nor had there been too much to eat at home anyway.

That Sunday morning cars picked up volunteers at various times. Eventually it was our turn. We piled into a van and headed off. This was my first visit to the North and it was the first time I saw an RUC man when I took a surreptitious look out of the almost blacked-out rear window of the van. Most of us had never been in the North. It was not only strange terrain, but also sectarianism, Orangeism and Hibernianism were terms that meant nothing to us.[2]

We reached our destination a few hours later. It was a house at the bottom of Orra More Mountain, halfway between Ballycastle and Ballymena. Our column was bedevilled from the word go. No real military preparations had been made. Dugouts and arms dumps should have been ready and safe houses prepared.[3]

We stayed in one small house and, although we slept five to a bed, it was clean, dry and warm. The bachelor owner had

---

2 'Orangeism' and 'Hibernianism' are references to the Orange Order and Ancient Order of Hibernians, both manifestations of a society deeply divided on religious lines and reflecting the mutual antipathy of Protestant and Catholic communities towards each other.

3 During this period the IRA relied on dugouts much of the time. These were literally underground shelters where volunteers could live while operating in an area where safe houses were not available. Arms dumps would normally be within easy reach of the dugouts.

laid in plenty of food, but as he was known to the RUC, once the campaign started his house would no longer be a safe place for us. With no safe house or dugout available to hole up in after an operation, we became uneasy. We would just have to make the best of it and we set out first thing next morning to find a suitable site for a dugout.

Our host, who had no experience of dugouts, suggested the top of Orra More. This was a couple of hours' march away and a twelve-mile march from Torr Head, one of our initial targets the following night. It sounded good to us. But we had no experience of dugouts either. The only snag we saw was that we'd have to leave his house before daylight and remain on the mountain until darkness, and then operate that night. In our innocence we said, 'So what!' Meanwhile our host told us stories about atrocities committed by the Black and Tans in the 1920s, and more recently by the B Specials. Not the kind of bedtime stories we needed.

Next morning at 6 a.m., after a good feed, and carrying our weapons, shovels and corrugated iron sheets, we set out for the top of Orra More. Tony Cooney headed off for a meeting with HQ personnel in Belfast, leaving Nolan in charge. It was brutally cold and there was a heavy mist. Half an hour into the ascent, the wind rose and it began to sleet. We were soon soaked to the skin and freezing. It took us two hours to reach the mountain top, the barest, bleakest spot I'd ever seen. We selected a spot at random and began digging. However, after we had gone down to a foot or two it filled with water. So we selected another location we thought looked better. It too began to fill with water as soon as we got a foot or so down. We tried another spot, with the same result.

The digging was becoming more difficult, not only because we were getting tired but also because we were frozen from the wind and sleet, which fell all day. Despite this, us Dublin men were prepared to keep going until we found a suitable site. But, after what seemed like a couple of hours of futile digging, the Cork men refused to dig any further, and they were right. Even as they laid down their shovels, the latest hole had begun to fill with water. Nolan, Donaghue and myself weren't too confident of finding a dry spot either, but we were prepared to continue searching for a suitable spot because we had been given to understand that this hole would be our only refuge after operating in a few hours' time and because we were trained to obey our officers. As far as I can remember, most or all of the Cork lads wore light civilian clothing and shoes that were totally inadequate for the appalling conditions. And, of course, none of us had gloves. If we had had sandwiches, flasks of tea, gloves and better clothing, the other lads might have acted differently.

Nevertheless, we were amazed at their insubordination. It was tantamount to mutiny. Nolan pointed this out to them, together with the fact that the dugout was our main, and perhaps only, hope of survival after that night's operations.

But they were either too demoralised with the futility of the dig or too frozen and physically exhausted to carry on. Nolan wisely decided to let them opt out of further digging, but made it clear that their refusal was a serious matter and would be reported to the OC, Cooney, himself a Cork man, when he returned to the billet from Belfast. He was expected back at our billet about the same time as us. We had to get back by 5 p.m. if we were to carry out our first operation as planned.

We continued searching for a dry site, without success, until 4 p.m., when dusk fell and the mist started to thicken. It was time to return to our billet if we were to operate that night. We could only hope to find a safe refuge afterwards.

I was impressed by Nolan's calmness and exercise of control under such adverse circumstances. He was an inspiration and an example of how one should behave in order to survive in such circumstances. I was glad he was in charge that day, and was the number 2 of the column.

The order to return was the most welcome instruction we'd been given all day and it didn't come a moment too soon. We couldn't have had a worse beginning to the campaign. Morale was extremely low, we were wet to the skin, frozen to the bone and the day wasn't even over yet. We shouldered our weapons and shovels, and headed fast down the mountain to our billet, to food and warmth and the chance to dry out our clothes and boots in the hour or two we'd have before heading off to our first target. Having marched for about an hour it was apparent that we had overshot our mark and were lost. We had reached the road that the house was on, but Nolan had no way of knowing whether it was to our left or right; nor had anyone else. He called a five-minute halt to rest and find our bearings.

This was almost the last nail in the coffin for our morale. There was a deadly silence. Phil and I were standing together and leaning against a low bank at the side of the road. After about a minute, however, my feet began to get so cold that I decided to take off my boots and socks and rub them back to life. Phil did the same. Then we wrung out our sodden socks, emptied our boots of water, and struggled back into them. Lacing the boots with frozen fingers wasn't easy. As we hunkered down beside the bank, hungry and exhausted, I was learning that idealism in itself was not sufficient to win, and that our leaders were not as infallible as I'd been trained to accept. But having been trained to endure hardship and accept that it was going to be a part of the struggle, Phil and I were perhaps better able to deal with it than most.

The five-minute rest was both too short and too long. As soon as the time was up Nolan ordered us to fall in and whipped us into some semblance of a column before leading us off to search for the house.

After what seemed like a couple of hours but was perhaps less than one, Nolan found the billet. 'This is it,' he said, in a tone that implied that he was never in any doubt. I was ecstatic, as, I'm sure, were the others. Minutes later, with the heat of a roaring fire and the smell of a stew simmering away, we made a rapid recovery. We immediately stripped to our underwear, placed our clothes, socks and boots around the fire to dry, and sat down to a life-giving hot meal. We ate the food in jig time without any kind of chat, nor was there any conversation during the hour or so that we waited for Cooney. There was also a lot of tension because of the day's events, particularly the insubordination of the Cork men and the physical unpreparedness of some of the column.

By the time Cooney returned, we had dried our clothes and boots – much of the former was scorched and the boots were as dry and brittle as tinder. Moments after he came in the door, probably sensing the tension, he said, 'Ye can relax, lads ... everything's okay, but the start of the campaign's been postponed for twenty-four hours.'

While this announcement wasn't greeted with cheers – that would have been unseemly – the sense of relief was palpable. I welcomed the postponement because, given the day's events, I felt that neither I nor the rest of the column were in any condition, physically or mentally, to operate successfully that night. I was also grateful for another night of freedom and life.

Some minutes later Cooney and Nolan adjourned to another room. I was called in and Nolan, in his usual calm and pleasant manner, asked me to 'describe what happened today ... you know, when we were trying to dig the dugout'. I recounted the incident exactly as it happened. When I had finished, Cooney thanked me and said, 'Okay, Mick, you can go back outside.'

The rest of the lads were sitting or standing around somewhat listlessly when I returned to the kitchen. There was still no conversation, not even the kind of inane banter that helps to pass the time and keep the morale up.

Shortly afterwards Cooney and Nolan spoke privately to the lads who'd refused to dig and I think they were mildly chastised for it. Meanwhile we were called to attention. Cooney apologised for the absence of a dugout and the other shortcomings. He went on to give us the details of the two targets we'd be hitting the following night. The first was the British Army barracks in Ballymena, headquarters of the Royal Ulster Rifles. We were to kill or disarm the sentries, take as many weapons and as much ammunition and food as possible, and then head on to our second target, the RAF radar station at Torr Head, which was about thirty miles to the north. The objective there was to take over the station, which had a garrison of six or so RAF soldiers, and destroy it. Then we'd head off to the Glens and safety. No maps or drawings of either target were produced.

Cooney asked if there were any questions. None of us, that I remember, had any questions, probably because we were too inexperienced to know what to ask. Moreover, I assumed our leaders were familiar with the layout of the targets and would give us the appropriate directions at the right time. There being no questions, Cooney went on to say that he had made some changes to the teams originally designated as the cover and assault groups.[4] He didn't give any reason for this; however, as soon as I heard the changes, it was apparent that they were the result of the lads' refusal to dig. Anyway, the change meant that Phil and I, who'd originally been appointed to the cover group, were now part of the assault group, and the lads who'd refused to dig were placed in the cover group. The change didn't please me one bit because, frankly, I was happy enough to be back a bit. But you didn't question orders.

The change also meant we would be travelling to the targets in a different order and in different cars. Liam Nolan, Phil Donaghue, myself and the other members of the assault group were assigned to McCarry's car. Cooney and the others were assigned to a van. As McCarry, our driver and guide, knew the roads like the back of his hand, our car would lead and the van would follow a quarter of a mile behind, near enough to keep us in view.

We spent the next day confined to the house, as it was unsafe to go out. That evening Cooney gave us a final briefing before we set out. It was good, but as I'd never seen either

---

4   A cover group provided supporting fire while the assault group carried out an attack. The cover group would also provide covering fire if the assault failed and the latter had to retreat.

target, or a detailed map, I had no real idea of the physical layout of either building. I assumed this must be the way things were done and, I rationalised, Cooney and Nolan were familiar with the targets and would be there to direct us every step of the way.

As this was my very first job, I kept my worries to myself. But while my confidence in our ability to succeed was affected, my determination to operate to the best of my ability was undiminished, and I'm sure the others felt the same.

The weapons and ammunition were distributed. This brought with it another surprise: because of a shortage of sub-machine guns, some of us were given Lee-Enfields. The Lee-Enfield is a long and cumbersome bolt-action rifle, excellent for long-distance firing but very unsuited for assault action at close quarters. We were instructed to load our weapons and prepare to move out. Some of the volunteers' training was so deficient that they had to be helped to load their weapons.

I recited a silent, fervent entreaty to the God I then believed in that he would somehow compensate for our deficiencies and help me live up to the example of the 'dead who died for Ireland'. Thus spiritually fortified, with a weapon in one hand, a haversack in the other and boots securely laced (I had a phobia about my bootlaces opening at the wrong time), I headed out the door with the others and we piled into the two vehicles.

With our car leading, we set off for the British Army

barracks in Ballymena, fifteen miles to the south. However, we were only fifteen minutes on the road when Cooney signalled our driver to stop. He spoke to Nolan and decided that – though we had left on schedule – we were too late to go ahead with the Ballymena job and should head straight for Torr Head. This decision pleased me and the rest of the column no end, because it just didn't make sense to try two jobs one after the other.

Torr Head was about twenty miles away. The van followed us, keeping out of sight most of the time, but the driver knew the route and, presumably, would catch up with us at an assembly point near the target. In those days, very few people had cars and we seemed to be the only ones on the road, though it was still only 9 or 10 p.m.

Everything was going well until about one or two miles from Torr, when our driver, McCarry, said there was something wrong with the engine. A few seconds later it died, and he steered the car into the side of the road and let it roll until it stopped. He tried to start it, without success. Then Nolan said, 'We better get out and get the others to stop.'

I thought, 'What else can go wrong? There's something wrong with this column: there's a jinx on it!'

Only a few seconds elapsed before the van emerged from a bend, whereupon Nolan and McCarry stepped out a few feet onto the road and, waving their arms in the air, signalled it to stop. To our utter amazement it didn't even slow down.

We all stood silent and incredulous as its lights disappeared from view. We all huddled down beside the ditch, on the other side of which was a forest. Nolan and McCarry exchanged an odd whispered remark, which I couldn't hear. The rest of us kept our thoughts to ourselves. Mine were too mutinous to voice! No amount of optimism could dismiss the conclusion that this was a disastrous start to our guerrilla days in Ireland.

While we waited for the van's return, McCarry tried to get our car going again, but to no avail. When the van failed to reappear Nolan decided that we should start walking towards our objective, but keeping off the road, walking inside the fence. Phil and I were carrying a fifty-pound mine as well as our rifles and packs. We began walking in the direction of Torr Head, expecting at any moment that we'd come across the van pulled in to the side of the road.

Minutes later we heard the unmistakable sound of gunfire. There were three or four bursts over the course of a minute; it sounded like a Bren light machine gun and it was coming from perhaps a mile away. Then there was silence. Nolan immediately called a halt and instructed us to hunker down in silence while he and McCarry discussed the probable cause of the gunfire. They reached the inevitable conclusion that our comrades in the van had run into an RUC patrol and had put up some resistance. Then Nolan told us, to our amazement, that all the other columns had probably hit their targets hours earlier and the British forces were now on full alert. This was the first I knew that the other columns had been scheduled to hit their targets before we even set out for ours. On the basis of this information and the fact that we'd no way of knowing what had happened to our comrades, the consensus was that our only course was to head for the Glens and safety, on foot, as we now had no transport.

It was now a very dispirited, demoralised and angry half-column. Our comrades in the van had probably been arrested, wounded, maybe even killed. We had all had to overcome our fears and doubts about risking our lives and liberty for the cause of Ireland, and to come to terms with the possibility of taking someone else's life. But now, after all the training and the soul-searching, we'd missed the best opportunity we could have hoped for to strike a significant military blow against the British in the North. Moreover, we'd lost the element of surprise, which was about all we had going for us. We were about to be hunted, once the RUC came across McCarry's car, without ever getting near to hitting either of our targets.

Our predicament was made worse because we were ope-rating in an area where there were few supporters prepared to billet IRA men after an operation. And who could blame them when they were mostly known to the RUC. Besides, the Antrim Glens had few roads, making it difficult to escape a British security dragnet, except by forced marches over the hills. While the upper slopes of the Glens were clear of under-growth and obstacles, facilitating a relatively fast marching pace, they offered little cover from observation, or the weather, making it necessary to move only at night. We were over seventy miles from the border with no nearby escape route. Lastly, we were isolated from the other IRA columns in the field and from the field headquarters of General Headquarters (GHQ), which was necessarily based on the border.

A fail-safe for a column such as ours that couldn't engage in border hopping was that we should head for the Sperrin Mountains, which stretch along the Tyrone–Derry border. These mountains are a traditional republican area where we would find succour and safety. But the Sperrins were over thirty miles away and the suggestion of 'heading for the Sperrins' soon became a joke whenever things were bad. Our immediate concern was to survive the intensive search operation that would be mounted at first light. McCarry decided that our only course was to head to Pat McCormack's house in Glenarm, where we'd be given shelter and food. Unfortunately, McCormack was known throughout the North as a Gaelic-Leaguer and republican.

Nevertheless, with McCarry leading, we set out at a rapid march towards our destination, until the unfit began to find the slog to the upper slopes difficult and slowed us down to a dangerous extent. It would only be a matter of hours before the RUC, B Specials or British Army found our broken-down car, which belonged to a known republican, and launched a search for us at first light. We would never make McCormack's by then at the current rate of progress, even after abandoning our fifty-pound mine.

A rest was called but we were only allowed to hunker down or stand, because the tiredness and cold would make it much more difficult to get moving again if we were allowed to sit or lie on the ground. During this first rest, Nolan, supported by McCarry, gave a brutally realistic outline of our predicament. We faced certain capture if we didn't reach McCormack's or some other shelter by daylight; and while McCormack's wasn't a safe billet we would at least be certain of food. Nolan also felt sure that the RUC or B Specials would not have expected us to travel this far on foot before dawn, particularly in view of the atrocious weather and terrain. He then called myself and Phil aside and told us to take up the rear and push, shove or do whatever else was necessary to keep the stragglers moving at the right pace. This was the kind of instruction we were glad to hear and carry out.

After this break, which lasted no more than ten minutes, we did what we could to shake the paralysing cold from our muscles and bones and fell into marching order, an arm's reach apart, and set off for our destination. The climb to the upper slopes was painful even for those of us who were fit, but it must have been excruciating for the others. There were frequent three or four-minute rests, which were always welcome. Once we reached the upper slopes, the going was somewhat easier but we were now exposed to an unrelenting north wind.

Our compasses and maps were not much use to us in this situation, but fortunately McCarry didn't need either. After a ten-hour march, thanks to his incredible sense of direction and grim determination, we finally reached McCormack's in the half-light of a misty dawn. With our blackened faces and army khaki, the McCormack family at first thought we were a British Army unit that was lost! However, McCarry soon convinced them that we were indeed IRA men on the run. Shortly afterwards we were stripped to our underwear again, our clothes strung out to dry around a fiercely burning stove and each of us was wrapped in a blanket absorbing the homely heat.

Then the woman of the house (I think she was the daughter rather than the wife), refusing all offers of help, prepared a meal for us. We ate so much that I'm afraid we ate virtually all the food there was, but our host didn't mind emptying the cupboards and the woman of the house set to baking more bread for us to take with us when we inevitably moved out.

After an hour or so, when our clothes and boots had dried out, we adjourned to the hay barn adjoining the house to rest until it was time to move out. We took turns watching and listening for the approach of a search party. The McCormacks' house was about fifty yards from the road and on the upward slope of the glen, not a bad position for a withdrawal, given the mist and a couple of minutes' warning of the approach of any search party.

Of course, none of us were able to relax, but now that we were sheltered and fed to bursting point, morale was better. Then we heard the BBC news reports over our 'portable' radio, a bulky four or five-pound instrument that the OC had bought on hire purchase in Belfast and it was my responsibility to carry and keep dry. It covered the previous night's IRA activities.[5] We learned of the capture of all but one of our comrades at Torr Head and once again experienced a deep sense of frustration and anger at their arrest. (They subsequently received sentences of between ten and twelve years each.) We were even angrier that we'd missed a great opportunity to successfully hit our targets. But because of the culture of unquestioning obedience towards HQ and our officers, we felt unable to voice our criticisms of whoever was responsible for this debacle. Another source of resentment was the discovery that some IRA columns operating in relatively safe border areas hit their targets up to an hour before the general strike time. We felt that if any column should have been given the advantage of a first strike it was ours, operating so far from the border.

5   Among the many other incidents on the first night of the campaign, the BBC transmitter in Derry was blown up, the courthouse in Magherafelt, Co. Derry was burnt down, an RUC constable was wounded during an attack on the Armagh telephone exchange and there was a gun battle outside the Royal Irish Fusiliers' barracks in Armagh. A Territorial Army barracks was also damaged by an explosion in Enniskillen, as were several bridges near the border.

After the news bulletin, Nolan and McCarry concluded that we were not safe in McCormack's, which was too well known to the RUC, and would have to move out at dusk, about 4.30 p.m. Meanwhile we geared up to be ready to move at a moment's notice, packing whatever bread and other food the family could spare. Our aim was to head south to a forestry hut on the upper slopes of Orra More, an estimated ten-hour march, where we should be safe for a few days, with time to reassess our position.

We cleaned our weapons and when it came time to depart, the woman of the house, who had cared for us as though we were her own sons, sprinkled us with holy water, gave each of us a miraculous medal and sent us on our way with 'God bless you all.' It was a scene that was to be repeated again and again over the next five years. I'll never forget her and the many other 'women of the house' who sheltered and cared for us.

So, in a mist-shrouded dusk, with visibility down to about twenty feet, we headed for the high ground in close order. When we were at a safe distance from the roads and the houses dotted along the road of the glen, and out of earshot of the dogs, we turned for Orra More.

The north wind returned with the snow and it fell throughout the night. We stopped for the now customary hunkered-down rest for about five minutes every half hour. There was always a yearning to lie down, even on wet ground, but to do so would have been fatal, as even the fittest of us would have succumbed to sleep. One consolation was that the wind was now at our backs. Although conditions made it impossible for us to see the lights of Ballycastle to the north or Ballymena to the south, McCarry, with his extraordinary knowledge of the Glens, brought us safely to the hut by daybreak.

Having established that it was unoccupied, we made a very fast descent through a forestry plantation. Once inside we set about lighting a huge, roaring fire, stripped off and once more started to dry our clothes. We ate the bread and, having bolted the door, set ourselves around the fire to discuss our situation. With no back-up organisation, no intelligence, no transport, no money, no dugouts and, according to news bulletins, house-to-house searches of republican homes in the Glens and twenty-four-hour roadblocks, our only hope of evading capture was to move out of north Antrim and live to fight another day. We drew up a roster for guard duty, lay down on the floor of the hut and tried to get some much-needed rest.

At about 2 p.m. we were wakened by the man on watch, who had heard a vehicle approaching. By the time we scrambled into our clothes, pulled on our boots and grabbed our weapons, a tractor had arrived at the hut. By then McCarry and Nolan had taken up position where they could view it without being observed. Instructing us to maintain absolute silence, they watched as the driver climbed down and approached the door of the hut. He tried opening it and then began knocking. Getting no response, he peered through the window and could see the fire in the grate. He then tried the back, and returned to try the front door again. Obviously perplexed by the fact there was a fire and the door was bolted from the inside, he walked slowly back to his tractor and, after a long look back at the hut, slowly drove off.

Why, one might ask, didn't we let him in, tie him up and hold him for a day or even a few hours? McCarry, acting on pure instinct, assumed that the visitor was a forestry worker, who, seeing the smoke, decided to investigate. In this area the man was bound to be a unionist, living somewhere nearby, and he most probably told his wife or a neighbour he was going up the mountain to investigate. If he hadn't returned home shortly, given the appalling weather, his people would have called the RUC or the Forestry Department.

That visit changed everything for us. It was still two-and-a-half hours to dusk and there was about a quarter of a mile of open ground between the woods and us. It had stopped snowing and, with clear skies and a full moon, there would be no real darkness that night. Then we heard on the radio that, having fine-combed the Torr Head area for us, the combined RUC, B Special and British Army search effort had been extended to create a 'ring of steel' around north Antrim. We decided that, given the Torr Head area had already been searched and it was the area McCarry knew best, our only hope for survival was to return there. Furthermore, McCarry knew of a cave known to only a small number of people where we would be absolutely safe. His father, who used it when on the run in the 1920s, had shown it to him.

So, despite the lack of any sleep to speak of, the hope that we might not only survive but be able to carry out an operation instilled new life into us. We packed our gear, removed all traces of our presence from the hut and doused the fire. With haversacks on our backs and our weapons slung across our shoulders using twine from the hut in some cases so that we could keep our hands in our pockets, we formed up in front of the hut for one last check to see that we had packed everything. Nolan and McCarry told us we would have to complete the long march back to Torr Head by daybreak next morning. No one would be allowed to slow us down. It would be a fourteen-hour trek through the snow, carrying weapons, haversacks and, in my case, a heavy radio.

We set off in the now accustomed order, single file, with McCarry and Nolan at the point (front), myself and Phil taking up the rear, and the remainder in the middle. In an effort to disguise the number of people who left the hut, we stepped into each other's footprints in the almost foot-deep snow before heading into the woods. We kept climbing the mountain long after we'd left the woods behind and stuck to the high ground throughout that long march. Being on the high ground meant we were exposed to that bitingly cold north wind, which blew so strong that we often had to lean far forward to remain upright. Even breathing became difficult and we had to take frequent breaks, hunker down, turn our backs to the wind and catch our breath.

We felt naked in the moonlight, although we were too high to be observed. We felt particularly exposed when, traversing the high shoulder of a glen, we'd see a car with headlights blazing far below being stopped by a waving red lamp, and after a minute or so the driver being allowed to resume his journey. The men on the roadblock would resume their vigil, lightless, motionless and soundless, like vital components in a web waiting for the unsuspecting flies. I couldn't help thinking how strange it was to know that barely half a mile below us were our hunters, and it was stranger still on those occasions when, with the wind gusting towards us, we could actually hear their voices. Fortunately, this was an era before night sights and sophisticated sound detection.

We had to make some road crossings at a safe distance from any junctions. There was virtually no cover, even on the lower slopes of the Glens, with the moonlight made brighter still by the snow on the ground as we made our descent and climbed up again to the high ground on the other side. We tried to walk in each other's footprints, with the last man brushing over the tracks with a furze branch.

About 6.30 a.m., an hour before full light and fourteen hours after we left the hut on Orra More, Nolan and McCarry halted us for a final rest by some clamps of turf on Torr Head. We then began the hazardous descent of almost perpendicular cliffs – or so they seemed – to our final destination. The trek down the cliffs to the rocks above the high-tide mark was treacherous, but what matter when it was going to mean the difference between capture and freedom! McCarry, demonstrating once again his incredible guiding skill, brought us safely down the cliffs along the rocky base and, after only a couple of tries in the predawn darkness, found the narrow fissure that was the entrance to the cave.

It was about twenty feet high and ten feet wide, cold and austere but safe. It had to be because there was only one way out! The permanent residents – pigeons – stayed away for the few days we were there. Once inside the cave McCarry, tireless as ever, described for us our geographical position. The entrance faced Rathlin Island, three miles distant. A British navy cutter was on permanent patrol between that section of the north Antrim coast, Rathlin, and the Mull of Kintyre in Scotland, which was only twelve miles away. They were watching mainly for smugglers. We would have to be extremely careful when leaving the cave to relieve ourselves. Though in view of our diet over the previous four days we now had very little in the way of bodily waste to deposit anywhere.

He then gave us the best news of all. We had a few sound supporters within an hour's walk. He and Nolan would call to one of them as soon as it got dark. With that, everyone set about finding a suitable place to sleep. As the floor was rather crowded, Phil Donaghue and myself opted to make our beds on a rocky shelf about seven feet above the floor and some six feet wide.

McCarry and Nolan left at dusk and arrived back some hours later with food, a bucket of water, a Primus stove for boiling water, some tea, cigarettes and candles. They confirmed what we had garnered from radio reports, that the RUC and B Specials had shifted their search to adjoining areas, but there were still permanent roadblocks and a 3,000-man 'ring of steel' around north Antrim to snare the rest of the Torr Head column.

Clearly we could expect further raids on supporters' homes, so we would have to content ourselves with life as cave dwellers for the time being. None of us were surprised, in view of our experiences since our arrival four days previously, which seemed more like four months. At the same time the proximity of a friendly house, the prospect of being able to call there for a dinner, or even a wash, gave us a lift. The smokers too were elated with the prospect of getting their first cigarettes in almost four days.

We spent the next twenty-four hours resting until it was time to make the hour's trek to a friendly house for dinner. On reaching it, we took the precaution of dousing our boots in basins of Jeyes Fluid in case a search party with bloodhounds arrived. Once inside the house there were brief handshakes all round and within minutes we were seated around the huge farmhouse table gobbling down an appetising dinner. For a while, which was all too short, we could relax while our host kept watch for the approach of raiders or a chance visitor.

Immediately after we had finished eating and been given packs of food to keep us going over the next day or so, as well as some more cigarettes, we made our return journey to the cave. Once more we were sprinkled with holy water and blessed as we left. As we formed up outside the house before moving out, I ruminated over what we had heard of the security situation and felt sure we had little hope of operating in the near future.

During the next few days we replenished our supplies with daily two or four-man trips to pick up food from the house that had provided the dinner and another house where a relative of McCarry lived.

Life in the cave was, of course, extremely restrictive and boring. We couldn't go out on the rocks in daylight for fear of being observed by the patrol boat or passing trawlers. It was also debilitating and brutally cold. There was no shortage of volunteers for the daily food trips, despite the hazardous trek along the rocks and the cliff climb to the plateau above, which could only begin at dusk and would take anything from two to three hours. A chance of recuperating in a warm, friendly kitchen made it worthwhile.

Morale fluctuated wildly. There was no happy medium;

it was either very good or very bad. When it was bad, we weren't willing to talk about it, or its causes. When it was good, we were euphoric and delusional. Some of us, on the strength of apparently spectacular IRA successes elsewhere, and wishing we'd had the good luck to be a part of those columns, reckoned we would probably succeed in 'freeing the North' in about three months. Some even thought that three months was a pessimistic estimate. These euphoric episodes were similar to the illusions of oases that appear to water-starved wanderers in the desert. But they were prompted by blind faith in HQ and an unshakeable belief that we would succeed because our cause was righteous. The only real question was when.

At the same time, we remained secretly angry at whoever was responsible for our situation. But we didn't know who exactly to blame and, even if we had, it would have served no useful purpose discussing it, only leading to further demoralisation. Adding to our frustration was the news each day of another spectacular attack by the border columns.

On or about the fifth day in the cave, Nolan called us together for a formal discussion of our situation. There were no really safe billets available, or, therefore, any real prospect of being able to operate, or even survive, until a back-up organisation could be created. Alternatively, we could return to Dublin and request reassignment. He spoke in his usual friendly way, encouraging us to give our opinions. He concluded by saying that those who chose to operate elsewhere would be welcome to come back to north Antrim whenever the area was reorganised. A consensus soon emerged in favour of reassignment.

Nolan and McCarry immediately set about organising transport. On the very next day McCarry, who had excellent contacts in the smuggling fraternity, had organised transport to take myself, Phil and some others to a safe house near Crossmaglen, Co. Armagh, a couple of miles from the border. I believe it was the home of a horse-breeder and his wife. They cooked us a feed and generally made us welcome for the couple of hours we spent there. We even had the luxury of having a thorough wash in a bathroom. Then transport was organised over the border by way of smugglers' routes into Co. Louth. That should have been a great relief, but we were too disappointed and angry that we had not been able to operate in north Antrim.

***

We reached Dublin a couple of hours later, at about 9 p.m. It was two days before Christmas and O'Connell Street was decked out in Christmas lights and decorations. It felt like another planet, having lived in a cave until ten or so hours previously. Before we separated – Phil to get a bus home to Ballyfermot, me to get a bus to East Wall – we arranged to meet a couple of days later at HQ, which was in the *United Irishman* office in Gardiner Row.

Neither I nor the rest of my family were given much to overt acts of affection, but, on this occasion, with the relief that I was all in one piece, we forgot our inhibitions and actually hugged each other. I have to admit that I was glad to be home, particularly at Christmas, but also because I wanted to be able to say a proper goodbye when I left again in a few days. Next time I might not be so lucky and there were things I wanted to say to my parents: a testament, if you like. That was the last time I saw my family until my arrest.

While I was part of an IRA column in the North, my mother had told Palgrave Murphy's that I was sick, and so Palgrave's had been sending my wages to our house. Fearing that she or I would be accused of dishonesty, she felt that I should return to work for a few days and then resign. I felt as she did and I was anxious to preserve the honour and integrity of the IRA. Anyway, in the six years I'd worked for Palgrave's, for slave wages, I'd never missed a day. So I agreed to return to work briefly and then resign. By the time I left Palgrave's at the end of December 1956, I was three months short of twenty-one and my wage was £3 5s 0d, about as bad as could be had at that time in Dublin.

Over the next few days, I made contact with HQ, reported what had happened in north Antrim and requested a transfer to another area and another column. The report was accepted without question, but no apologies or explanations were offered, nor did I seek any. I was told I would be assigned to a column in a matter of days and to report for further orders.

In fact my first reassignment was as part of a guard of honour for Seán Sabhat, who was killed in the Brookeborough raid on New Year's Day 1957, as his remains passed through Dublin en route to his native Limerick for burial. I had taken extreme precautions for two years to remain a secret member of the IRA and this assignment meant it would end, seriously reducing my effectiveness. But I reasoned that HQ knew what it was doing. Besides, I was glad to be asked, proud in fact.

Up until the Brookeborough raid the IRA had held the initiative, enjoying some successes – even the failures had been spectacular. They evoked the sympathy of the people and within the IRA there was a kind of euphoria and sense that we were winning. However, with the deaths of Sabhat and Fergal O'Hanlon, who was killed in the same raid, the sense of invincibility among volunteers came to a screeching halt. But, for the moment, it served to harden the resolve of most of us to remain on active service. How could we abandon the campaign and the cause our comrades had died for? They had kept faith and so must we.

Brookeborough was, of course, a debacle, militarily speaking. Both mines placed against the barracks in the Co. Fermanagh village failed to go off and the lorry from which most of the fire was directed was too close to the barracks for volunteers to aim at the upper-floor windows, whereas the RUC could fire directly into the back of the vehicle below. Three weeks into the campaign someone, whether the column OC or HQ, should have anticipated the need to vary tactics when making repeated attacks on RUC or British Army installations, where security had been tightened up.

On or about 10 January 1957, Phil Donaghue and myself were assigned to the column operating along the Tyrone–Donegal border, along with Bertie Murphy, another Dubliner whom I had trained with before the campaign. We were picked up the next day and I earnestly hoped it would provide an early opportunity for action. Our journey to the column's camp was made in three stages and took about seven days. Our first stop-over billet was Master McGowan's home in Kinlough, Co. Leitrim. (He was called 'master' because he was a teacher.) It was a joy to walk into that warm, welcoming and supportive house. The master, his wife and their adult children welcomed us, somewhat embarrassingly, like heroes. Mrs McGowan immediately set about cooking a meal for us, the first of many. The food was great and the chat was just as good. Shortly afterwards our driver departed, saying we'd be picked up the next day and taken to the column. We offered to help with the washing-up, but Mrs McGowan wouldn't hear of it, another experience that was to be repeated often over the next few years.

That first night in McGowan's was as pleasant as we could

have hoped for. With stomachs full and hunger sated, we sat around a roaring fire listening to the master's interesting and provocative views on Ireland's history, as well as his account of his own IRA activities during the War of Independence and later. We listened to some old records on the wind-up gramophone and not alone had the McGowans a gramophone, but they also had a radio. Few rural homes had either. The records we played most were 'The Hills of Donegal' and 'The Green Glens of Antrim'. The hours flew and soon the settle bed, which was in the kitchen, was opened out and drawn up in front of the still-burning fire.[6] Having experienced the warmth and comfort of a settle bed during visits to my grandparents' homes in Louth and Meath as a child, I looked forward to sleeping in it. Mrs McGowan sprinkled ashes over the fire to keep it going until morning.

We woke about 6 a.m. No one else was stirring. We folded the settle bed and placed it in position along the wall to give Mrs McGowan room to carry on with her busy daily work schedule. Having breakfasted royally, we offered, once again, to help with the washing-up. Mrs McGowan again demurred in her quiet, dignified way. The master went off to school and we adjourned to the 'room', that is the parlour, to avoid accidental discovery by neighbours making unannounced

---

6 'Settle beds' were settees that opened out into a bed and were a common household fixture of the time.

visits, which was a common occurrence in those days. We sat by the fire, chatted or browsed through the master's many books and played the wind-up gramophone.

The McGowans' house was of the old kind, with solid, eighteen-inch-thick walls, strategically situated in the lee of a hill to give maximum shelter from the prevailing winds. We couldn't have been more comfortable, yet we were keen to join the column. We spent the day in anxious expectation of our lift. When it hadn't turned up by 11 p.m. we went to bed, disappointed but convinced it would arrive the next day.

Eventually, at dusk on the fourth day, we were picked up. The driver did not explain the delay but told us we had to leave within minutes. We interpreted the urgency as meaning that we were joining the column that night, perhaps to participate in a job. We thanked our hosts for their hospitality and, as we headed out the door, Mrs McGowan gave each of us a religious medal, sprinkled us with holy water and said, 'Ye're welcome any time. God bless ye.'

We were an hour on the road when our driver, in response to a question about what time we would reach the column, said, 'Eh, you won't be going that far tonight. We're just going as far as Convoy, and ye'll be staying there … and then tomorrow ye'll be picked up and taken to where the column is.' We were deposited at the home of Frank Morris in Donegal, who would bring us on to our billets. Our driver departed with the promise that we'd join the column the next day.

Frank Morris was a very disillusioned man, with little faith in HQ. It didn't do much for our morale to hear Frank, a veteran of the 1940s campaign, recount how he'd been tortured by the RUC and sentenced to a flogging with the cat o'nine tails, every stroke of which was meted out. He then spent eight years in Crumlin Road Jail, Belfast, because of a betrayal by an informer in HQ. I had never heard, or read, anything about floggings, torture, or an HQ informer. Frank didn't mention the name of this informer or the details of his activities. It was six months later that Jack McCabe, another victim of informers, filled in this gap in my education.

Frank, however, had every faith in the ordinary volunteer. And he proved it. He did everything that was asked of him, and more. He fed us, provided us with cigarettes and other treats, and had us billeted in safe houses that night and for several nights after because our driver's promise that we would join the column next day failed to materialise.

Phil and myself were billeted in the home of a widow and her daughter. As their small house was beside the road and both women were away most of the day, we had to confine ourselves to the bedroom for almost the entire three days and nights we spent there. Each morning, before they left, the daughter would bring us breakfast and a basin of water to wash ourselves. And, thankfully, there was a chamber pot kept under the bed for 'minor calls of nature'. The 'major' calls were dealt with outside and after dark. 'We're going out to the fields at the back for a bit of a walk', we'd say, this being an age when you couldn't mention any bodily function in front of women.

Both women were extremely nervous or embarrassed, or perhaps both, by our presence, but they cared for us as if we were their own. And perhaps our impatience and frustration began to show, having spent over a week cooped up in billets without much exercise. We were eventually picked up by an elderly man, Paddy McCallig, in his Ford Anglia. The two-hour drive to our destination was made in the early after-noon, so I saw for the first time the lovely hills of Donegal and the majestic Barnesmore Gap. Paddy, a veteran of the War of Independence and an avid student of history, regaled us with stories and anecdotes about the history of the places we passed through. And I saw for the first and last time the Londonderry to Lough Swilly bus-train heading north on its narrow-gauge track along the southern slopes of the gap.[7]

Finally, Paddy drove us through an impressive but dilapi-dated gateway and down an overgrown lane to a large, two-storey house, which was the column's base camp. A bonus of arriving safely was the discovery that I knew the OC, who was Bearnárd Ó Riain, another Dubliner. I also knew most of the

---

7   Rolling stock was replaced on the Londonderry to Lough Swilly line with buses, which were mounted on the rails. This cheap and efficient transport system was to fall victim to the cost-cutting policies of Todd Andrews, chairman of CIÉ, and a War of Independence veteran.

column, who were all in high spirits. The rest of that night was spent swapping stories about our experiences in the campaign so far. At some point, having asked what supporter was so generous as to give us this big house to billet in, I discovered that the owner was a retired British Army officer, a Colonel Snodgrass, who didn't know that we had 'commandeered' it. He now lived a few miles away and paid only occasional visits. He wasn't due to call for another few weeks. I was brought on a tour and was amazed to find every room was fully furnished. There were photographs and pictures on the walls, and the colonel's service medals and uniforms were stored in what I took to be his bedroom.

After sandwiches and pints of tea, everyone went to bed. There was an air of relaxed abandon in this billet. There was no instruction about what time we should rise the next morning and no word about operations. The next few days were similarly spent in idleness. Then, on about the fourth night, the OC called us together to tell us we would be going to the border that night – to operate, we assumed.

Sometime after dark we formed up in the spacious kitchen. We were each given a weapon and ammunition; some of us were also given a couple of primed grenades. These were made by our own engineers and often proved a greater danger to us than the enemy, but still we packed them in our pockets. We moved outside to board our transport, either a Ford Anglia or Prefect of the old box type with a drop-down boot. There were six of us, plus a passenger, Piaras Ó Dúghaill (later Fr Ó Dúghaill), who was on his way to south Derry or Tyrone. We piled into the Ford, weapons, ammunition, grenades and all, with two sitting on the dropped-down leaf of the boot.

We were in a reasonably light-hearted mood, even though we hadn't a clue where we were going or what we were heading into. Some of us, out of a sense of bravado perhaps, were using that old and trusted four-letter word a bit too frequently. Our passenger, however, put a damper on our bravado with, 'I don't want to hear any more of that bad language – that's the language of the Tommy.'

We reached wherever it was we were going and dropped off our passenger. Then, instead of heading on for an operation, as we were led to believe, we discovered that we were heading back to Colonel Snodgrass's house and a situation with which Phil and I were growing increasingly disillusioned. There was virtually no discipline, and no apparent purpose to our existence, which may have been due partly to the OC's inability to impose discipline and partly to the failure of the local organisation to supply him with operational intelligence. This did not help either the OC's morale or his sense of purpose.

Nevertheless, having lain around aimlessly for two weeks with no prospect of operations and no apparent intention on the part of the OC to push harder for them, Phil and myself decided to tell him of our dissatisfaction and request a transfer to an active column. He apologised for the absence of operations, which, he said, was due to a lack of reliable intelligence and back-up. He understood how we felt and agreed to our request for a transfer. However, as he didn't know how to go about contacting the other columns, he felt we should return to Dublin and get HQ to arrange our transfer. He understood, of course, that we would have to tell HQ our reasons for requesting a transfer, with its implied criticism of his leadership.

Two days later a car arrived at the house to take Phil and myself on the first leg of our journey to Dublin. However, moments before we were due to leave, the look-out reported that someone was approaching the house on horseback. The OC immediately ordered the doors closed and locked. All of us were to remain in the house, out of view and maintain silence. The horseman was, of course, Snodgrass. He rode slowly and deliberately to within six feet of the front door. He gazed at the house and grounds – including the parked car – for several moments before dismounting. Then he slowly walked to the front door, tried to open it and, failing to do so, walked back to his horse and remounted. After a final lingering look at the house, he rode back the way he had come. Undoubtedly he had been told there were 'some people' there and, just as obviously, he would assume that those people were IRA men. So the OC organised an immediate evacuation.

During the few days it took us to get back to Dublin,

Phil and I discussed our experiences and the way we felt the campaign was going. Though the campaign was only six weeks old, the IRA in the North had been virtually wiped out through widespread arrests. There was now no possibility of large columns operating deep within the North, or even along the border. Phil and I agreed to propose to HQ that teams of between two and four men carry out sabotage operations on selected targets, and that we would volunteer for such service in north Antrim.

Having reported to HQ on the situation in Co. Donegal and why we wanted a transfer, we went on to explain our idea for sabotage teams and volunteered to return to north Antrim on active service. HQ accepted our report and agreed to our request to return to north Antrim, surprised that anyone would be willing to operate so far from the border. But, as we explained, we had total trust in McCarry's guiding ability and wanted to redeem the debacle of the opening night. HQ was also delighted because our activity would give the lie to British claims that this was only a 'border' campaign.

Things moved surprisingly fast, and efficiently, for a change. Within a week, HQ had contacted our partners and guides. Frank McCarry, who had come south as well after the previous operation, would be working with me in the Torr Head area, and another excellent guide, Jack, would partner Phil to the south of us. Frank and the other guide went in first, while Phil and I were collected at pick-up points in

Dublin at the appointed hour, again much to our surprise. Our transport to Belfast was a taxi. More surprising was the discovery that we were to be accompanied on the journey by an elderly priest.

In the expectation of being stopped and searched at RUC or B Special roadblocks between the border and Belfast, Phil and I carried only our boots and heavy socks in brown paper bags, stowed under the seats. At that stage in the game, our safe passage was virtually guaranteed by the presence of a priest in the front seat, especially in the light of the Catholic hierarchy's condemnation of IRA violence and the edict excommunicating members.

Phil and I settled in the rear seat for what we expected would be a straightforward three-hour drive to our transfer house in Belfast. However, when we reached the outskirts of the then village of Swords, ten miles north of Dublin, about 10.30 a.m., the priest turned to us and said he had to make a stop to visit his aunt, if that was all right by us. Of course it was, we replied. We pulled to a stop and the priest, having asked us if we needed anything, left the car and entered the doorway to his aunt's house, which was beside a bar. He emerged about fifteen minutes later, apologised for the delay and we resumed our journey north.

About twenty minutes later, as we were approaching the outskirts of Balbriggan, the priest turned about and asked us if we minded him making a stop to see another aunt. Once again, we said we didn't mind, not at all. So we stopped in Balbriggan and he entered another doorway near a bar, emerging about fifteen minutes later. This time, though, he had a paper bag in his hands, containing three or four bottles of beer, and had a bottle of beer in each of his jacket pockets.

When he had settled himself comfortably in the front seat, he told the driver to go ahead. The driver started the engine and we headed towards the border again. A few minutes later the priest turned to us and, now with somewhat slurred speech asked, 'Will ye have a bottle of beer?' We demurred, politely, as he was a priest, and because neither of us drank anyway. The priest, with a shrug of his shoulders, faced forward in his seat and proceeded to systematically down his beers, almost as if his life depended on it.

Stops to visit various aunts were made in Drogheda, Dunleer and Dundalk. But he was under strict instructions not to make any stops with us once we crossed the border. The driver of the taxi, who was from the North, never uttered a word throughout the entire journey. He knew exactly what routes to take and he got us to our destination, a very large house in the northern suburbs of Belfast, without incident.

It was about fifty feet in off the road and surrounded by tall hedges, which made for a great deal of privacy. The exterior of the house and the grounds were in such immaculate condition that I thought the driver had made a mistake. But this was indeed our stop-over before we headed to north Antrim. The driver let us out and then drove off with the priest. The door was opened to us by the woman of the house, Mary Brown.[8] Her enthusiastic welcome immediately put us at ease. It was about 3 p.m. Her ageing but very active father and her husband were at home, but the latter worked the night shift in a bakery and was asleep. Three of her children were at school, and the eldest, Mary, who was eighteen, was at work.

She sat us down before a roaring fire in a beautiful living room and offered us a drink and cigarettes, which we declined. Having chatted for a few minutes she excused herself to 'make a cup of tea', which turned out to be a sumptuous dinner that we consumed ravenously, but with a bit more decorum than was our custom. Soon afterwards, the children arrived home and were brought in to meet us. They, having already been told who we were, were understandably deferential, almost awed, but still friendly. They'd also been warned not to say a word to anyone about 'the visitors'. And I know they didn't, because I stayed there off and on throughout 1957 and the house was never raided.

At 5.30 p.m. Mary Óg arrived home from work. She was a beautiful but shy girl. I was equally shy and we had little to say to each other, but it was love at first sight, on both sides, though it was a love that was not expressed at first, other than through mutually admiring glances. Anyway, I was kind of

8   This family's names have been altered to protect their identity.

going with a girl in Dublin and I couldn't bring myself to 'betray' her. However, I was so convinced that Mary Óg and I had fallen in love, or would shortly, that I determined to break off with my current girlfriend as soon as I got back to Dublin, assuming I ever made it back.

During those first two days I spent in her home there was no attempt to give physical expression to my love, by a kiss or otherwise. And there was an unwritten rule that prohibited volunteers from becoming involved with anyone in a house where we stayed. And while I was at times consumed by desire, at twenty years of age I'd never had a sexual relationship. This was due in large part to my Catholic upbringing, a fear of dying in sin and the belief that 'patriots' didn't degrade or sully Irish womanhood, or the cause, by having sex outside marriage. There was, of course, the added inhibition of making a girl pregnant. I'd heard of 'French letters', but only 'dirty sailors and prostitutes in pagan England' used them, so I never considered procuring them, even if I knew where they could be got.[9] The 'pill' hadn't been invented, nor had the Catholic Church produced its 'rhythm method'.[10] Mary would make her feelings known to me later on, during a walk on Cave Hill, and her mother also gave us her blessing, but I was committed

---

9   'French letter' was a colloquial term for a condom.

10   A traditional method of birth control promoted by the Catholic Church, based on a woman's menstrual cycle and avoiding sex on dates when she is most likely to conceive.

to the campaign and, besides, I felt that Mary Óg was far too good for me. I think she later married a teacher.

Meanwhile, two days into that initial stay at the Browns' house, our transport to north Antrim appeared, but Phil and I had already become attached to this wonderful family. Just before we left, Mrs Brown gave me a prayer book and a silver whiskey flask, and Phil received medals and a set of rosary beads. She walked us to the door, embraced us and, with tears in her eyes, bade us goodbye. She told us we were welcome to stay any time.

I arrived in a safe house in the Torr Head area that night. Phil was dropped off safely in his operational area and linked up with his guide and operating partner, Jack. The next morning Frank and I discussed potential targets. Given that there were only two of us, we were restricted to the sabotage of installations rather than anti-personnel attacks. We settled on an attempt on one of the giant wooden pylons on which RAF radar equipment was mounted at the highest point of the Torr Head plateau, where they were spaced at intervals of a quarter of a mile and within a one-mile radius of the guardhouse to the RAF radar installation.

A night or two later we made the first of a couple of re-connaissance trips to the pylon that was best positioned from the point of view of a successful attack and withdrawal. We established the thickness of the seven-foot chain-link fence, the strength of each of the four twelve-inch square stanchions, the position of the trip-wire that activated the warning flares and the approximate frequency of the two-to-four-man jeep patrols. About every half an hour the jeep drove over the rough road to allow the patrol to check the pylons. The jeep would pause for a few seconds at each pylon to establish all was well and the patrol would return to base in about ten minutes.

We assembled our gear: two short arms and ammunition, a couple of pounds of the high explosive gelignite, some detonators and fuse, insulating tape, matches, and pliers for cutting the chain-link fence. It was still in the depths of winter when we set out for Torr Head. The time was about 8 p.m., which allowed for the hour's march and another hour to check that the intervals between the patrols had not changed, plus the ten to fifteen minutes it would take to cut through the fence, drill the stanchions and place the charges. This should leave us eight to ten hours to reach our safe billet ten miles away before daylight.

When we set out that night, things never looked better for carrying out a job. We had excellent intelligence, all the gear we needed, the night was dark, we were fit and we had a reasonably safe billet for after the job. With Frank leading, we made our way towards the pylons, whose silhouettes we could see despite the darkness. When we were a quarter of a mile away, we heard the unmistakable sound of the jeep setting out on its patrol. We hunkered down and watched its headlights blazing as the patrol completed its tour and returned to base.

We resumed our march at a faster pace, until we were about a hundred yards from the pylon. We lay down in the somewhat sparse cover to await the next patrol. Because the pylon and the road leading to it were at a higher elevation, we were safely below the jeep's headlights and line of vision. The pylon was easily accessible on three sides and, as soon as the next patrol departed, we ran to the pylon, cut a hole in the fence, stepped carefully over the trip-wire, unslung our haversacks and began to work fast.

Frank began boring through the first stanchion with his brace and bit. The process took longer than we had anticipated. We were becoming a little apprehensive and, as we were in the process of boring through the last stanchion, Frank touched the trip-wire. Immediately the warning flare burst into life. We stood in stunned silence for several seconds; then, after a rapid whispered exchange, we decided to finish the job. As soon as we had the fuses lit, we grabbed our haversacks, scrambled through the hole in the fence and ran like the hammers of hell. I began running in the direction I thought Frank had taken, but in fact I was heading for the cliff and Frank had to shout a warning.

Even as we were going through the fence, we saw the headlights of the jeep heading for our pylon. We continued running southwards as fast as we could and about a minute later we heard the sound of the charges exploding. The flare having burned out, we slowed to a fast walk. Behind us the jeep could be heard heading towards the pylon and, though they were not pointed in our direction, we were conscious of its headlights penetrating the dark. In another minute we lay down to catch our breath and seconds later the patrol members switched off the jeep's lights and began firing sporadically. Then they began sending up flares, turning night into day. Although we were probably out of range of their sub-machine guns, we were still well within range of the flares. Even running between the flares, we covered the first mile in record time. Once out of range of both the firing and the flares, we lay down, exhausted, for perhaps five minutes, then marched steadily for the next eight hours, until we reached our safe billet shortly before daybreak.

Our 'hosts' were members of a prosperous Catholic family and had no idea that we would be seeking refuge in their house. We approached it from the rear. Frank lifted the latch of the back door (no doors were locked in those days) and silently pushed it open. We entered on tiptoe and made our way silently to the kitchen. We pulled a couple of chairs up to the stove and sat down to wait until the occupants got up, when, hopefully, we would be invited to stay for a day or so.

We promptly fell asleep and didn't waken until the woman of the house came down to the kitchen. She was surprised, amazed really, to find us sitting there. Frank greeted her with a laugh and an apology for taking the liberty of entering the house while they were asleep. He asked if it would be all right for us to stay until nightfall. Though the residents were not supportive of the IRA, they wouldn't refuse us shelter. They made us breakfast, and by 10 a.m. we were sleeping soundly in freshly made beds. We slept right through until we were wakened at dark about 6 p.m., as we'd requested. After another good feed, during which the conversation was carefully restricted to safe subjects, such as how the lambing was and the weather, we said our goodbyes and headed into the friendly darkness for another billet some five or six hours' walk away.

We always travelled light. Each of us packed a spare pair of socks, underwear, a shirt and a groundsheet, and we had one revolver between us with a few spare rounds of ammunition in our small British Army haversacks. The revolver was old but in good condition, though we wished the ammunition was of a more recent vintage. We had no holsters, so the weapon was usually stowed inside the flap of the haversack when we were traversing the Glens.

The weather was intensely cold that February and March, but mainly dry. We'd have worked up such a sweat half an hour into a march that we'd stop to take off our heavy woollen pullovers. Either then, or at some point every day, I'd say a silent prayer. On Sundays, wherever we happened to be, Frank and I would kneel, or hunker down, depending on conditions, to recite a rosary – sometimes fast, sometimes slowly – but always in whispers, despite the utter remoteness of our position. Saying the rosary was a comfort. But it also brought on feelings of loneliness and isolation, particularly on clear nights when we could see far below us the lights of a house, the occupants in our minds' eye sitting around a fire, chatting or listening to the radio, safe and secure, warm and comfortable. There were, after all, only the two of us, and I would become disconcertingly aware of the virtual impossibility of what we were attempting: to free Ireland with so few of us, Frank and myself in the northern sector, Phil and Jack somewhere to our south and west, and only two or three local men in the entire area willing to operate with us.

However, I'd indulge in these depressing thoughts for only a few seconds before reminding myself that I'd volunteered in the full knowledge that this was the situation. Obviously I would have preferred a 1916 or War of Independence-type situation, with dozens of comrades beside us. But I wondered if we were any worse off than the men who rose in 1848 or 1867? Hardly, though Michael Doheny's trek through Munster to Cobh, described in *The Felon's Track*, seemed much more romantic.

When we reached our next billet we heard the depressing news that our attempt to fell the pylon had failed. It had, however, keeled over to one side, and I think it had to be dismantled because of our work. As far as I know, the attempt was popular with the Catholic and republican people of north Antrim, as was the fact that those who carried it out got clean away.

Over the next few days, Frank and I discussed what we would do next. There wasn't a wide choice, with no reliable intelligence organisation and only the two of us. We came down on the side of carrying out another job on Torr Head. We considered another attempt on the pylons but rejected it as too risky, because we couldn't get fresh intelligence on what new security measures had been put in place. That left us with only one possible target, the pumping station that supplied water to the RAF barracks. It was not as spectacular as a pylon, but was far riskier as it was no more than 150 yards from the guardhouse. The tank and pumping machinery were sunk into the ground, surrounded by the same protective fencing as the pylons, including the trip-wire. The pumping station was checked every half hour and completely exposed.

We gathered whatever gelignite was available, about forty pounds, and reconnoitred the area before settling on a night to do the job. We used a shed about 200 yards from our billet and about a mile from our target to make up the mine and use as our jumping-off point. We arrived just before dawn on the day of the job and remained there until it was time to set out. We packed the forty pounds of gelignite into a milk churn, the best 'mine case' available and primed it with detonators and fuses. Though priming the bomb before we'd reach the target was somewhat risky, we had no option, given its exposed position.

We remained in the shed until dark, and after one last

check on the mine, we walked the mile to the target, each of us taking a handle of the churn, which now weighed about sixty pounds. The going was extremely slow. We hadn't anticipated the weight and the awkwardness of the bomb, and had to stop every fifty yards or so to rest and change sides. More disconcerting was the emergence of a full moon so bright it cast shadows, or as Frank put it, 'You could pick pins off the ground.' The clouds cleared and the Aurora Borealis made an appearance. It was my first and only sighting of the Northern Lights. And with not even the barest wind, there was a weird and worrisome silence; the kind of still night when a cough could be heard a hundred yards away.

We stopped to discuss whether we should wait for a dark night but decided to trust to our luck and continue. It seemed brighter than ever by the time we reached the high, coverless plateau, where what appeared to be a couple of dozen search-lights were shining skywards. For the last quarter of a mile we scurried forward, twenty yards at a time, keeping the churn only inches off the ground. A hundred yards from the tar-get we heard the sound of laughter coming from the guard-house. While we were making the next twenty-yard dash the bottom of the churn struck a protruding stone with a clang. We immediately dropped to the ground, lowering the silver-coloured churn onto its side. We waited, barely breathing. It seemed an eternity in that awful revealing moonlight, but was perhaps five to ten minutes. Long enough for the sentries to have sent a patrol down to the pumping station to investigate if they had heard us.

We were lying face down, on either side of the churn, our bodies pressed as close to the ground as possible, our faces about six inches from each other and we exchanged a thought: what if they had heard and were just waiting for us to make our move? Will we, or won't we? The rest was an instinctive understanding. Up we got. We stood the churn silently upright, grasped a handle each and moved forward in fifteen to twenty-yard stretches until at last we reached the fencing. With Frank cutting a link at a time, and me holding each side of the cut to prevent the very taut wire from flying back with a loud twang, we made a hole large enough for us and the churn to squeeze through. We moved fast to the man-hole cover, lifted it off as quietly as we could, still listening to the banter and laughter of the guards, then lowered the churn slowly into the tank. Frank held it still while I struck a match, lit a cigarette and ignited both of the two-minute fuses, which we fervently hoped would burn under water, as they were supposed to.

The instant we were sure the fuses were burning we let go of the churn, which sank with a soft thud. We scurried back to the hole in the fence, climbed through and ran for our lives. We ran until we heard the explosion. We threw ourselves full length on the ground to await the first flare, which came about half a minute later and was immediately followed by the sound of gunfire. An already bright night was transformed almost into daylight for the half minute it took for the flare to burn out. As soon as it did, we jumped to our feet and ran for the few seconds until we heard the 'pop' of the next flare leaving the gun, when we hit the ground again. And so on for about a mile, ten minutes or so until we reached the cover of lower ground. There we took a short rest, then set out at a fast pace until we crossed the first road and reached the high slopes of the glen. There we took a good long rest before resuming our ten-hour march to what we hoped would be a safe billet.

We spent the next day in that billet, which was an empty house. Then, having learned which homes had been raided in the adjoining glen, we headed there and spent the next few days safe and secure. The following Sunday we returned to the Torr Head area to see what else we might be able to do. We set out in high spirits, at nightfall as usual. As was now customary, we stopped half an hour or so later to take off our pullovers and put them into our haversacks. We hunkered down on the sheep track for a few minutes' rest before continuing our journey over the relatively easy going of the well-worn sheep and shepherds' path on the high shoulder of the glen.

With Frank leading, a few feet in front of me, we resumed our silent trek. We'd only gone a further half mile when we simultaneously saw, about a hundred yards to our left, what appeared to be the light of a torch move towards us. There wasn't even a whisper of wind that night and we hunkered down dumbfounded under the cover of a small clump of furze. Frank, with his back to me, indicated with his hand for me to open his haversack and take out the revolver. While I silently slid the restraining straps through the buckles, Frank was peering through the bushes and watching the progress of the light as it came towards us. We both had the same thought: no shepherd would need a torch on a night like this.

I reached in for the revolver, which should have been lying handy just under the flap of the haversack. It wasn't there. I felt further down, until I reached the bottom of the haversack and realised we must have forgotten to put it back when we stopped to take off our pullovers half a mile back. I tipped Frank on the shoulder. He turned his face to me and I indicated with my hands that the revolver wasn't in the haversack. He stared at me for a few disbelieving seconds until I convinced him, wordlessly, that the revolver wasn't in his haversack.

At that point, we resumed our fascinated observation of the light beam as it made its way towards us. Then, when the light was about twenty yards away it went out. We remained as we were, silent and unmoving. But, long and hard as we looked, there was no one to be seen and no sound to be heard. Moreover, the sheep that were lying down in the path of the light, and which should have been disturbed by it, lay unmoving and unperturbed.

We rose just enough to peek over the top of the furze bushes and see what the holder of the light was up to. But there were only the sheep and lambs lying motionless and contented. Having satisfied ourselves that there was no one there, we back-tracked to the place where we took off our pullovers and the revolver was lying just as we'd left it. We stowed it in one of our haversacks and were just about to resume our journey when it occurred to us, simultaneously, that this was a Sunday and that we'd said no prayer. We also speculated about the mysterious light we'd seen and, I think, we both took it as some kind of warning that we had left the revolver on the path. Neither of us said as much, but we recited a fervent rosary before continuing on our way to the next billet.

We had now been operating in the area for about six weeks. It was approaching the middle of March and the nights were getting noticeably shorter. We were still trying to get intelligence on possible targets a few days later when we received word to return to Dublin. I think HQ felt we were pushing our luck. Phil and Jack received the same instruction. So, towards the end of March 1957, we travelled to Dublin via Belfast. I spent a very pleasant couple of days in the Browns' home, where I became more convinced than ever that it was indeed a case of love at first sight with Mary Óg.

I had just turned twenty-one and was at the peak of physical fitness and optimism.

A day or so after I reached Dublin I met with HQ, who were pleased with our performance but indicated that it would be some months before we'd be going back to the North.

4

REGROUPING AND RETURN TO THE NORTH, 1957–58

I spent the next few months training recruits in the Dublin Mountains at weekends and helping the Dublin 'engineer' manufacture time-bombs. This man, George, loved his work and was a perfectionist to boot. He was a hard but fair taskmaster.

During this period, about thirty IRA men were arrested at a camp in Glencree, including Seán Garland – who was attached to GHQ at the time and still recovering from the injuries he suffered when he took part in the Brookeborough raid – and other prominent and experienced fighters, to their eternal embarrassment. They were sentenced to from three to six months' imprisonment in Mountjoy. When internment was introduced, on Friday 5 July 1957, they were transferred to the Curragh after their sentences ended and were held there for up to another eighteen months.

I had been training recruits at Ballinascorney, in the foothills of the Dublin Mountains the week internment was introduced and was unaware of what had happened. When I returned to the city at 7 p.m. on the Saturday it was still bright and I decided to call to HQ in Gardiner Row. Just as I reached the corner of Parnell Square and Gardiner Row a member of Cumann na mBan, Gwen Jones (Gwen and I had 'done a line' for a few months), stopped me and said the Special Branch were in the *UI* office and were holding anyone who went in. I thanked her, turned around and headed for a safe house that night. It was only the next day that I heard that a couple of hundred members and supporters, including almost the entire Ard Chomhairle of Sinn Féin, had been arrested and interned in the Curragh.

A few days later I was staying in Jack and Máire McCabe's home in Finglas. Despite Jack's record of IRA involvement in the 1940s, this was a safe billet.[1] He had spent eight hard years in English jails for his part in the 1939–40 IRA bombing campaign. I asked Jack if he could put me in contact with HQ, or what was left of it. Both Seán Cronin (now chief of staff) and Charlie Murphy (adjutant-general), having become suspicious of the inordinate volume of Special Branch activity, had taken the precaution of going on the run and therefore evaded the round-up. The following day Jack drove me to

---

1   The Special Branch and the RUC in the North would have had records of suspected IRA activists, which would include men imprisoned in the 1940s both in Ireland and in England. Jack McCabe was killed on 30 December 1971 making explosives in his garage for the Provisional IRA.

Tadhg Lynch's house in the then rural area of Santry, where he thought we'd be able to make contact with either Murphy or Cronin. They were both there and were amazed to see us arriving at their super-safe billet.

Some days later I met them again and was asked if I was prepared to go back to north Antrim to operate, preferably with the aim of conducting an ambush of the RAF garrison at Torr Head. I said I was, but only if Frank McCarry, now working as a bus driver in Dublin, was prepared to go with me. For some strange reason I assumed from the beginning of the conversation that their plan envisaged only myself and Frank going in to carry out the ambush. Perhaps there was no one else available, or no one else prepared to go into north Antrim. By now, July 1957, some ninety-five per cent of volunteers who had battle experience since the start of the campaign were in jail, as was ninety-nine per cent of our northern support organisation.

Frank and I, who hadn't seen each other for almost three months, were brought together to discuss the proposed operation. If it came off it would contradict Free State, unionist and British propaganda that ours was merely a border campaign, being mounted from the South with no support in the North (although this was, of course, fairly true). We agreed to try it and so a week later we were on our way back to Torr Head via Belfast. Although there were just the two of us, we felt reasonably confident that we could do this on our own.

Ambushing an RAF armoured jeep patrol was far riskier than anything we'd attempted previously, but we were keen to get it done as soon as possible, while making thorough preparations.

The weather was beautiful, the kind of balmy days that made it difficult to contemplate death or to accept being locked in our billets for the week or so it took us to gather intelligence for the job and assemble the gear. The latter wasn't the best but it was all that was available: one Thompson sub-machine gun, for which there was only one magazine; one revolver with one fill of ammunition; twenty pounds of gelignite; half a dozen electric detonators; two 4½-volt batteries; a hundred yards of flex (electrical cable); and a bucket that would have to do as the mine container.

The gelignite wasn't in great condition. More worrying still was the type of flex provided. I felt that the colour of the flex would make it easily visible at night and highly visible in the lights of a car, but other opinions prevailed. Anyway, it was pointed out to me, 'since the jeep will be approaching our position from the other direction, it won't have to pass over the flex'. Another negative was that there were only about five or six hours of darkness, from 10 p.m. to 3 or 4 a.m.

I spent the last two days before the job locked away in an upstairs bedroom, because the rest of the house was being painted. I read the classic Australian novel *Robbery Under Arms*, perhaps not the best choice for a relaxing read but it was all that was available.

Two weeks after we arrived in the area, we were as ready to operate as we were ever going to be. The intelligence was that the jeep patrol always took the upper road from Ballycastle to Torr Head to a regular schedule. We decided to hit it on a Sunday night. The ambush site was reasonably good. It was at a T-junction about half a mile from the Torr Head radar station. Our firing position was immediately behind the ditch on the south side of the road that formed the head of the T and directly in line with the stem road, which headed north and was the road the jeep would take immediately it reached our position (assuming it would approach from the west, and on the upper road). While our position didn't afford any cover from fire, the ground behind us sloped sharply downwards. Anyway, the five occupants of the jeep wouldn't be in any shape to fire back once we detonated the mine. Success depended on a number of factors: that the jeep would approach the T-junction on the upper road, that it would approach from the west and that there was only one vehicle.

The weather was ideal on the night. It was very dark with a steady drizzle as we left our billet for the hour's march to the site. We laid the mine in a clay bank just under a telegraph pole, which was our marker for detonation. It was about twenty yards up the road from the T. This meant that the mine was about thirty yards from our firing position. As a precaution against the flex being picked out by the headlights as the jeep approached we laid it across the road some thirty yards to our right and east of the junction. We then threaded the flex along the inside of our ditch and up to our firing position. I connected one wire to a terminal on the batteries and placed the other wire safely out of accidental touching distance of the other terminal. Then we lay, prone and silent, to await the arrival of the jeep, which was due within an hour. There was no wind. It was so quiet I could hear the drizzle in the hedges on both sides, dripping from leaf to leaf.

About half an hour into our vigil, we heard the faint but unmistakable sound of the jeep's approach. It was almost right on schedule. We immediately settled ourselves for the two or three minutes it would take it to reach our position. But a minute later, the sound of the jeep began to diminish, until we could hear it no more. We spent the next couple of minutes wondering what had happened. Our questions were answered when, to our amazement, we heard it coming from behind. 'Jesus!' said Frank, and we turned and saw the lights of the jeep. 'Jesus Christ, they've taken the lower road!' whispered Frank.

Tonight, of all nights, the patrol had chosen to take the lower route. This ran half a mile behind us and was at a slighter lower elevation. The lower road then turned north and joined our road a quarter of a mile east of our position. This meant, of course, that it would now pass over the highly visible flex. A minute or so later we saw a second jeep following the same route. This meant we were sandwiched between them and in danger of being taken prisoner.

It was impossible to carry out a successful ambush and get away. Frank immediately indicated to follow him. We rose quickly to a crouched position and ran fast and silently eastwards, to our right, inside of the hedge, which took us out of the immediate line of fire. We'd travelled only thirty feet or so, and were attempting to climb over a barbed-wire fence, when the patrol opened fire and simultaneously fired off a night flare illuminating the sky like daylight for thirty seconds or so before it fizzled out. We heard some rounds hit a corrugated iron shed beside us.

Having scrambled over the fence, we lay flat. As soon as the flare expired, we upped and ran, still inside the hedge and heading east, for another thirty feet or so, until we heard the now-familiar pop of the next flare being fired. As soon as the second flare died, we began running downhill and south until we heard the pop of the next flare leaving the gun. South was the direction we needed to go, but while this took us out of view of the first jeep, we were now exposed to detection by the second one, some 300 yards ahead of us and somewhere along the road we had to cross to gain the safety of the fields and glens beyond. We continued to hit the ground the instant we heard the pop of a flare and lie completely still until it fizzled out before leaping to our feet and heading up the hill to the road.

What was really worrying us now was whether the occupants of the second jeep were lying in ambush for us, or could see us lying on the ground when the flares lit up the area. We had no choice but to keep making our way downhill between the flares to the bottom of the field, then repeat the exercise running up the far slope to the road, the road we had to cross to get out of immediate danger along which were the occupants of the second jeep.

We decided to crawl the rest of the way, until we were within twenty or thirty yards of the road. Then we stopped to get some idea of the position of the second jeep. Having waited a long minute or two, with time running out for us, we heard the crackling of the jeep's radio some twenty yards to our right. This was one of those moments when one's sense of hearing was of paramount importance.

Now, having established the position of the cut-off jeep, and assuming that its occupants were lying in ambush close to it, we bear-crawled fast to our left for about fifty yards, a sufficient distance to put us out of sight and hearing of the occupants of the jeep. Then we crawled up to the side of the road. We waited there until the latest flare burned out, climbed over the bank and dashed quietly across the road. We crossed the bank at the other side and walked fast up the slope of the hill until we reached the safe high ground about fifteen minutes later. After a five-minute rest, we set a fast pace for the five-to-six-hour march to reach our billet before daylight.

About half an hour before dawn, and while we were on

the upper slopes of a glen, Frank called a halt. We hunkered down for a few seconds. He pointed to a house that lay along the glen road far below us. 'That's our billet,' he said. 'We'll head down now.'

We made a fast descent down the bare slope of the glen until we reached the back door of a well-appointed two-storey house, not the kind of one expected to house IRA activists or sympathisers. Frank lifted the latch and we moved silently into a small pantry. He closed the door, paused for a few seconds, then whispered, 'I don't think we should stay here … We'll go on to the next house; it's only a quarter of a mile on.'

Trusting Frank's uncanny judgement about billets, I followed him. Now that it was growing light, we jogged the quarter of a mile. Again, we entered by the back door and made our way to the kitchen, where we sat by the stove waiting for the rising of the household.

At about 7 a.m. we heard someone stirring in the bedroom above the kitchen. A few minutes later, the man of the house entered the kitchen. He stopped short as soon as he became aware of our presence in the dimly lit kitchen, but when Frank announced who we were he bade us welcome. A short time later, we were sitting down to a good breakfast with the family. Afterwards he led us upstairs to one of the bedrooms and, indicating a freshly made bed, said, 'There y'are, boys. Have a good sleep … We'll keep a watch out for the Bs,' meaning the B Specials.

We laid the weapons on the floor, stripped, got into bed and were asleep in minutes. Half an hour later we were awakened by the sound of our host and his daughter as they burst through the door shouting, 'The Bs are raiding next door.' He added, 'Get up, quick! ... You'll see them from the window.' We leaped out of bed and could see the B Specials searching the outhouses of the other property, while, presumably, another party searched inside. 'They'll be here next, what do ye want to do?' the man of the house asked.

We wanted to avoid capture, but how? It was full daylight, with absolutely no cover on the lower slopes of the glen, so escape on foot was impossible. Our host, realising our dilemma, made the amazing and heroic offer to drive us out of the glen towards Ballymena. There was a good chance of a B Special or RUC roadblock somewhere along that road, but if we were prepared to take the chance, he would drive us, on condition that we didn't carry our weapons! It was a generous gesture indeed. Things would go badly enough for him if we were caught in his house, but much worse if we were arrested in his car. We opted to be driven out, hoping our luck would hold.

Only two or three minutes elapsed between our being awakened to our accepting the offer of a lift. Our host gave instructions to family members where to dump the weapons. We sat into the car, grateful to our host but also very mindful of the risk. We were very dependent on luck.

And our luck held. There was no roadblock at the end of the glen, nor anywhere else on the road to Ballymena. On reaching the town, we split up. Frank was dropped off at the home of a friend who would put him up 'at a pinch' but no one else; I was dropped off at the bus depot, where I caught the next bus to Belfast. I made my way to the Browns' house, home of my beloved Mary Óg, where I spent a very pleasant week before returning to Dublin.

***

It was now late August 1957. HQ asked me on my return if I was prepared to volunteer for service on the Leitrim–Fermanagh border. In a matter of days I was on my way there in the company of the chief of staff, Seán Cronin, who was going to take personal command of a column that had been assembled.

Desperately in need of a successful and spectacular operation against the British Army to revive morale and stimulate resistance within the North for the coming winter, HQ had assembled a fifteen-man column of virtually all the active service men who had survived the round-ups. Its main task was to ambush a British Army patrol that operated along a particular stretch of the Leitrim–Fermanagh border. The plan called for splitting the column following the ambush into three separate units, each with the capability of operating independently, but able to come together for large strikes when called upon. It was a competent plan, though it didn't work out quite like that. My main task was assembling and manning two of the six mines to be used in the ambush. Apparently, I was regarded as something of an explosives and mines expert, or so I was informed when I asked why I was being seconded to an already strong column.

Cronin and myself were dropped off at Miss Mac-Dermott's cottage, in the townland of Corranmore, near Kiltyclogher, Co. Leitrim. She was the sister of Seán Mac Diarmada, the 1916 leader. After an all-too-brief introduction to this grand woman, Cronin and myself adjourned to the parlour to change into our 'working clothes': boots and uniforms. While Cronin was pulling on his boots he said, somewhat passionately, 'You know, Mick, this country is on its knees!' When we finished dressing, we went back to the kitchen, said goodbye to Miss MacDermott and set off with our guide to join the column a half hour's walk away.

In the matter of good leaders, experienced volunteers, reasonably good weaponry and the plan, the column had all the ingredients for success – by the standards of December 1956 that is. But much had changed in the intervening months.

After a brief meeting with the column commanders I was brought to where the main body of the column was billeted, a hay barn on the property of a bachelor small farmer. During the few days I spent there, Cronin, an avid admirer of German

martial music, played a Nazi band record from dawn to dusk
on a wind-up gramophone. Our cook, Joe Conway of Newry,
anxious to give us a treat, decided to make some damson jam
as there was an old damson orchard beside the barn. It tasted
good but left our teeth as black as soot.

A couple of days later we were brought to the assembly
point for the operation that night. Cronin briefed us, distributed the weapons and allotted tasks. Three of us – myself,
Paul Smith and another lad called Bill – were made responsible for assembling a pair of twin mines each and detonating
them at the ambush site. Shortly before we moved out Cronin
informed us that we'd be accompanied by a journalist from
New York, a man named Ford, who wanted to report on the
IRA in action. He had previously been covering the Algerian
war of liberation.

The British Army target that night was a patrol consisting
of an armoured car and two other vehicles, which, according
to our intelligence, travelled a particular road between
midnight and 2 a.m. After about one-and-a-half hours' march
we reached the ambush site. And an ideal position it was. The
fire position was behind a four-foot clay bank and at the apex
of a hill overlooking, and about seventy yards from, the road.
The road curved at that point, which meant, of course, that the
convoy would have to slow down, thereby giving us a better
chance of hitting them with the mines. There were haystacks
scattered about the field below us, but they didn't impede

either our view or our field of fire. So we would have cover, both during the ambush and in the course of our withdrawal.

The night was dry and moonless. I felt very confident about the outcome of the operation, given the weather, a column where almost all had some combat experience and the fact that we had competent, determined leaders, good weaponry and an adequate supply of explosives.

As soon as Cronin had set up the fire positions, he instructed the mine men to go down to the road. The three of us and three other volunteers carried the mines. After pacing out the appropriate distance between each pair, we set about digging them into the ditch. As soon as my partner and I had dug our twin mines, I sent him back to the fire position to report to the OC that our mines were ready and that I was now going to wire them, in accordance with our instructions.

I connected the detonator wires of my mines to my flex and, playing out the cable carefully behind me, I made my way back to the fire position. Having sealed off one terminal of my battery to prevent an accidental detonation, I connected one wire of the flex to one terminal of the battery. I reported to Cronin that my mines were ready and took up my position.

At about the same time, Bill reported that his mines were in position, which meant that we were only waiting for Paul Smith to complete his mines. However, after a long ten minutes had elapsed Cronin instructed me to 'go down and see what's holding him up ... help him out'.

I went back down to the road and found Paul. I told him the OC was getting anxious about the delay. He said he was almost ready. He'd only to connect the flex to the switch. But when I saw that not alone was he using a push-button switch but that he also had the flex wired to both terminals of his batteries (which he was carrying in his pocket), I insisted that we go back into the field to take cover before he made his final connection because there is no way of knowing when a push-button switch is on or off. I also tried to dissuade him from using the switch, but he insisted, saying, 'Look, I know what I'm doing ... the switch is off.'

However, he did agree, reluctantly, to come with me into the field and take cover behind a haystack while he made the last connection. The instant he did so his twin mines exploded with a thunderous bang, almost levelling our haystack and showering us with debris. We were blackened and somewhat shocked, but otherwise unhurt. We were only twenty feet from the mines, which were placed to explode outwards.

I was too angry for words. All I said, when we'd recovered from the shock, was, 'We'd better get back up to the fire position and tell the OC what's happened.' Paul merely nodded his head, too shocked to respond.

When we reached the fire position, we were greeted with a whispered chorus of 'What happened?' from the lads. The OC took us out of earshot of the others and asked me what happened. I said he had better ask Paul. After Paul had given his report, including the fact that I had tried to dissuade him from using the push-button switch, Cronin, who must have been extremely angry at the premature and potentially disastrous explosion, asked, 'Are ye all right? Are ye fit to carry on?' We said we were. Then he asked me if my mines were still all right. I told him they were and that Bill's were too.

Cronin decided we would wait in ambush for as long as we could and that the journalist would be told, if he asked, that we had blown the mines as a decoy, to draw out the British. In fact, the last thing we needed was to give them warning of our presence in the area. Ford did ask, and was very impressed with this piece of cheek on our part. He then settled himself down for a quiet smoke in his secluded cover.

Although our main weapon, surprise, was gone, we waited in the ambush position for an hour or more. Eventually, when the time at which the patrol should have reached our position had long passed, and time was running out for our withdrawal to the border in darkness, Cronin ordered us to explode the remaining mines before our withdrawal to the border. Ford joined us at that point, roundly cursing the British Army as cowards for not responding to our 'decoy' explosions.

The withdrawal would be a fast one, now that we were not hindered by the burden of 300 pounds of gelignite, together with the fact that we were racing against the impending dawn. As soon as Bill and I exploded our mines, the column scrambled over a high moss-covered stone wall, which was at right angles to our fire position, and assembled there to await the arrival of the last man over the wall, myself, before heading out.

As soon as the second-last man, Joe Conway, saw me make for the wall, he sent the word up the line to the OC to move on. However, the wall was somewhat weakened after thirteen or fourteen men had scrambled over it and, when I grasped the top with my left hand (I was holding my rifle in my right) the wall gave way. I fell backwards and a couple of large stones fell across me. They were so heavy that I was unable to move my legs. I sat up and tried to push them off, but failed. I then spent several precious seconds trying to pry them off with my rifle, but they were too heavy.

I whistled in the hope that Joe would realise that I wasn't behind him and luckily he heard me. He halted the column and came back looking for me. Maybe a minute after I had sent out my whistled appeal I heard him calling out, in a tone between a whisper and a normal speaking tone, 'Mick, Mick, where are you?'

'I'm over here,' I called from my position behind the bank.

Joe, nicknamed 'Gee Boy', because of his habit of prefixing this to everything he said, looked over the bank and said 'Gee, boy, what's up?'

'I can't fuckin' well get up!' I said.

He came over the bank and in a matter of seconds had prised the stones off my legs. Joe was as strong as an ox. After a few more whispered 'Gee, boys,' we scrambled across the bank and set off at a fast pace to catch up with the rest of the column. I explained to Cronin what had happened and the rapid march to the border resumed. My left leg was badly gashed, but that was the least of my worries.

Our journalist-guest was not quite up to the pace and, after falling into a river, had to be half-carried the rest of the way. Well, it wasn't so much a river as a ten-foot-wide, three-foot-deep drain, with muddy ground on each bank. The column had no trouble clearing it, but poor Ford, who was extremely tired and wearing wellingtons, couldn't get up enough speed to clear the drain and landed smack in the middle. The sight of him thrashing about was so amusing that some of us couldn't help laughing. But Cronin wasn't amused and quickly put an end to the show with a curt 'Pull him out.' Joe and myself, his official minders, had to pull him out and help him to the border.

We reached our billet, a barn a few hundred yards south of the border, just before daylight. We dug ourselves into the hay at the back and settled down to rest. No one really slept. We were too disappointed with the way things had turned out.

Up to then, I hadn't had time to dwell on the gash in my leg; now, however, I began to worry about a tetanus infection, as the wound was covered with mud and dirt. I told the number 2 about it and he immediately set about washing it.

He opened a naggin flask of whiskey or brandy, carried for medicinal purposes, and pouring a few drops over the gash to disinfect it, he said jokingly, 'This is an awful waste … but we've no iodine.'

We spent a couple of inactive, depressingly boring days in the barn. Then, in keeping with the original plan, the column split into three sections, or two-and-a-half, as two volunteers had been sent home sick. One section remained in the Leitrim–Fermanagh area; another section, headed by Paul Smith, was sent to the Louth–Armagh border; and the third section, comprising myself and Christy Sullivan, was allocated to the Swanlinbar section of the Cavan–Fermanagh border.

On 11 November Paul Smith, three other volunteers and the sympathiser in whose house they were staying, Michael Watters, were killed in an accidental explosion at Edentubber on the Louth–Armagh border. It is thought that they were in the process of assembling a time-bomb when the explosion occurred. I've often wondered if Paul was still using a push-button switch.

By then Christy and myself had been transported to a billet in Elphin, Co. Roscommon, where we were to await the arrival of two new volunteers to form a column. As usual it was after dark when, on a day in November 1957, we arrived at Scotts of Elphin. The house, which was on the outskirts of the town, was extremely impressive. I subsequently discovered that it was formerly the Protestant archbishop's palace. We entered a cavernous hall, where our driver introduced us to Mrs Scott, a tall, stout, severe-looking woman, who merely nodded her head in acknowledgement. There was no smile, no handshake. Not a good omen, I thought! Then with, 'I'll be back tomorrow to take them away', our driver left.

Mrs Scott let the driver out the front door, where she stood for a second or two before locking and bolting it. She turned back to us and said, 'Come with me … I'll make you some supper.' We followed her into a cavernous kitchen, where she indicated we should sit at a ten-foot-long table. Fifteen or so conversation-less minutes later we were eating a welcome feed of porridge. Christy and myself sat at one end of the table and Mrs Scott at the other with her son Seán, who was about thirty and had just come in. Other than introducing ourselves to Seán, no word was spoken during supper. The embarrassing silence was broken only by the occasional sound of someone's spoon scraping his or her porridge bowl.

The kitchen was in semi-darkness, lit by a single oil lamp. There was no electricity in the house, which was common in rural Ireland at that time. When we'd finished, Mrs Scott rose, quietly made her way around the table to pick up the dishes and brought them to the sink, where she began to wash them. We remained sitting at the table, waiting for some signal to move. A few minutes later she turned around and, addressing her son, said, 'Show them up to their room.' Seán walked across to the cupboard, lit a candle and brought us upstairs, past a couple of bedrooms to our room.

As with everything else in that house, the room was large and austere. There was an unmade iron-sprung single bed along the left wall and our bed was along the opposite wall. Beside our bed was a small table on which there was a candle, a jug of water and a porcelain basin for washing, as was customary. The chamber pot sat discreetly under the bed. While I felt there was something weird about this house, I was grateful to our hostess for putting us up in her clean, warm, dry home. My partner, Christy, being more superstitious, couldn't shake off the eerie feeling he had about the house. He insisted on sleeping on the inside, against the wall. Just as I was about to blow out the candle, Christy said, 'Jeez, this is a strange house.' Not wanting to add to his worries, I said, 'It's strange, but it's all right, and it's safe.'

We spent the next couple of days in unaccustomed comfort. We were well fed, the house was dry and warm, and we had a comfortable bed. But sitting down to our meals at that huge table, in that cavernous kitchen, with no word being spoken by either Mrs Scott or Seán, was an ordeal. I couldn't help wondering why this woman, who so obviously resented our presence, had agreed to put us up.

On the third or fourth day, a courier called to tell me that I'd be picked up the following day and taken to Dublin to attend the army convention. I looked forward with excitement to the prospect of attending my first convention. Christy, however, wasn't too happy about being left on his own.

We went to bed that night at our usual time, about 10 p.m., and talked for half an hour or so before going to sleep. Like most men on the run, we were light sleepers. After perhaps three or four hours, we both woke on hearing the sound of the latch being lifted. We both lay still. It could have been Seán coming to warn us of an impending raid, but we knew instinctively that it wasn't, and it most certainly wouldn't be his mother. We heard a slight creak as the door opened and the sound of the latch again as it closed. The intruder walked slowly to the unmade bed, where the footsteps stopped. After a few seconds, we heard the bedsprings creak as he lay down. Then there was silence.

Christy lay stiff and silent beside me. And while I too thought there was something very strange happening, I decided that this stranger might be a comrade on the run so, turning towards the other bed, I whispered, 'Who's there? Who's that?'

But there was no response.

Again I called out, but somewhat louder, 'Who's there?'

Still there was no response.

I let a minute or so elapse and then I reached across to the table for the matches and lit the candle. I couldn't see clearly enough to the bed at the other side of the room, which was so big that a single lighted candle couldn't illuminate it properly. I got out of bed, took the candle-holder in my hand and walked very slowly to the bed. There was no one in it. Nor was there anyone elsewhere in the room.

Throughout my search, Christy was silent. I walked back to our bed and set the candle back on the table before getting back in. Then Christy whispered to me, 'Jeez, Mick, I'm not staying here on my own. This is a very strange house.' We didn't sleep another wink that night. What we had heard and experienced defied rational explanation. It also reminded me of the strange light that Frank McCarry and I had experienced in north Antrim some months previously.

Next morning, we rose at our usual time and went downstairs to the kitchen for breakfast. Christy in the meantime remained adamant that he would not remain in the house another night. He was going to insist that the driver who'd be taking me to the bus take him to another billet, any billet.

After breakfast, as we were going upstairs to pack our gear, I asked Seán if I could have a word with him. I told him what had happened during the night. He paused for a few seconds and then said, 'Ah, don't worry about that. It's all right. That kind of thing happens in this house at odd times.'

He refused to say another word.

Our driver arrived, and after I explained Christy's feelings, he dropped me off for a bus to Dublin and took Christy to another billet. I arrived in Dublin late that evening, where I heard the tragic news of the five lads blown up in Edentubber.

I attended the convention, which was held in a huge mansion on the south side of the city. Much of what went on was beyond me; all I remember was a heated discussion about whether to continue the campaign.

The next day I was brought to Swanlinbar, Co. Cavan, where I was billeted in the home of Pat Barney McGovern, where Christy Sullivan was already settled. Pat, a man in his late fifties, was an affable, wise 'old' man. He was a great storyteller, and from him I first heard the legend of the Black Pig's Dyke and other folk legends. Deeply religious, he would have us kneel down in the kitchen every night to say the rosary. He kept his home in spotless condition, somewhat unusual for a bachelor in those bleak times.

Again we awaited the arrival of the 'two or three volunteers' needed to make an operating section. A few days later we were brought on to another billet in Co. Cavan, which was equally good, and were provided with the same promise that the rest of our section would join us in a matter of days. Another week went by with no sign of the promised reinforcements. Our new host, who was married (it was always a joy to stay in a house where there was a woman), was another great storyteller, with the most marvellous capacity to embellish what might have been an insignificant happening into an outrageously incredible saga, with him usually at the centre of the story.

After yet another week or so I was told to return to Dublin. A local man, Peter Albert, waited while I packed my few bits of gear and then we set off on a two-mile walk over the fields to his house, where I'd be picked up the following morning. On our arrival at his house, his wife made tea and we chatted away about things in general. At some point in the conversation, and while himself, his wife and myself were sitting around the fire, he asked, 'How did you like that billet? He's a great character, isn't he?' I replied, 'It was a really great billet … but can't he tell some lies?' With that, Peter laughed and said, 'You have it right there!' Turning to his wife, he added, 'Now, I'm not the only one thinks that your brother is a notorious liar!' I shrivelled up with embarrassment. Peter's wife, however, took it in her stride, used as she apparently was to her husband's comments about her brother.

In Dublin, HQ asked me if I'd go again to north Antrim with Frank McCarry in early December. I agreed, as did Frank. The purpose of this trip, HQ explained, was purely propagandist: our only task was to poster as much of north Antrim as we could with a manifesto commemorating the first anniversary of the 'Campaign of Resistance', which also set out the objectives of the campaign. It was hoped that postering the area would help stimulate local resistance.

Frank and I travelled separately to north Antrim with the manifestos. But as soon as we met to discuss where best to start, it was clear we were both sceptical about their value, a scepticism we had felt when the project was put to us but hadn't expressed, because it wasn't the thing to do. We also knew that the RUC would soon mount searches for the 'outsiders' responsible. However, as we'd given our word to HQ, we proceeded to carry out the exercise to the best of our ability. We spent the next three or four nights footing it over the now familiar Glens of Antrim, pinning our manifestos to telephone poles and wherever else they'd be seen along the main roads in a ten-mile radius of Torr Head and Ballycastle. Having completed this task, and with nothing else to do in the area, we split up and headed off for our respective new destinations. I got a lift to Ballymena and a bus to Belfast. I spent a couple of days there before catching the train to Dublin a day or so before Christmas. I spent that Christmas in Jack and Máire McCabe's hospitable home in Finglas, as it was too unsafe to return to East Wall.

In early January 1958 the chief of staff asked me to take charge of a three-man section that would operate against the British Army in the Omagh–Lisanelly area of Co. Tyrone. He went on to say that the other two men had already agreed to the idea. They had spent some time in the area and were experienced. There was a good local guide, some local assistance available with transport and billets, a safe dugout, some gelignite and good weapons in the area. Or so he was informed.

The three of us were transported to a house in north Monaghan. Mrs Mooney's was a great billet but was very much overused and there were already six other volunteers billeted there. Among them were some determined and hardened operators, who had spent most of the previous couple of months kicking their heels in idleness, like myself and Christy Sullivan in Co. Cavan. They would have been more than willing to join us to make up an operating section, but communications being what they were, this potential was missed.

Come bedtime, all nine of us adjourned to a large upstairs room, where, after much bantering and bargaining, we each secured a fair share of blankets or a sleeping-bag, picked a good spot on the floor, and lay down. We did not go to sleep for a long time, however, there being too much chat and too much unused energy and tension.

My section was driven to an isolated and long-abandoned cottage in the Lisanelly area of Co. Tyrone. The dugout was under a pigsty, which was about twenty-five yards from the house. The floor of the sty was concrete, with an access manhole snugly fitted in the part of the sty most frequented by the pigs. We lowered ourselves into the five-foot vertical hole, and then crawled horizontally for four or five feet until we entered the dug-out proper. We lit a candle, shouted to the guide that we were okay, and with a 'See ye in the morning, lads!' he replaced the lid and departed for home. How I envied him!

The dugout, which hadn't been used for six months, was very damp, lice-ridden and obviously frequented by rats. It was about five feet in height from floor to ceiling. We laid our blankets and sleeping-bags down on the bed, railway sleepers covered with straw, and settled down to chat a while and, hopefully, sleep. After about an hour or so, however, the flame of the candle began to flicker; and a minute or so later it went out. Not realising that the candle had expired because of a lack of oxygen, and thinking there was a faulty wick, I asked one of the lads to strike a match and light another candle. He, however, being familiar with the vagaries of this dugout, said, to my consternation, 'There's no point, Mick. There's not enough air.' It turned out there was only one ventilation hole.

We never slept a wink that night, what with the lice, the possibility of rats paying us a visit and the lack of air. Instead we chatted, carefully avoiding any reference to oxygen or rats. At some point, however, when the air became very bad, we decided that we'd have to raise the lid. Being the tallest, I felt my way to the tunnel and, standing almost upright, began pushing with all my might to lift the lid; but, much as I tried, I couldn't move it. A pig was probably lying on top. So I reluctantly abandoned the effort and crawled back to the 'bed'.

Early next morning we heard the welcome sound of the lid being lifted by our guide. We rushed outside to breathe the lovely air and then pick a spot where we could relieve ourselves. By the time we ambled back to the shed that adjoined the pigsty, our guide, who had brought a Primus stove, a kettle and a frying pan, was cooking breakfast. Soon we were sitting down to fried eggs, fried bread and tea. This was to be our daily diet for the three weeks we spent in the dugout. After the first week I threatened each morning that I'd never eat another egg, but hunger being the best sauce, I'd have eggs for breakfast, dinner and tea, regardless.

I told the guide what we hoped to do, namely, carry out an attack against the British Army – a soldier, soldiers, a patrol or whatever – and that to carry out our assignment I needed three reasonably safe billets within a two or three-mile radius of Lisanelly or Omagh. We would each spend a week or so gathering intelligence on British Army movements in the area, then meet, compare notes and decide on the best target. We'd also need detonators and some gelignite, a safe billet for after the job and a safe car to transport us between jobs.

Our guide, a courageous and committed supporter, listened politely to what I had to say and said with some embarrassment, 'Well, Mick, I'll do my best ... but I've got to be honest with ye ... There's only myself prepared to do anything around these parts now. There's one family that I *think* would drive you around to Omagh and that, and they'd put you up before a job ... but their place wouldn't be safe after a job and their car is likely to be stopped if there's a stranger seen in it. If you want to take the chance in their car, I'll ask them. But the only really safe place is the dugout.' He also reported that there were no hand grenades or gelignite in the area. I told him to do his best.

He returned a few days later with news that a car would be available for intelligence runs but when it came to doing a job, he'd have to drive us. A few more days elapsed before transport could be arranged. We were now about ten days in the dugout. We were becoming debilitated from lack of sleep and a diet of just eggs, bread and tea. Only the lice were thriving and we were beginning to get on one another's nerves.

Without explosives we were effectively reduced to a sniping job and further restricted by orders to operate offensively only against the British Army. We could, of course, defend ourselves against the RUC or B Specials. Moreover, as none of us was familiar with the Omagh–Lisanelly area, we were completely dependent on one-inch Ordnance Survey maps to gain any sense of the local geography. After a week's search for a suitable target, and in the absence of any local intelligence, we settled on a sniping attack on the sentry at the gate of Lisanelly Army Camp. Lisanelly at that time was more rural than urban, but there was a small group of council houses on rising ground about two hundred yards from the camp gate. The road into the estate was directly opposite the gateway.

The sentries were housed in a sandbagged pillbox (a fortified post) to the right of the gate and were armed with Sten sub-machine guns and a Bren light machine gun. Their drill was to remain in their emplacement until one of their vehicles stopped at the gate. One sentry would remain in position behind the Bren, while the other checked the credentials of the driver. It was this sentry that we selected as our target.

We picked our night at random, were driven to the estate, took up positions in the back yard of one of the houses about 150 yards from the target, which was as close as we could get, and waited for a vehicle to approach the gate. We were armed with two bolt-action Lee-Enfield rifles and one Thompson sub-machine gun. We also had short arms, but they were ineffectual, as indeed were the rifles and the Thompson at that range at night. We gave no thought to the possibility that the occupants of the nearby houses might be unionists. We were too anxious to get this job done to enquire.

We had just taken up our fire positions, standing between two houses, when an armoured car drove up to the gate. It took us by surprise, as we were accustomed to waiting for hours in positions for an ambush, but we decided to go ahead there and then. We waited until the armoured car went through the gate then opened fire on the sentry as he made his way back to the pillbox. But even as we began firing, I was conscious of the fact that, given the range, our lack of firepower and the difficulty of sighting in the darkness, we'd need an inordinate amount of luck to hit him. In the couple of seconds it took the sentry to dash back to the safety of the pillbox we managed to fire only a few shots. I thought we'd hit him, but the British Army press statement said there were no casualties.

We ran back the few yards to where the car was parked

and scrambled in. The driver, who had started the engine as soon as we began firing, sped off as we closed the doors. We were already on a back road, but our driver, anticipating a chase, took us over even poorer roads – bog roads, really – as he brought us towards the dugout. After fifteen minutes, he dropped us about a mile from the dugout and got away safely.

The next day our guide told us we hadn't hit the sentry, but the job had stirred up a hornets' nest. There were widespread searches for us and the RUC was certain local people had not carried out the job. He reckoned there was no chance of doing anything else in the area for a long while and that we'd be better off 'getting out of it'.

I asked him to call back the next day, to give us time to assess things. We had to face the facts of our situation. We had no safe billet, no gelignite, detonators or grenades, no local intelligence, no transport and no local volunteers available to join us in an operation. All the volunteers from the area were in jail or interned. Although the dugout was relatively safe, life there was beginning to wear us down and we had no money with which to buy food. Besides, our host, poor as he was, couldn't risk being seen buying anything he wasn't used to buying. While there were people who would have supplied us with other food, he didn't want to risk asking them, for fear that they'd talk, thus jeopardising our security.

We decided to get to north Monaghan, thirty miles to the south, and then to Dublin to receive further orders. Next day our guide said our only course was to cross the mountains and fields to John X's house, ten or twelve miles to the south.[2] It was a safe billet and, as no operations had taken place between John X's area and the border in a long time, we should have no problems getting across the border.

We took his advice and our host, without waiting to be asked, said he'd return after dark to walk with us to John X's house, twelve miles distant. Delighted with this offer, I said, 'That's great. We'll see you tonight.' True to his word, he arrived back just after dark. However, one of the lads, Johnny McAlinden from Lurgan, who had been over the route once before, said he knew the way. We only had to go 'right for about a mile, until we reach the electricity pylons. Then all we need do is to follow the pylons south until we reach John X's house. Right?'

Our host paused for a moment before agreeing, adding that there was even a pylon at the house we were heading for. However, he cautioned us with, 'That bit of country is very awkward, so why don't I lead you to the line anyway?' I agreed, but McAlinden insisted there was no need to put him to such trouble as he knew the way. In the face of such certitude, and because there was already some tension between us from living in the dugout, I agreed, against my better judgement.

---

2   X has been used here and later in the text, when the author is unsure of the name.

We left the rifles and the Thompson with our guide to be dumped. Having checked our gear, and with each of us still carrying a short arm, we shook hands with our guide and said goodbye. It was about 8 p.m. as we set out at a leisurely pace for the pylons. The night was nicely dark, the weather was crisp and dry, we were travelling light and I was looking forward to a relatively easy hike. McAlinden led, as he said he knew the way, the other volunteer was in the middle and I brought up the rear. After about an hour, I called a halt to ask how things were going. McAlinden estimated, 'We should get to the pylons in fifteen minutes or so.' I thought I detected a bit of uncertainty in his tone, but let it go. I didn't want to upset his concentration or his confidence.

After marching for another half an hour or so, during which time McAlinden stopped three or four times to get his bearings, there was still no sign of the pylons. I called another halt and asked, 'How are we doing? Do you know where we are?'

He said he wasn't too sure and I asked if he had 'any idea where you think we went wrong?'

'I think we should've headed to the right sooner … So if we start heading right now we have to reach the pylons soon.'

With that I said, 'Let's go ahead and do that.' Having marched for another hour there was still no sign of the pylons. I called another halt. This time McAlinden admitted he was lost. I decided that the only way to establish our position was to march towards the lights of the nearest town, which was three or four miles away and find a main road. Somewhere on that road, we'd find a signpost. I had a compass but it was virtually useless until we discovered where exactly we were.

After another three hours we reached the main road. It was a toss-up which way to go and I think we turned left, away from the town. We made our slow, laborious way along the inside of the ditch because of the risk of a B Special or RUC ambush. We finally reached a crossroads, and a signpost to discover that after a six-hour march we were only a mile or so from the dugout. It was now 3 a.m. and we couldn't possibly reach our new scheduled billet, which was at least eight hours' march away, before dawn broke. We had no idea what was a friendly house or an unfriendly house. But at least we now knew where we were and in which direction to head for the pylons.

There were really only two choices. One was to head for the pylons and hope we could reach them before dawn, and then find good cover for the day. The other was to hide out in the nearest good cover and resume our march at dusk, fourteen hours hence. I chose the latter course. We were tired and demoralised. Moreover, I wanted to consult my map before I walked another yard and we had no torch, so I needed daylight. We headed back up the rising ground from the road for perhaps half a mile, until we found reasonably good cover: a thick grove of furze bushes. We crawled into the centre of the thicket, which was about ten feet across, lay down and settled ourselves for the long wait until dusk. I was angry and frustrated with McAlinden but held my peace. Recriminations would achieve nothing.

We hardly spoke throughout that long day. Virtually the only sound was the barking of a dog and the occasional sound of someone calling across the fields to a neighbour. These sounds of people engaged in normal human activity were a sharp reminder of our predicament and made us lonely for the company of friends and the warmth of a safe house. And what with the cold – we had no blankets or sleeping-bags – and the hunger, we even discussed going down to the farmhouse to seek shelter, but decided against risking it. With the way our luck was running, it was probably the home of a B Special.

Those hours under the furze bushes passed exceedingly slowly. After 10 a.m. I refused to consult my watch any more. Nature would take its inexorable course; night would follow day, of that at least we could be certain. I had experienced worse cold and hunger, but what made this experience different was being lost. Come nightfall, we crawled out of the bushes, spent several minutes shaking the stiffness and the cold out of our joints, then headed off at a fast pace in the direction of the pylons. After a long study of our maps, I was happy that we were now headed in the right direction. Sure enough, McAlinden finally found his bearings. After less than an hour, we finally reached the pylons. Our morale restored, we stopped to celebrate with a cigarette. Then, sticking like glue to the line of the pylons, we set off at a cracking pace for our destination.

After about eight or nine hours McAlinden stopped and said, 'I think this is it.' He walked slowly towards the dark outline of a house and outbuildings about a hundred yards distant. After five minutes, or maybe less, he returned and stood for a moment, trying to locate us in the dark. I called him over in little more than a whisper and he said, 'We're there.'

I could have hugged him but I just said, 'That's great, Johnny. Let's go.' And we followed him as he led us through a couple of gaps in fences and a barnyard to the door of our friendly billet. It was now about 5 a.m. He silently lifted the latch of the door and pushed it open. We entered and followed him silently, sinking gratefully into chairs around the stove. We lit the last of our cigarettes and settled down to wait for our unsuspecting host to get up.

But he was a light sleeper and had heard us. He shouted down the stairs, 'Who's there?' McAlinden, who had stayed in the house before, replied, 'It's me, Johnny.'

'That's okay, Johnny ... I'll be down in a minute.'

John came down to the kitchen a couple of minutes later, pausing for a moment as he peered across the kitchen at us in the dim light of the Sacred Heart lamp. 'Jesus, Johnny, it's yourself,' he said. 'How are ya doin'? Are ye in trouble? Ye're welcome anyway.' He shook hands with McAlinden and, after the latter introduced us, shook our hands as well, saying, 'Ye're welcome, boys. Are ye hungry?' This was the kind of welcome you prayed for.

And while we were telling him of our experiences, *and* of our hunger, he made breakfast. Soon we were sitting around the kitchen table devouring eggs, homemade bread and tea. With our stomachs full and sitting in the warm kitchen of a friendly host, our morale was restored. We then got down to asking if he could arrange a lift for us across the border into north Monaghan. John thought for only a moment or two before saying he could arrange it that afternoon. He wasn't bothered about the risk or by the fact that we had short arms with us. We went to bed until it was time to go.

In the early afternoon our lift arrived. I sat in the front with the driver and my two comrades sat in the back. We carried the short arms in our pockets. Our driver and John felt that we wouldn't encounter any roadblocks. Aughnacloy was where we'd be crossing and there had been no IRA activity in the area for a long time. Right enough we encountered no roadblock on the twenty-mile drive to Aughnacloy. We drove through the village without seeing a single policeman or soldier and heaved a sigh of relief. However, just as we approached a crossroads half a mile south of Aughnacloy and only a hundred yards from the border, we saw that an RUC jeep was approaching the same crossroads from our left.

The driver asked, 'What'll I do?' I told him to just keep driving at the same speed and stay calm. Personally, I felt anything but calm as four men in a car was somewhat unusual in that place and at that time of day. We had only short arms, and the patrol had sub-machine guns.

We were travelling at no more than twenty miles an hour; the RUC jeep was moving just as slowly. Expecting the patrol to stop us, we had pulled our short arms from our pockets, but instead of blocking the crossroads, the RUC jeep stopped about five or ten yards short of it while we drove through. Again I told our driver, who was becoming more nervous with each passing second, to hold his speed as it was and about half a mile further on we crossed the border. We took the back roads and reached our next safe billet without further incident.

**

After a couple of days in north Monaghan I made my way back to Dublin, where I reported to HQ on our escapades in Co. Tyrone. A few days later I was sent to train some new recruits who had volunteered for active service and were billeted in a house in north Meath, where they'd been for a week or more awaiting a training officer. In fact, they had been waiting for about six months to be trained before their arrival in Co. Meath. I spent a week or so training them in weaponry and tactics. In a week of twelve-hour days you can teach anyone all they need to know about the tactical use of a Lee-Enfield rifle, a Thompson sub-machine gun and a Bren gun, as well as how to strip and assemble them. It began to get boring; the lads wanted to see a bit of action.

I committed an awful faux pas in this house. Assuming that our host, who was in his seventies, and our hostess, who was about thirty-five, were father and daughter, I turned to the woman in the course of a chat one night and said, 'By God, your father's a great man for his age.'

'He is, isn't he ... but, you know, Bill is my husband,' she said, without a trace of embarrassment, as she turned affectionately towards him.

I tried to mumble something appropriate. Bill was clearly not pleased with my observation, but said nothing. Now I knew why he had been watching over her with more than a fatherly concern. We had made no effort to conceal our admiration for this attractive woman.

After about a week in Bill's house, a great billet, a driver from HQ called and told me to pack all the gear as we were moving immediately to another area. The lads, assuming they were at last heading for the border, packed enthusiastically. We said goodbye to Bill and his wife, piled into the car and headed off.

Half an hour later, our driver turned into the yard of a house alongside the road but to the south of our previous billet. 'Well, lads, ye'll be here for a day or so, and then ye'll be taken up the road,' he said, implying that we'd be heading for the border. We spent the next few days going through weapons training, ad nauseam. Then we were picked up by another HQ driver and taken to another billet, which was only twenty miles north of Dublin. This was Easter Week 1958.

On arriving at this house I found waiting for me another three young volunteers who had spent the previous two weeks anxiously waiting for the arrival of a training officer to give them a final run-through on weapons and tactics before they were sent into action. These new recruits had already received a good basic training in weapons and tactics. They had been waiting for six to twelve months to be called for active service. I gave them some talks on the theory of explosives, which weren't much use as I had no actual materials. Anyway, they weren't too anxious to handle them as there had been too many accidents, resulting in the deaths of six of our men. However, I went ahead and devised a training programme that would concentrate on tactics, strategy and outdoor exercises.

I was two days into this course when, on Good Friday, a driver from HQ arrived with a message telling me I was to leave immediately for the Lifford area in Co. Donegal, where I was to join Jim McKillican's five-man column for a 'special operation' against the British Army on Easter Saturday or Sunday. Jim was from Limerick and had been a friend of

Seán Sabhat. He needed me to make the mines and handle them during the operation, as apparently none of his team had any real experience handling explosives. I was told I'd be brought back to complete the training of the lads as soon as the operation was over.

I was angry at the short notice and the disruption to the training camp. But, discipline being what it was, together with the fact that the operation sounded like a worthwhile one – and McKillican had a good, experienced crew – I appointed one of the lads to take charge in my absence. I changed into my travelling apparel, a good suit that had been a present from Mrs Brown in Belfast the previous year, and packed my 'working' gear of boots, military trousers and jacket into a brown paper bag. Less than half an hour later the HQ driver and myself were on our way to Co. Donegal.

After an uneventful five-hour trip we arrived at my drop-off house. The driver introduced me to the man and woman of the house and then, without even waiting for a cup of tea, headed back for Dublin. An hour or so later I was brought to the house where Jim McKillican and the rest of the column were billeted. McKillican and I, not having met previously, introduced ourselves. I knew everyone else, except for Tom Dixon. We sat around chatting for a few minutes; then, anxious to get the details of the operation, I indicated to McKillican that I wanted to have a private word with him.

We adjourned to another room, whereupon he told me he

had had to abandon the special operation because he didn't have enough gelignite. He had come up with an alternative job, which was all he could think of at such short notice. The chief of staff was anxious that he organise some kind of operation over the Easter weekend.

I was amazed to discover that there was no gelignite, and further astonished to discover that the alternative operation was an Easter commemoration in the village of Clady, Co. Tyrone, a hundred yards north of the border. I pointed out that HQ had taken me away from a training camp specifically to make and man the mines and that he hardly needed me now.

'Oh, I do,' he said, 'because you never know but we might run into a patrol.' In the unlikely event that we encountered an enemy unit, the odds of success without any gelignite for a mine, or the element of surprise on our side, were extremely slim. But he was the OC, so I'd no alternative but to remain.

The next night the five of us assembled for the briefing and distribution of weapons. The briefing was simple: we'd be driven to the bridge at Clady, walk across and assemble the residents to hear the 1916 Proclamation. We'd hoist a tricolour, then return to the bridge, where we'd wait for a short while in case a British Army patrol showed up.

When we arrived in Clady, a mainly Catholic village, a couple of volunteers moved to the north end of the village to keep watch for the approach of any patrol while the rest of us

went door-to-door asking people to attend our Easter commemoration. One of the lads had 'dismantled' the telephone
in the public phone kiosk as a precaution.

It wasn't easy to come up with an appropriate formula of
words to explain our errand to the villagers. 'We're the IRA,
and – eh, we're holding an Easter commemoration at the
bottom of the village ... and we'd like ye to come down and –
eh, listen to it ...'

The first few people who answered their doors to my
knock were amazed to see this armed man asking them to
attend an Easter commemoration, but they said they'd attend.
However, when I knocked on the door of the last house in
my section, which happened to be the post office, I received
an entirely different reception. I didn't know until afterwards
that the family was Protestant. The woman who answered the
door, assuming perhaps that I was a British soldier as I was in
military clothes, didn't fully understand what I was saying and
motioned me into the kitchen.

Here there were half a dozen men and women sitting
around a table, playing cards. Most of them were neighbours,
in for their Saturday night game. I repeated my message and
they all looked at me as if I had two heads. No one said a word.
I repeated it again and this time they turned for some kind of
response to the man who was apparently the postmaster and
the owner of the house. He looked at me in what I took to be
a belligerent way. So I directed my message to him, but still he

said nothing. Then someone said, 'He's deaf: he doesn't know what you're saying.'

This was all I needed! Now they were beginning to get agitated. I couldn't afford to leave them in a house that had a phone. I poked one man with the weapon, told him to tell the head of the house that I wanted everyone outside. No harm would come to them, but they were all to get out, now! I herded them out and walked them down the street near to where the 'commemoration' was about to begin. This was not to force them to attend but so that I could keep an eye on them and be near enough to the rest of the column in case a British patrol arrived.

The Proclamation was read to the surprised villagers. The reader thanked them for listening, we fell in and marched back to the bridge, about a hundred yards distant, where we took up cover positions in the pedestrian alcoves that were at intervals of ten yards along its fifty-yard length.

The OC's decision to take up ambush positions on the bridge came as a surprise to me. However, we awaited the arrival of a British armoured patrol car, which, according to intelligence reports, *always* arrived at the same time and took up a stationary position fifty yards from what was now our position. It was already overdue by a couple of minutes. We waited a long ten minutes before Joe decided, wisely, to withdraw. We fell in and, as we marched south across the bridge we met three or four girls who were on the way north, to a dance in Clady. They stopped and called out, 'Hey, who are ye? Are ye the IRA?'

'Yes,' said someone.

'Up the IRA!' said the girls as they continued on their way.

We arrived at our car and were brought back to our billet.

After a hearty supper and a chat, we adjourned to bed in our safe house. At dawn the following morning the Special Branch awakened us. The five of us were arrested in our beds. I've seldom felt so embarrassed or angry in my life. We were taken to Letterkenny Garda Barracks to await transport to the Curragh Internment Camp, where most of us spent the next twelve months.

***

I was furious at being arrested in such ridiculous circumstances and for an ineffectual stunt. We were virtually the last remaining active service unit. I was determined to make some effort to escape, at the slightest opportunity, refusing to accept the prevailing wisdom that a jailed IRA volunteer was an asset in the struggle for freedom.

The only real opportunity to escape occurred while we were in Letterkenny Barracks. We were taken into the day room, where, having given our names and addresses, we were formally charged. The Special Branch men then left the room and we remained under the charge of a uniformed sergeant, who was a decent sort of man. About half an hour or so later we heard the sound of the Special Branch men leaving the barracks.

We spent the next half hour sitting around the fire and chatting to our garda minder, who was standing in front of the locked door that led into the hall. I thought if we could get through that door we'd be only six feet from the hall door and freedom. I caught McKillican's eye and indicated I was about to try something; he indicated that he understood. Then I looked at the sergeant and said, 'Look, sergeant, we'd love to have a shave and a wash … and – eh, to go to the toilet as well … Is there any chance you could arrange it for us?'

'Well,' said the sergeant, 'I'll see what I can do.' A couple of minutes later he came back and said, 'Okay, but only a few of you at a time.' He unlocked the door, and myself, Jim McKillican and Tim Nicholls followed him out into the hall. He locked the door and said, 'You have to wait here for a minute.' He was obviously waiting for another garda to accompany us to the washroom before he returned to the day room to mind the rest of our comrades.

The sergeant was standing beside McKillican, who was near to the front door. Nicholls and myself were together opposite them and only two feet away. I signalled to McKillican to make a dive for the front door. He made a dash for it, spent a couple of seconds pulling back the locks, and then he was outside. Instantly the sergeant shouted a warning to his comrades and made to grab for myself and Nicholls.

We grappled for a few seconds. I managed to reach the door before being grabbed again by a number of gardaí who had arrived on the scene. Nicholls and myself were bundled unceremoniously back into the day room. The sergeant, who was extremely annoyed over our abuse of his relaxed regime, said, 'That's it. Ye've lost your privileges,' as he slammed and locked the door of the day room. A few minutes later the door reopened and Jim McKillican was flung in. He had been captured a few hundred yards from the barracks.

About two hours later, around 2 p.m., the door was unlocked and McKillican was called to the hallway. A few minutes later I was called out. The hall was filled with plain-clothes men. One of them had handcuffs in one hand and read out a document he was holding in the other. 'I'm arresting you, Michael Ryan, under Section 21 of the Offences Against the State Act.'[3] He then handcuffed me and directed another Special Branch man to lead me outside, where I was placed between two others in the back seat of an unmarked car. The same ritual followed with the rest of my comrades.

About fifteen minutes later, we were all securely hand-cuffed and ensconced in the back seats of our various cars.

---

3   Section 21 of the Offences Against the State Act made it a criminal offence to be a member of a proscribed organisation such as the IRA.

With a scout car leading and a reinforcement car taking up the rear, the seven-vehicle convoy set off for the Curragh. My participation in the 'first phase' of the campaign was unceremoniously, ignominiously and unnecessarily over.

5

INTERNMENT AND REORGANISATION, 1958–59

I was interned for just over a year. It was by no means a difficult year. On the contrary, as internees we had three square meals a day, freedom of association, an unlimited supply of letters, weekly visits and other privileges. But it was a wasted year. And it was still jail.

Most volunteers seemed to have a cavalier attitude to being jailed, as though it were fulfilling a useful purpose. The movement's own propaganda glorified those who served time – the longer one served the greater the glory. In the minds of the naïve, like me, this was eventually translated into assuming that such people were highly principled, able and courageous. And a person who had served a long period in jail was almost assured of a leadership position at local or national level. That is not to suggest that anyone went willingly to jail. But the belief that the cause was being served as much by those imprisoned as by those who were active on the outside

MY LIFE IN THE IRA

was illusory. Imprisonment and internment had brought the campaign to its knees.

Worse still was the fact that those in prison were divided, mainly on the question of the feasibility of an escape. Our own OC, Tomás Mac Curtáin, opposed a breakout through the wire at the Curragh, because he felt it would surely result in the deaths of the escapers. He believed that a tunnel escape, which was already well in train, offered a greater and safer chance of success. Charlie Murphy, on the other hand, believing that Mac Curtáin wasn't serious about any kind of escape, orga-nised a mass escape of men. This breakout attempt took place on 2 December 1958 and, to everyone's surprise, it succeeded.

While Murphy's intention in breaking men out was sup-posedly to rejuvenate a flagging campaign, this didn't happen. When the campaign was revived in the summer of 1959, fol-lowing the release of all the Curragh internees, only three of Murphy's escapees took part and he was not among them.

By the time I was released, in April 1959, the camp was like a ghost town. Men had been released regularly over the previous months and it was to be closed a week later. There were only about twenty of us left. We were too few and too long together to provide each other with any kind of surprises or mental stimulation. In fact, we were bored and beginning to get on each other's nerves. The close confinement, forty men to each hut, meant there was no privacy and, to many, a cell in Mountjoy would have felt preferable.

170

The morning I was released was one of those beautiful spring mornings, crisp and dry, with only the barest touch of frost on the grass. It was more beautiful still when I was told I was being released. I was given an hour to pack my belongings. It took about two minutes, given that most of them were on my back, and the rest of my things fitted into a small brown paper bag. I said my goodbyes to comrades and to the OC, Mac Curtáin, and our quartermaster, Andy McDonnell, to whom I owed two shillings for cigarettes, which I promised to repay as soon as I got a job. At about 11 a.m. I was escorted to the gate by a military policeman, then brought to a room and searched for hidden messages. I was then ushered to the nearest bus stop inside the army camp to await the arrival of the next bus for Dublin. When it arrived, I was handed a voucher to cover my fare; when I was placed safely on board, my escort and my bus departed.

That was the best bus trip of my life. I was free after thirteen months of internment and it was a beautiful morning. I'd have loved a companion to share my joy, but I was the only Dubliner released that morning. I'd have loved a smoke too, but I'd neither a cigarette nor the money to buy one. I hadn't even the money to get the bus from the Dublin terminus in Store Street to my home in East Wall. So, having stepped off the bus, and after a brief wait to see if by some miracle there was someone there to meet me, I set out with my brown paper parcel under my arm on the walk home.

It was a thrill to be free. But I couldn't help thinking that it was a far cry from the dream of my homecoming when the campaign began in 1956: the dream of coming home victorious, the British gone from the North and Ireland united. Looking back, I could see that it was the dream of an innocent and inexperienced idealist.

The news of my release had been broadcast on Radio Éireann, so my father, being an avid radio listener, was keeping a vigil at our door when I turned the corner into Caledon Road. My mother was working in a shop in Stamer Street, off the South Circular Road, so she couldn't be there. There were no bands, no bonfires and no celebrations. A neighbour was standing at her door and, as I drew close, she said, 'Michael, it's so long since I saw you! Have you been in England or what?' She didn't know I'd been interned and I was too embarrassed to tell her. Nonetheless, it was a lovely day.

Within a week of my release I had been contacted by three different people, each claiming to be acting on behalf of 'official' HQ, asking me to attend separate Dublin unit reorganisation meetings. One meeting was being organised by Gerry McCarthy of Cork, one by Charlie Murphy and the third by someone who turned out to be the representative of the 'real' HQ. I attended none of them.

Seán Garland contacted me a week or so later. We agreed that the only thing to do was to rejoin the official HQ, regardless of who was in HQ, and begin to reorganise the campaign. He asked me who I thought was prepared to participate and I told him that Phil Donaghue and Tommy Nixon were anxious to be active again. The four of us duly met at the Belvedere Boxing Club in Mountjoy Square and agreed to 'row back in'. At the time, I was penniless and living at home, as I wasn't entitled to the dole. I spent most of my time visiting the National Museum, and it became a meeting-place for some of us ex-internees because it was interesting and free.

Any northern volunteers living in Dublin were receiving financial support from An Cumann Cabhrach (the Republican Aid Committee, which was set up for the relief of republican prisoners and their dependents) and from their local organisation.[1] While I could have applied to the fund, my mother wouldn't hear of it, although she was now a member of its central committee. She felt that the movement's funds should go only to those in real need, not realising that some recipients were far from needing it. Not alone that, but she used to travel to fund-raising meetings as far away as Limerick when she finished work in the small grocery shop.

A couple of weeks after our meeting in Mountjoy Square, Garland contacted me and said that the Army Council had decided to reopen the campaign that autumn. A training

---

1   Local organisations in this case included the likes of the IRA, Sinn Féin or individual members of either group. An Cumann Cabhrach handled applications centrally.

camp was being organised for those prepared to volunteer for active service and the main emphasis would be on developing leadership capability, as most volunteers already had a good deal of weapons training and combat experience. When the camp was over (after only two weeks), we would form a very effective twenty-man column that would be transported to the border to carry out a significant operation. The intelligence had been gathered and it was hoped that its success would stimulate resistance in the North so that we could break up into smaller groups to form the nuclei for a new campaign. Lastly, but most importantly, there was the promise that some long-awaited bazookas would arrive before Christmas 1959. What he had told me, particularly about the bazookas, was music to my ears. Some of us had been seeking them almost since the start of the campaign.

The camp wouldn't begin for another month, but in the meantime four or five of us were assigned to reorganising IRA units along the border. I was assigned to the north Louth and south Armagh area, with Dundalk as my base. I lived openly in a good, homely billet in a housing estate. This was two months after internment had ended in the South, so I wasn't, strictly speaking, on the run, though I was of course under Special Branch surveillance, as were other border organisers.

My objective was to re-establish the North Louth unit, which had been badly divided as a result of the Curragh split and was bedevilled by personality problems. If that was not possible, I was to establish who in the area was prepared to help us when the campaign reopened. I did not attempt to conceal my meetings with the OC and known members in the area, while I met secretly with others. I had Mark McLaughlin's car for non-secret meetings, and a bicycle, which I used at night to contact the few people living along the border who might provide billets, dumps for weapons and materials, or act as guides.

Full-time organisers, such as myself, were supposed to get £1 per week from HQ, but this never materialised. As I had no money, I 'lived off the people'. While that was fine in theory, I was billeted in the home of a man who was working long hours for low wages, and had a wife and three children to support. However, he and his wife somehow managed it, as I was never hungry. Neither they nor their children ever complained about my presence. Moreover, they always made me feel welcome, showing great dedication and commitment at a time when our cause seemed hopeless.

After two or three weeks I was stopped in broad daylight on Dundalk's Main Street by Detective-Garda Joe Donovan and another Special Branch man. Donovan was about six foot in height and had an athletic build. He searched me, then said he was taking me to the garda barracks for questioning. The same thing was happening to other organisers along the border. Given the style of my arrest, it was obvious that I wasn't going to be charged or jailed, so I did not attempt to escape.

When we reached the barracks, Donovan, who had a token grip on my arm, led the way into a room and said, 'We'll wait here till the super is ready to see you.' He invited me to sit and I declined, saying I preferred to stand. We stood there for perhaps a minute in silence. Then Donovan said, 'Mick, you look very fit. Are you as fit as they say?' I made no reply. 'Well, Mick, maybe someday I'll try you out.' His remarks were a portent of things to come.

A minute or so later I was brought in to the superintendent. He signalled for Donovan to leave. His name was, I think, Fitzpatrick. He was sixtyish and seemed a decent sort. He asked me to sit down, which I did. He said, 'Mick, I'm not going to ask you what you're doing here, because, firstly, you're not going to tell me. Right?' I said nothing. 'And, secondly, I know what you're trying to do here: you're trying to organise for another go. But I want to tell you that you're wasting your time. It's not going to work … Why don't you be a wise man and go home, get yourself a job and settle down?' He delivered this in a fatherly tone.

I made no response, in accordance with our drill in such circumstances. But I listened politely and waited for his final word. 'Well, Mick, I see you're not going to take my advice. But I'm going to give you a chance, and don't say you haven't been warned! I'm giving you a couple of days to get out of town and go back home. But if you're still around after that, you'll be picked up and you'll be charged under Section 21 of the Offences Against the State Act, and you know what that means. You'll do six months in Mountjoy for refusing to account for your movements. You'll be doing six months for nothing.' This was a new form of internment as it meant if you didn't say where you were for the previous twenty-four hours, you'd be automatically sentenced to three or more months' imprisonment.

The super called Donovan and told him to let me go. That evening I changed billets as the first step towards going on the run, at least until my business was completed in Dundalk.

A few days later I had the first of many confrontations with Detective-Garda Donovan. I was now living as much as possible under cover, which wasn't much given that I was now known to most local gardaí and had a limited number of safe billets, and virtually everyone I needed to meet was a known member or sympathiser.

One of the latter was sceptical of the threat of arrest against me and arranged for me to meet a border contact on the corner of Main Street and Church Street on a Saturday afternoon. I waited in Church Street, stepping around the corner into the Main Street every few seconds to see if my contact had arrived. After a while I peered around only to see Donovan and his partner no more than fifty yards away. They spotted me almost simultaneously. I immediately turned back into Church Street, grabbed hold of a bicycle, one of many parked there, and began pedalling like mad.

I'd gone only a few yards, when I discovered that the back wheel was flat. I jumped off and began running as fast as I could. I made it safely back to my billet and told my host what had happened, but he, sceptical as ever, said, 'You've nothing to worry about; they're only trying to scare you out of town.'

Come Sunday morning, and my host made ready for 12 p.m. mass in the Dominican church, opposite the garda barracks. 'Come on,' he says. 'Are you right?'

I told him I wasn't going, as it would be too risky.

'Come on,' he said. 'You're not that important.'

I didn't think I was 'that important' either but I didn't want to go to jail for nothing.

'Anyway,' he said, 'we've a lift up to the church, so who's going to see you? And Mick, you can't stay here unless you're going to go to mass.' After the lift up to the church, my host made his way through the crowded rear of the church to find a seat. I stayed among the crowd standing just inside the door, under the choir. I listened, entranced, to the singing. It carried me back to when I sang the mass in St Laurence O'Toole's church every Sunday. And thinking of Seville Place reminded me of John Mitchel, Joe Brady the Invincible, and home.

As the mass ended there was the usual crush at the doors and two young men took a grip of my arms. The one on my right said, somewhat nervously, 'You're Michael Ryan ... and we want you to come over to the barracks for questioning.'

My very first thought was to curse my host and my second

was that I wouldn't be going to jail this easily. The crush was still too dense to make a run for it as those leaving the church mingled with those coming for the next mass. I said to the two detectives, 'Okay, but just let me tell that woman there that I won't be back for a few hours.' The ruse worked. They released my arms and I walked slowly towards the woman. As soon as I was out of the crush, I bolted.

I sprinted down the hundred yards or so from the church to the Pearse Park housing estate. Having made certain that I'd lost the two detectives, I ran up a side path to the back of a house. I knocked on the door and, without waiting for an answer, walked in. I explained to a very surprised woman who I was, or rather what I was, that I was escaping from the Special Branch and asked her if I could stay in her house for a few hours.

'Oh, son, you've given me an awful shock!' she said as she sat down. I apologised for bursting in the way I did. Then she said, 'Yes, you can stay … Oh, you gave me a terrible fright … I'm here on my own; my husband and the children are at mass.'

I thanked her – I could even have hugged her – and sat down to wait. She offered me a cup of tea, which I declined. I spent the next few minutes trying to put her at ease. I told her that no one had seen me come in and that I had done nothing wrong.

About ten minutes later there was the sound of the front

door being opened, and she said, 'That'll be my husband and the children.' And so it was. One of the children ran into the kitchen, shouting, 'Mammy, Mammy, there's guards all over the road ... They're looking for someone that escaped.' On seeing me, however, a total stranger sitting in their kitchen, they went shyly silent.

A moment later, the husband entered the kitchen and was about to say something when he saw me. He paused and looked from me to his wife with a 'who's this?' look. Meanwhile the children had moved close to their mother to tell her, more quietly, the news from the street. I went over to the husband and, out of hearing of the children, told him my story.

He listened calmly to what I had to say and then said, 'Come on into the parlour.' There I explained my situation in detail and asked him if I could stay in his house until dark. He said, 'I don't support the IRA, but I'm no informer and there was never any in my family. I'd never turn anyone away. Yeah, you can stay till dark.' He went on to ask me if I was sure I hadn't been seen entering his house. I reassured him on that point, although I pointed out that they must have seen me run into his street. 'If I thought there was the slightest chance that they'd seen me come in here,' I said, 'I wouldn't stay.'

'Yeah,' he replied, 'they must have seen you coming into the street all right, because they're going through the back gardens. And they've blocked off the end of the street.'

I discovered later that the gardaí did indeed search

the back gardens and searched the three or four houses of sympathisers in the estate, including the one I'd stayed in before my arrest two weeks previously. The search was called off a couple of hours later.

My 'host' then said, 'I'd better go and tell the kids that you're an old friend of mine, in case they're wondering who you are.' A minute or so later he came back and said, 'Come on into the kitchen, but don't say a word about anything.'

I joined the family in the kitchen, chatted about everything – except politics that is – had a great dinner and spent the rest of the daylight hours chatting or listening to the radio. As soon as it fell dark, I said my goodbyes and gave my heartfelt thanks to my hosts. I left by the back door and made my way from back garden to back garden until I reached a safe billet.

I spent the next week really underground and trying, without much success, to get something done by way of re-organisation. Then I received word to return to Dublin as the 'special camp' would be starting the following week.

***

Twenty of us, including the OC, Seán Garland, and his number 2, Dáithí Ó Conaill, attended the camp. It was held in the Slieve Bloom mountains. Of nearly 200 young volunteers who had passed through the Curragh, these were virtually all who had volunteered for service again. The camp was supposed to last two weeks and cover all aspects of training from weaponry to field craft, attack and defence tactics, survival, leadership and so on. The weather was glorious, which was a bonus as we were living under canvas. The food was reasonably good, for an outdoor camp. There was an adequate supply of weapons. And, much to my surprise, there was an allowance of ten cigarettes a day, which was maintained most of the time. The only drawback was that it was a forestry plantation and midges plagued us.

The first two weeks saw us build up a tremendous spirit of camaraderie and confidence in each other. We even managed to overcome the antagonisms that had existed between those who had taken opposite sides in the Curragh split. However, much of what we were doing was old hat and by the third week we were beginning to feel stale and disgruntled. At the beginning of the third week, it was decided to embark on a real survival course. We were divided into three sections, each carrying a minimum supply of food and weapons, with one man appointed to each section who could use a map and compass to cover prearranged routes to an assembly point. The exercise would take five days, at the end of which the sections would rendezvous at the home of a friendly forestry worker. We were then to be brought to an assembly point for a final briefing by Seán Cronin and sent immediately to the border.

All three sections made the rendezvous and we were given

a great feed before being transported to the forming-up point for the journey to the border. However, things didn't work out quite as planned. Instead of the twenty-man column, now in the peak of physical and psychological preparedness, moving straight to its operational area, we spent another two weeks moving aimlessly around the midlands. Food was in short supply, as were cigarettes, which was particularly difficult for the smokers. None of us had any personal money and it was obvious that HQ's finances weren't good either.

Finally, we were told that things were ready. We'd be moved immediately to Charlie Prendergast's house in Athboy, Co. Meath and the day after we would be moved to the border. It wasn't that we were madly enthusiastic about resuming the life of the guerrilla, but as we had opted for that course of action we wanted to bring an end to the tension that aimless waiting inevitably causes.

We arrived in Athboy that night. We were now under the command of a new OC, Dáithí Ó Conaill. I was appointed number 2 as I was one of the most experienced volunteers still at liberty. Prendergast's, it should be noted, was a well-known IRA house.

The next morning, when the other lads and I assumed we'd be preparing to move to the North, Ó Conaill, with characteristic arrogance and stupidity, instructed me to immediately erect barbed-wire entanglements at all the gaps in the yard that surrounded the house, and on top of the walls.

Having at last come to the realisation that not all IRA leaders were competent, intelligent or capable, and having reached the end of my tolerance for nonsense orders, I asked him why he wanted this done. Not being used to someone questioning his orders, Ó Conaill looked at me as if I had two heads. He said, 'If we're raided it'll make it difficult for them [the gardaí and the Special Branch] to get in at us.'

'Yes,' I responded politely, 'it would slow them down in getting in to us; but we wouldn't be able to get out. And the appearance of the barbed wire on the walls would be observed by the postman and locals, who would surely speculate that the IRA were back in Charlie's.' I suggested instead that we introduce a strict regimen to restrict the movement of the men in order to prevent observation.

Ó Conaill merely said, 'Start erecting the wire immediately. That's an order.' He then told me that he was leaving to arrange transport to the border. He would return the following day, or the day after at the latest, and I was to take charge of the camp in the meantime.

I assembled the lads and relayed the instruction about the erection of the barbed wire. I told them of my objections, but that these had been overruled. We began to erect the wire. One of the lads, Tim Nicholls, asked privately, 'What kind of idiot is he?'

Four days later Ó Conaill returned, but he only stayed long enough to tell me to move everyone to Brendan Lynch's house in Ráth Cairn, five miles away. We would be taken from there the following morning to the border. When I asked him what transport was available to carry out the transfer, he told me to 'use Brendan Lynch's car'. Brendan was an IRA member, a fact that was well known locally and therefore added to the risk factor.

I then told him that Charlie Prendergast, our host, who was deaf but 'heard' things, had mentioned that people were beginning to talk about the 'strange goings-on' at his house and felt it was only a matter of time before we were raided. In which case, I said, as Lynch's was an equally well-known IRA billet it would also be raided. We would be better getting out of the area altogether.

Ó Conaill dismissed Charlie's concerns as pure rumour and ordered me to proceed to Lynch's, where we'd be picked up first thing next morning and taken to the border. Having inspected the wire, he left to organise transport for the pick-up the following morning. In accordance with instructions, I borrowed Brendan Lynch's car, a Volkswagen Beetle, which was well known locally, and began ferrying the lads and their gear to Lynch's as soon as it was dark. The lads groaned with disappointment and disbelief when I told them that the billet we were transferring to was only five miles away. They felt it was another con job.

After Tim Nicholls, who was doing the driving, had made six or seven trips to Lynch's, there was only one more load to

MY LIFE IN THE IRA

go: myself, Nicholls and the last remaining items of gear. It was about 1 a.m. when the two of us, heaving a sigh of relief, set off on the twenty-minute journey to Ráth Cairn. As we approached a bridge on a back road about two miles from Brendan Lynch's house, a garda stepped into the middle of the road, waved a torch and signalled us to stop. This being a most unusual occurrence at that out-of-the-way place and time of night, we decided not to stop. However, as the garda was standing right in the middle of this narrow road, Nicholls slowed down as though he was going to stop. When the garda stepped aside to approach the driver's side, Nicholls accelerated and we drove like the hammers of hell for Lynch's.

As soon as we reached the house, ten minutes later, I called the lads together and told them of the checkpoint and the likelihood of a raid. We spent the next five minutes packing and distributing the gear. Then, as we'd no safe transport, we headed out across the fields, with our host, Brendan Lynch, leading, until we reached a small copse half a mile away. I told Brendan to explain to Ó Conaill why we had moved and we settled down to wait.

About an hour before dawn, we heard someone approach. It was Brendan. 'Ó Conaill just came back,' he said. 'I told him why you'd moved out to the fields, but he said it was nonsense, and that you and the rest of the lads were to come back to the house immediately, that the transport would be arriving any minute.'

We returned to the house, where Ó Conaill reprimanded me and said the transport would arrive any minute. I told him that all our gear was packed and we were ready to go. Despite Ó Conaill's attitude I was so convinced that a raid was imminent that I placed Tommy Farrell at the gate on watch. About an hour later the first of our cars arrived, followed a few minutes later by a van. Farrell remained on watch at the gate, which was thirty yards away, while we began packing the gear and ourselves into the transport. Five minutes later, we were ready to go.

A few of the lads and myself were sitting in the rear of the van, right up against the back doors. Beside me was Phil Donaghue, and we were looking out the back windows to direct the driver as he reversed to leave the yard.

Just at that moment Tommy Farrell came running, shouting, 'The branch! The branch are coming up the road!'

With that, Phil grabbed the inside handle of the door, but it wouldn't open; then he pushed his arm through a broken window, grabbed the outside handle and flung the door wide. As we clambered out, we saw two or three Special Branch men running towards us. We ran across the yard and through a gap into the first field, which was newly ploughed and made for heavy going. We began running, followed closely by the rest of the lads who had managed to get out of the cars and by the Special Branch men.

When Phil and I were about fifty yards from a very tall

hedge that bordered the field, I glanced around to see what was going on behind me. I saw Nicholls and another volunteer being grabbed by a few Special Branch men, and that another couple of them were chasing myself and Phil.

Although Phil and I were very fit, we were exhausted by the time we hauled ourselves across the ditch and through the hedge into the next field. I paused to get my breath back and saw that Phil was having difficulty getting across. Just as I reached out to grasp his hand, a Special Branch man grabbed his legs. However, Phil kicked backwards, knocking the branch man to the ground. I discovered afterwards that the reason he had difficulty was that his belt caught momentarily on the barbed wire strung through the hedge.

Ó Conaill had also escaped the net into the field where we were, which was about five feet higher than the one we'd just left, so we were able to see that many of the lads had been captured. Our pursuers were catching their breath just at the other side of the hedge.

Phil, Ó Conaill and I jogged on for another fifteen minutes, then decided to seek shelter in the next house we came across. It was now 7 a.m. and full light. The house was a new bungalow, situated alongside a road. Not being familiar with the area, we'd no clue about the political orientation of the occupants. But beggars can't be choosers and luck was on our side.

After repeated knocking, the door was opened by a man

in his thirties. We told him who we were, what had happened and that we were seeking shelter for a few hours. We were really seeking shelter until nightfall, at least, but we didn't say that. We needn't have worried, as he was a supporter of the IRA campaign. 'Sure I'll put ye up,' he said. 'Come on in for God's sake.' A few minutes later we went up into the attic, in case the Special Branch decided to carry out a spot check.

We were supplied with plenty of tea and sandwiches throughout the day. The Special Branch set up a roadblock right outside the house, mainly to check the occupants of cars. Not surprisingly, there was very little conversation among the three of us as we waited in the dark attic for nightfall. Phil and I were sitting somewhat close to each other, while Ó Conaill sat some distance away. I was too angry with him to engage in any conversation whatsoever.

Come nightfall, and the Special Branch having ended their roadblock some hours earlier, we came down into the kitchen where we devoured a big fry. Our host agreed to arrange transport to Jack Guiney's, a safe house in Dunboyne, ten miles or so further south. Our driver was Pat Goggins.

We discovered the full extent of the catastrophe the next morning. Eight of our comrades were arrested at Lynch's and another four at a Westmeath camp a few miles away, after the Special Branch found a map in Lynch's house marking its location. For reasons best known to himself, Ó Conaill had left a sealed envelope containing written instructions for a driver who was to call to Lynch's later that day on how to get to the Westmeath camp. The twelve lads were sentenced to terms of imprisonment in Mountjoy. So, for these twelve volunteers, more than half the column, all the training, the waiting, the frustration, were for nothing. Brendan Lynch was also arrested and sentenced to six months in Mountjoy Prison. The 'crack column' ended up a shipwreck, due entirely to Ó Conaill's intransigence over erecting barbed-wire 'defences' at Prendergast's, his refusal to acknowledge the likelihood of the raids and a decision to leave written details of the Westmeath camp with Lynch. We also lost all our camping gear, tents, blankets, utensils, Primus stoves, spare clothing and footwear, a considerable loss considering the chronic state of IRA finances at the time.

The lads who escaped were so angry about Ó Conaill's behaviour that they asked me to convey to HQ our dissatisfaction with him and request an inquiry. The big snag was that my only contact with HQ was Ó Conaill. As it happened, a few days later Ó Conaill told me that the chief of staff wanted me to supply a written account of the raid and that he would bring it to him that night. I wrote the account, including my criticisms of Ó Conaill, and handed it to him. That was the last I heard of it. I was never asked to make a verbal submission, nor was there ever an inquiry.

The following morning, I was collected and told that I was going to Co. Clare, where I'd be assisting Ó Conaill in the running of another training camp. Ó Conaill was OC and I would be his number 2 again. Not a pleasant prospect for me, but I went anyway as, if I refused, I risked being dismissed from the IRA.

The only sustaining element of that camp was the fact that it overlooked the mystical Lough Greaney, the Loch Gréine of Brian Merriman's epic poem, 'Cúirt an Mheán Oíche'. The camp was attended by about six trainees and lasted ten days. The weapons – a Bren, some Lee-Enfields and some Thompsons – were all serviceable, but the training was the same old stuff. It was as if the previous two years' experience had never happened. The one 'innovative' idea was introduced by Ó Conaill, who advised recruits that 'When operating in the North it was a waste of time and energy walking the fields and mountains. Instead you should use the roads.' Within two months of giving this piece of advice, Ó Conaill walked into a B Special ambush while he was walking a road in Co. Tyrone. He was seriously wounded, but survived and was jailed for several years.

While the view was enchanting, our living conditions were primitive. We had no tents, only one blanket or a sleeping-bag apiece, the barest cooking utensils and one Primus stove, and I had no change of clothing because of the capture of all our equipment at Athboy. Ó Conaill's answer to the shelter problem was the construction of a crude lean-to hut from materials in the wood. 'The guerrilla must be resourceful at all times!' he said. I thought to myself, *The guerrilla must also be intelligent enough to avoid this situation.*

After several hours of pulling and hacking, because we had no saw, we completed the shelter, which was no more than a dozen or so uprights roofed over by as many thick-leaved branches as they would support to keep out the rain. But the branches of pine trees don't afford much protection from the rain, and it rained continuously for the ten days of the camp. Moreover, the ground was already damp, so with no groundsheets and no protection from above, we were constantly wet.

Afterwards the trainees were dispersed to various areas. Ó Conaill went to Co. Tyrone and I was assigned to Garland's four-man column on the Leitrim–Fermanagh border. I was first brought to Ballinamore, Co. Leitrim, where I spent a very comfortable day. The following evening, I set off on a borrowed bicycle in the company of a local girl who acted as my guide on the ten-mile trip to Swanlinbar, where Garland's section was billeted. A very dedicated member, she then had to cycle the ten miles back to Ballinamore, having dropped me off at midnight.

The small house was about fifty yards in from the road, and whoever was on guard duty emerged from the darkness and brought me into the kitchen, which, for security, was unlit. Only the glow of the fire revealed the lads who were quietly sitting around it. We greeted each other in whispers and room was made for me at the fire. One of the lads mentioned that when the woman of the house and her husband got up in the morning we'd be able to sleep in their bed. It was music to my ears to hear that there was a woman in the house, as it usually meant it would be clean and well-kept. Just as importantly, her mere presence would have an elevating influence. A short while later Malachy McGurran, who was from Lurgan and had a wry sense of humour, asked, 'Are you hungry?'

'I'm starving!' I had my fill of lovely homemade bread. I noticed, however, that none of the others were eating.

Come first light I was able to see the kitchen in some detail. I didn't like what I saw, but I held my peace. At about 8 a.m. there was the sound of our host getting up. After a few minutes a very unkempt man emerged from the bedroom and, with 'Hello, lads', proceeded to the kitchen door that led outside and urinated. This was Andy Eliza. When he finished, he turned back inside, put water in the kettle and put it on the fire to boil.

Then I heard the woman of the house – who had obviously taken a little bit longer to dress – open the door of the bedroom and I waited for her appearance with welcome anticipation. To my surprise, it wasn't a woman who emerged but a man – a man, moreover, who appeared to be somewhat 'simple'. I looked at the lads, who were grinning from ear to ear at the success of their joke.

There was no woman, only two bachelor brothers, one

of whom, Bernard, was the cook. He went outside to relieve himself as well, then came back and announced, 'I'll make the bread.' He proceeded to throw flour and other ingredients into a basin and mix the lot with his unwashed hands. Now I knew why the lads hadn't partaken of the 'delicious homemade bread' and opted to eat the shop bread. Nor were we in any hurry to go to bed. But we were still grateful to these two men for putting us up, grateful for their hospitality and for sharing their meagre resources with us at a time when few were willing to do so. I'm not condemning these two bachelor brothers for the primitive state of their home. I only wish to illustrate the fact that in September 1959, thirty-seven years after the establishment of an independent Irish state, there were still people living in conditions that were more appropriate to the middle of the nineteenth century.

Andy and Bernard were not unique, especially in the economically depressed areas of rural Ireland. They were living in penury. Their few acres were swampy, because of high rainfall and poor drainage, and they were lucky to get a few cocks of hay each year. There were no local industries and, as the surrounding land was made up of similar smallholdings, there was little or no labouring work available. Moreover, Bernard wasn't capable of working. Virtually their only source of sustenance was the few pounds' unemployment assistance they received each week. Together with a bit of bartering, the few weeks' work Andy got during the harvest season in

Co. Fermanagh and a few pounds from distributing poitín, it enabled them to exist. They lived mainly on bread and tea, potatoes and eggs. Vegetables and meat were luxuries. They would have mutton stew, without vegetables, about once every ten days.

Their cottage was about a mile from Swanlinbar. There was no path from the road to the cottage, not even a scattering of gravel. The kitchen floor had stone flags, but the bedroom floor was bare clay. There was no running water, no indoor toilet, or outdoor toilet for that matter and, of course, no bathroom. An indoor tap, as in many other areas of rural Ireland at that time, would have been a luxury. An indoor toilet or bathroom was a rarity, even in some urban areas. They had no electricity; they couldn't have afforded it anyway. So they used candles and an oil lamp for light. They didn't have a radio because they couldn't afford one. Their only contact with the outside world was the local weekly paper, *The Anglo-Celt*. Water for drinking, cooking and washing had to be carried in a bucket from the well, which was fifty yards from the house. (No wonder there was little washing-up done!) Now here they were, despite their poverty, putting the five of us up and sharing their meagre rations with us. And we ourselves had no money. Not a penny.

We soon discovered that if we wanted reliable intelligence on RUC and British Army activity we would have to get it ourselves, because the handful of supporters in the area were in no position to spend night after night for a week, and it would take a week, watching for patrols. Like our hosts, they had a hard enough struggle to live without the added burden of going without sleep for nights on end, not to speak of the added hardship of an hour or two's trek from home to a watch point.

Years after the campaign ended, one of these local supporters confided to me: 'Mick, there was many a time I dozed off when I was lying behind the ditch. A patrol could have passed and I wouldn't have known it. But to be honest with you, even when I saw a patrol I didn't want to tell ye about it, because ... sure the campaign was lost, and I didn't want to be sending ye to your deaths or to jail for nothing. And that's the way the rest of the people, the people who supported us, felt too. They supported ye, but they didn't want to see ye dying for nothing.'

So there was a long, tedious and risky pre-operational phase when we made reconnaissance trips to those border roads that patrols could reasonably be expected to use. And, with a heavy garda and Free State army presence on the southern side, we were restricted to hitting a target from three hours after dusk to within two hours of dawn, allowing time to approach and withdraw under cover of darkness.

We were wet most of the time, for not alone was it generally raining but the ground was swampy. We also had to wade the Swanlinbar River up to our waists on every reconnaissance trip because of the permanent garda roadblock on the only bridge for miles around. We didn't notice the wettings so much while we were on the move; it was only when we'd have to stop in one place for a few hours that it would get to us. Then we'd become uncomfortably stiff with a paralysing coldness that induced lethargy and eroded morale. On such occasions someone would always groan, 'This is fuckin' terrible, but we could be worse off. We could be dead!'

What sustained us was a commitment to the campaign, a deep feeling of comradeship, knowing we could rely totally on each other, and a sense that we were an integral part of the historical tradition of resistance to British rule in Ireland. We had an obligation to those who had struggled, suffered and died in the cause. What was our sacrifice compared to theirs?

I would be conscience-stricken by images of the ruthless exploitation of the Irish people over the centuries by the English and by images of the heroes and heroines who had suffered and died in their attempts to free our people – of Wolfe Tone dying alone in his cell, of Robert Emmet and Sarah Curran, of John Mitchel, deported for life to Van Diemen's Land, of Constance Markievicz, of Patrick Pearse, Seán Mac Diarmada, John MacBride, James Connolly, and all the rest of those great people. But even this motivation and comradeship couldn't compensate for poor operating conditions, not just in this area but many others as well. Problems included the absence of the right kind of equipment or an adequate support infrastructure, the hunger and the constant wettings, the absence of a few shillings to buy cigarettes or whatever, sleeping in barns and other crude shelters for days at a time and the inadequate food supply because most of the time we'd arrive unexpectedly at homes where our hosts just wouldn't have enough food on hand. There was always an adequate supply of tea and bread, however, for which we were thankful.

Because this was part of guerrilla life, we had a built-in psychological tolerance of the conditions. Nevertheless, over a protracted period, physical deterioration and a concomitant erosion of morale occurred, particularly as awareness grew that the campaign had been over in all but name as far back as February or March 1957. But while a few succumbed for one reason or another, the rest continued to do their utmost, regardless.

Because of these difficulties, we could hit only the weakest possible targets, and even to do that meant waiting for the enemy to present us with such an opportunity. As a result, we spent an inordinate amount of time awaiting the rare opportunities. After a couple of weeks spent in a fruitless effort to establish intelligence on a regular patrol, Garland decided, rightly, that we should set up an ambush on a road where there was an occasional night patrol. Following this attempt to ambush a patrol, we would disperse to other areas and establish new active service units around individual members of the column, regardless of the outcome of the attempted ambush. This would prove to be wishful thinking that reflected our aspirations rather than the real world around us. Anyway, from a security standpoint, we'd already spent too much time in the area.

We assembled the weapons, ammunition and gelignite essential for the job and spent several hours cleaning the weapons and the ammunition, which had been dumped in a dampish place. Myself and another volunteer assembled the mine, sixty to seventy pounds of gelignite packed tightly into a large wooden butter-box. Our weapons consisted of a few Lee-Enfield rifles and a couple of old, but still serviceable 1920 Thompson sub-machine guns.

As soon as it was dark, we took a circuitous route to the border and the ambush position. We took turns carrying the mine, which had to be hoisted onto one's back and strapped on with a rope harness. Having made the mine, I felt reasonably confident that it wouldn't explode prematurely, but there was always a nagging doubt, particularly in view of the poor state of the gelignite. Some sticks were 'weeping', the nitro-glycerine seeping through the wax cover, which meant that too much vibration might cause an explosion.

The going was slow. Moreover, it was a pitch-black night and we had to stay within arm's length of each other to avoid being separated and to be sure of hearing the guide's warnings, whispered from man to man down the line, of the presence of obstacles.

After about an hour plodding through the fields we eventually reached a disused railway line, which we took for a mile or so and made for relatively easy going as the tracks and sleepers had long ago been removed. But it was laborious, having to move at the pace of the slowest, the man carrying the mine. There were increasingly frequent stops to transfer the mine from one back to another, as men grew tired.

Of course we all complained intermittently, and in our own individual way: 'This is some army', 'We're like mules', etc. In fact, it might not have been a bad idea to borrow a donkey to carry the mine, though none of us had thought of it in time.

Our journey along the railway line was uneventful, although there was nearly a disaster when we crossed the fence at the end. The guide was in front, the OC was next and I, who happened to be carrying the mine at that point, followed. The guide turned to us and said, 'Be careful here now.' But he didn't elaborate about why we should be careful. He crossed the fence. Then Garland, who was directly in front of me, stepped across and disappeared from view. There was a ten-foot drop from the fence to the floor of a cattle-loading pen, and he had fallen into it. I, with the sixty pounds of gelignite on my back, was about to follow him over when I heard him shout, 'Mick, stay where you are! Don't move!'

'Where are you? What's happened?' I asked. It was pitch-dark. Realising that I was carrying the mine, and aware that if

I fell on top of him even if the mine didn't go off the weight of it would kill him and probably me, he shouted again, 'Stay where you are!'

So I stayed where I was until we ascertained the situation; then we helped him out of the pit. Fortunately, he only injured his knee and he insisted he was fit to carry on.

We resumed our trek to the border, which for us was the Swanlinbar River, and reached it about an hour later. The river was only twenty yards wide but in flood from the incessant rain. The guide waded into the middle of the river to test the depth and waded back to the southern bank to tell us that it was 'only' chest-deep in the middle and safe to cross.

After much cursing and swearing we eventually succeeded in hoisting the mine high up on the shoulders of the man whose turn it was to carry it. We secured it with ropes to his body and with a couple of us supporting him on each side – while at the same time holding our weapons and ammunition clear of the water – we set out to wade the river. It was easier said than done. The bottom was stony, so there was much slipping and sliding. I couldn't help thinking about how we wouldn't be in much fighting condition when we reached the other side. Even if we weren't spotted we were going to have to lie for hours sodden to the skin in the hope of encountering the occasional patrol.

Once across, the mine-carrier was relieved of his burden and we hunkered down on the bank for a few minutes' rest.

Some of us took off our boots and socks to drain them of water. It was a subdued break.

The mine was then secured to the back of the next carrier and we plodded uphill to the ambush site, about a quarter of a mile away. It was on the Derrylin road and we reached it about 11 p.m. It wasn't a great ambush position, but it was the best available. Tommy Nixon and myself found a suitable position for the mine in the clay bank, dug a hole, placed the mine, wired it and returned to the column some few yards away.

The rest of the lads, having readied their weapons, were standing in a tight circle, stamping their feet to keep warm. We settled as best we could to await the patrol. The rain fell incessantly and, because we were already soaked, we remained standing, stamping our feet and generally moving in place to keep ourselves warm. There was hardly any conversation. Malachy McGurran, always good for a joke or a laugh, was uncharacteristically quiet.

We waited and waited. But it was in vain. At about 3 a.m. we had to leave if we were going to make it back across the border before first light. The OC had no option but to abort the operation. But what were we going to do with the mine? The usual drill, if we were remaining in an area, was either to conceal its position, leave it somewhere near at hand, or dig it out and take it with us for safe dumping and another try. However, as this was our final attempt at an operation in the area, the device was unstable and fully primed, and carrying it back would take too long, Garland decided there was no option but to explode it. As soon as I did, we began our hasty withdrawal.

There were, of course, British Army patrols in the area, but they were usually too big to hit without the advantage of a mine, unless we wanted to commit suicide. Bazookas might not have been a total answer to our problems but they would have made a critical difference to the scale and frequency of operations we could have mounted – but, despite promises from HQ, they had yet to materialise. Travelling without the mine we reached our billet an hour or so later.

It was still another hour to dawn, so we were somewhat surprised to see a light in the kitchen. We went into the barn while one lad crept up to the window to see what was going on. He came back saying, 'It's that wee bastard Charlie the Hare ... He's sitting at the fire, and he's likely to stay there most of the day.'

Charlie the Hare was a local petty thief, who had done time in jail. He was regarded as a simpleton by some local people, but as a shrewd and cunning informer by others. We went along with the latter assessment. There was nothing for it but to find a hiding place at the rear of the barn, in case Charlie decided to come in. We stripped to the skin, burrowed into the hay and tried to get the dampness out of our bodies and some heat back in.

A few hours later, we heard him shout his goodbyes to

Andy and Bernard. By now we were so bone-tired and muscle-stiffened from the cold, the damp and the hunger, that it took us several minutes to shake ourselves back to life and return to the cottage, where we spread our clothes and boots around the fire to dry, and huddled as close to it as we could get. Half an hour or so later, after a cup of tea and eating whatever bread there was, we felt almost human again.

Meanwhile, Andy and Bernard were breakfasting, word-lessly, at the table. When Andy discovered that there was no more bread, he told Bernard to make some, whereupon Bernard proceeded to do just that. This time I didn't mind if he drooled into the mix or not. Then Andy said, 'Boys, Charlie the Hare said he'd be back tonight ...' On hearing this we decided to go to bed and get a few hours' sleep before dark and then march to another billet to arrange transport to our future destinations.

We arranged for the safe dumping of the weapons and ammunition before our dispersal to new operational areas. Mine was south Armagh, but first I would have to go to Dub-lin for instructions. I cycled to Ballinamore, where John Joe McGirl, with his usual generosity, supplied me with cigarettes, a couple of quid and a couple of drinks. Then he organised a car to take me to Carrick-on-Shannon railway station, where I caught the train to Dublin.

***

I found a safe billet in Dublin at Madeleine Heffernan's house on Leinster Avenue, Rathgar. I arrived there in the company of fellow volunteer Maurice Fitz; and that was a bad beginning, for Madeleine had no time for Maurice. She said she didn't like his eyes. 'That fellow can't look you straight in the face, and I don't like that in anyone' was the usual reason she gave. But the real reason was that she had caught Maurice making a swipe with his boot at her dog, Terry, who greeted Maurice the first time he called to Madeleine's with a couple of make-believe growls, combined with a few not-too-convincing barks. This guardian role was Terry's justification for living, and a very good life he had too. Madeleine's first loyalty and love was reserved for the dog, and everyone else came second, including 'that brother of mine', which was the way she usually referred to her brother Myles. I was to stay in this billet numerous times throughout the rest of the campaign.

Madeleine had a love-hate relationship with us. One day she would be all over us and the next she would be complaining about those 'layabout republicans' who were great at thinking up excuses for not working and reasons why they had to stay on the run in her house. 'And I wouldn't mind if they'd help me out with a few pounds now and then towards the firing and food,' she'd say. 'They're as bad as that drunken brother of mine; it's no wonder he's no money, between drinking and gambling and lending the rest of it to those no-good wasters

Brendan Behan and Paddy Kavanagh and their dirty pals. That McDaids ought to be burned down.

'I don't know how Myles fell in with that crowd of foul-mouthed bums – and that's all they are. Writers and poets how are you! Sure Behan and Kavanagh hardly went to school at all, and Myles even went to Clongowes, and what did it get him? I'll tell you what it got him. He got a good job with the New Ireland Assurance Company and was doing all right till he joined the bloody IRA, and that New Ireland was full of IRA men. Sure wasn't it started by them so-called patriots Thornton and O'Reilly?[2] And what was Thornton only a turncoat! Didn't he turn Free State and murder some of his best friends during the Civil War! And now he's the best of pals with them that was his enemies at that time – sitting on the same board of directors with them, with O'Reilly and the others.

'Ah, by God, they knew which side of their bread was buttered. Codded the people, they did, with their patriotic founding of the New Ireland Friendly Society, which would keep your money in Ireland, don't be sending it out to England,

2   Frank Thornton and William O'Reilly were 1916 veterans who helped found the New Ireland Assurance after their release from Frongoch to offer an Irish alternative to British insurance companies. They had the support of Michael Collins and, like most of his close associates, took the pro-Treaty side in the Civil War. Nevertheless, the company had a policy of recruiting former IRA members down on their luck well into the 1960s.

our enemy, by insuring with the Royal Liver. Insure with us and you'll be serving your country and yourself by keeping your money at home. Oh, yes, they did, but Thornton and O'Reilly then, when the society, which was a co-operative, began to get the poor stupid people of Dublin to take out their burial policies with them, didn't those two rats convert the society into a company overnight, without a by-your-leave to anyone. No one was the wiser, but that pair became rich men overnight and they've never stopped making money since. But that stupid brother of mine can't see the kind they are. Just because they give him a fiver for the IRA or the prisoners every year he won't have a word said about them – and them millionaires! You won't find them gambling and drinking their money away or risking their necks in the IRA now.'

Myles, however, seldom heard much of this, as Madeleine could never work up the courage to tell him what she really thought, so she'd say these things only to me and a couple of her trusted friends, and of course only when we'd be in her good books.

Myles, who was then about fifty-two and no longer actively involved in the movement, would arrive home every night at about 9 p.m. He was usually well jarred and always carried a parcel of meat under his arm and a baby Paddy in his pocket. He would come into the sitting-room, studiously ignore Madeleine and greet me with, 'Well, Mick how're things? Okay, I hope,' all the time picking his way carefully around Madeleine's knitting or magazines while he made his way to a vacant armchair. Madeleine would be just as careful to avoid greeting Myles, except to glance up at him, nod her head as if to say, 'Look at him, drunk as usual, and I suppose he'll expect me to get up and cook that pound of steak he's got. Well, I will not, not tonight. I'm just going for once to sit tight and do my knitting and see the television without interruption from him.'

But after a couple of minutes, during which time both of them would be engaging me in conversation while ignoring the other as though they weren't in the room, the hunger and impatience would eventually force Myles to capitulate, and he'd open up with, 'Well, Mick, did you have anything to eat today?' And even though I might not have eaten, I couldn't very well admit it, as that would be an insult to Madeleine or her larder, so I'd usually say, 'Yes, thanks, Myles.'[3]

'Well, you're lucky. I hadn't a bit all day and here I come home and I suppose I'll have to cook the bit of meat myself,' and still not even a glance in Madeleine's direction.

But that was usually enough to draw Madeleine's fire. 'You'd have eaten if you hadn't spent the last four hours in McDaids with them tramps or them bloody IRA men,

---

3   'Larder' refers to a small room or cupboard which provided a cool storage area for items such as milk, fish or meat in the pre-fridge-freezer era.

drinking your money; and now you come home and expect me to cook your dinner and me only in a few hours from work too, working for that bloody robber Joe McGrath – another patriot, another one of your IRA men. I'm bloody well fed up with the IRA, and you can go and cook it yourself.'

Upon which Myles would look suitably annoyed at the insult to his friends – and, unintentionally, to me – even though Madeleine would never insult myself or any of the others who were on the run. 'That's a disgraceful way to talk of my friends,' he'd say. 'You see what I've to come home to, Mick? It's no wonder I stay in the pub.' And that was as good an excuse as any as far as Myles was concerned. He'd then rub his hands together in barely controlled anger and frustration and say something like, 'Well, Mick, that's a nice thing for anyone's sister to say about a brother, what? By God, if only my mother could hear that! She'll be turning in her grave to think that her own daughter wouldn't cook a bit of dinner for her own son.'

At that point, Madeleine would usually give in. She'd fold her magazine, carefully and deliberately and as slowly as possible, cease her knitting and pack it in its bag, and then without a word move into the kitchen, picking up the parcel of meat with a look of distaste and close the door with a mild slam. From the kitchen you'd hear her comments, and the sound of plates and cutlery being noisily clattered. Then there would be the sound of the meat frying, usually accompanied by a shouted comment, 'Why don't you come in at a proper time for your tea, like any decent Christian?' – which seldom brought forth a response from Myles, other than to whisper to me, 'Isn't that an awful way to be treated by your own sister?'

Madeleine, whose anger would have dissipated somewhat, would bring in the fry, place it convenient to Myles and, by way of a truce, say, 'That's a lovely bit of steak.' And Myles would respond with, 'Ah, that looks great, Madeleine.' Madeleine would return to her knitting, or whatever she was doing, and we'd spend the while before bedtime chatting.

It was a world away from the cottages and farmhouses on the border, and yet there was the same unstinting support for those of us on the run that never sought any reward other than the achievement of the Irish republic that we had all been taught was our common birthright.

If Madeleine could appear a scold at times and Myles a waster, they had a generosity of spirit you could not fault. Myles was certainly more sinned against than sinner; he pulled me out of a couple of awkward holes. He had a wonderful command of English and was a great conversationalist. He was also instrumental in getting me a job with the New Ireland Assurance Company after the campaign finished. When he was broke, he'd borrow from anyone who was able to lend him 'half a sheet' (a ten-shilling note); when he was flush, he would freely lend money to his friends.

Because of Myles' propensity to attend the funeral of

every demised employee of New Ireland, he came to be known as 'the chief mourner'. However, in 1968, when his health began to deteriorate rapidly – cancer was diagnosed – the chief mourner himself became the mourned. He spent the last month of his life in a nursing home. On the last occasion I visited him he was in great form. 'Mick,' he said, 'I'd an amazing experience last night. You won't believe what I'm going to tell you!'

'What's that, Myles?' I said.

Myles gleefully rubbed his withered hands together, his skeletal face broke into a frightful, incongruous grin, and he said, 'You're not going to believe it, Mick!' He wrung his hands slowly, in anticipation of what he was going to relate. 'Last night, just before I went asleep, I told the nurse, a grand nurse she is too, that I'd love to see my brother Tom, who's in Boston. And she said to me that I would see Tom. And, Mick, you're not going to believe this, but just when I was about to go asleep, what do you think? A helicopter landed right outside my window! The pilot got out and said, "Myles, we're going to take you to Boston to see your brother." I thanked him very much and then he tied my bed onto the back of the helicopter with a rope, and a few minutes later we were in Boston, and I was talking to Tom.'

Realising that Myles was hallucinating as a result of the painkilling drugs he was on, and not wishing to destroy his last remaining illusion, I said, 'That's great, Myles!'

'Wasn't it?' said Myles. And with that he fell asleep. He died that night.

Madeleine was determined that Myles would be buried with 'military honours'.

'Now, Mick,' she said, 'I hope you and all the boys will be at the funeral, and that he'll get the tricolour and the shots over his grave.'

This presented quite a problem, as it would be extremely difficult to give Myles the full treatment. He owed money to all and sundry – the publican, his bookie, his friends and colleagues – from one pound to hundreds. But, as Myles would say at those times when Madeleine would chide him for spending all his money on drink and for always coming in drunk, 'What are you worried about? I'm well covered and there'll be plenty of money there to look after you and my creditors whenever I go,' which usually produced the response from Madeleine, 'Oh, there's the great IRA man!'

On the day of the funeral, we put on the guard of honour, complete with flags and everything went fine until we got to the graveside. Madeleine kept asking me when the firing party was going to do their firing, that Myles would love it and that he deserved it. Still I hadn't the heart to tell her that he wasn't going to have one.

It seemed no time at all, and the prayers were over and we were making our way down to the gate, when suddenly, from the far side of the graveyard, there came the sound of a volley of shots. It was like a bolt from the blue – and the answer to a fervent prayer – for the shots didn't come from any of Myles's comrades. As luck would have it, there was a funeral of a Free State soldier going on, and he of course had a firing party. Madeleine was overjoyed at the sound of the shots and squeezed my arm in appreciation. She looked around at her relatives and friends as if to say, 'There, now, didn't I tell you Myles' friends wouldn't let him down!' And until the day she died Madeleine thought her brother had his firing party.

Myles' death had a devastating effect on Madeleine. She still loved him, despite all his transgressions. Moreover, she could always depend on him to 'deal effectively' with their landlord whenever their rent was overdue, forgetting, or ignoring, for the time being at least, that the rent or rates would be overdue because of Myles not having contributed his portion of either to Madeleine.

The landlord was Jewish, which was a stroke of luck for Myles and a misfortune for the landlord. Not that Myles was anti-Semitic; it was just that he was able to exploit the fact that the landlord was Jewish as a golden opportunity to demonstrate to his sister that he still cared for her.

I couldn't help overhearing Madeleine's reply to the landlord when he phoned her one day. 'How dare you! How dare you threaten me, threaten to take me and my brother to court! We've lived here for thirty years! How dare you threaten to evict me and my brother and my guest! I'm going to tell my brother about you annoying me like this, and I'll have you know that my brother is in the IRA. So you just watch out. How dare you threaten me! And I'll have you know too that I have friends who're very high up in the IRA!' I winced at this. 'I'm going to get my brother to talk to you as soon as he gets in tonight!' And that ended the conversation with the landlord.

'Mick,' she said, 'hadn't he some cheek! Didn't I do the right thing?' This was a rhetorical question, luckily.

That night Myles arrived home at his usual time, opened and closed the front door with his usual deferential quietness, and entered the sitting-room with the customary parcel of meat under his arm and with that usual expression of trepidation on his face – in anticipation of Madeleine's customary greeting, 'Drinking with your drunkard friends again!' On this night, however, and to Myles's visible relief, Madeleine looked up at Myles and, with a welcoming expression on her face, asked him if he'd had a good day. 'Are you hungry? Do you want me to do a fry for you?'

Myles' face lit up like a full moon. 'I'd a very good day and I'd love a fry. I've some lovely sausages and pudding here, enough for the three of us.' Myles, who couldn't believe his luck at this turn of events, was positively gushing towards Madeleine and carefully, and with apologies, negotiated his way over her wool and patterns, which were strewn across his path, as he made his way to his chair. Madeleine, having graciously taken possession of the parcel of meat, went out to the kitchen to cook it.

Myles, as happy as a pig in clover because of this unaccustomed welcome, sank into his chair with relief and gratitude. With his usual good nature, he asked how things were with me.

A couple of minutes later Madeleine, anxious to get Myles to stay the landlord's hand, came into the room and told him about the landlord's demands. Whereupon Myles, in an appropriately angry tone and turning to me but addressing us both, said, 'There's no one going to talk to my sister like that. Excuse me for a moment, Mick, but I have to talk to this Jewboy and tell him a thing or two.' So he went out to the hall, where the phone was, to call the landlord.

'This is Myles Heffernan here … Just one moment. How dare you threaten my sister with eviction, you, you bastard! Look, if my sister said you threatened to evict her then you did. I believe my sister before I'd believe the word of a – a – a Jewboy landlord. And in case you don't know, I can get the IRA on to you … Well, I'm glad you understand that, but don't you abuse my sister again with your threats!' He slammed the phone down and turned to me and said, 'Well, Mick, that's given that landlord something to think about! … Now, Mick, don't get me wrong. I've nothing against Jews – I've some very good Jewish friends – but that landlord is one of the worst types of greedy Jew.'

All of Myles's confrontations with Madeleine took place when he'd arrive home promptly, but well jarred, at 9 p.m. And, of course, she couldn't be blamed for that, as Myles was contributing little or nothing to the household expenses, leaving Madeleine to run the house on her meagre weekly wage of £10 from the Irish Hospitals Trust, probably Ireland's worst employer. However, after each tirade, Madeleine would heap an equal amount of abuse on Myles' 'drunkard friends', whom she ultimately blamed for his drink problem. It was not surprising then that Madeleine, a normally compassionate woman, couldn't find it in her heart to be compassionate to Myles' friends, alive or dead.

On the evening of the day on which a dear but indigent drinking partner died, Myles didn't get home until 11 p.m. Madeleine, used to him coming home about 9 p.m., was worried lest he'd had an accident. 'Do you think should I ring the guards?' she asked me several times during the two-hour wait.

'No, Madeleine, don't,' I said. 'If Myles had an accident, or was involved in any trouble, the guards would have contacted you by now. So let's wait a while longer.'

Myles' friend, Joe, had been a fellow-student at the exclusive Clongowes Wood College. Having finished school, Joe, at the behest of his parents – but against his own better judgement – enrolled in the College of Surgeons. Being a desultory student, however, he failed exam after exam over the ten years he was there. Having decided at last that the medical profession wasn't for him, he finally left the college.

By now he had been drinking heavily for about three years; moreover, his wife of two years, shocked at his heavy drinking and disappointed at his failure to graduate, left him. In the absence of financial and psychological support from his wife and his parents, Joe turned to his drinking friends for solace and worked at any and every odd job that provided him with enough money to satisfy his own drinking needs and also allowed him to buy a round of drinks for his friends.

At about 11 p.m. Madeleine and I heard Myles' customary struggle to open the front door. 'Thank God,' said Madeleine, 'he's all right.' Her relief soon turned to anger, however, when she discovered the reason for Myles' late homecoming. When he entered the sitting-room, very drunk, he stood exaggeratedly erect for a moment or two and then made his way carefully to his chair. Madeleine, seeing that Myles was even drunker than usual, kept her peace, for the time being at least.

Myles wrung his hands, nodded his head from side to side, and after succeeding in focusing his glazed eyes first on me and then on Madeleine, said, 'You won't believe what I've been through!'

'What happened, Myles?' said Madeleine.

'Don't interrupt me, now, Madeleine,' said Myles. After another great effort to focus his eyes on myself and Madeleine he said: 'Madeleine, Mick, my great and dear friend Joe

Leonard died today, and I just left him, lying on a cold slab in the morgue, friendless, except for me, his only friend.'

'Well,' said Madeleine, who regarded Joe as one of those who led Myles astray, 'if he's such a great friend of yours why aren't you down there in the morgue with him?'

Myles looked at Madeleine for several seconds before he came up with a suitable reply. 'Madeleine, I can't believe that any sister of mine could be such a cold, unfeeling bitch.' And, turning to me, he said, 'Mick, isn't it terrible what a man has to put up with in his own home, and from his own sister!' Then he stood up and said, 'I'm going to bed, Mick.' Looking towards Madeleine he said, 'I hope you can sleep with your conscience. If my mother could only see you now, see the way you treat me, she'd – she'd turn in her grave.'

Just as he went to go out the door he turned and, in a last desperate effort to provoke a response from Madeleine who, like me, had held her tongue during this tirade, though for different reasons, looked in my general direction and self-pityingly said, adding further to my discomfiture: 'I hope she doesn't treat *you* like this. Good night, Mick.'

While this tirade was going on, I was looking at Myles with an expression neither of agreement nor disagreement, for Madeleine was all the while focusing her gaze on me and watching for my reaction. As soon as she had made sure that Myles was indeed on his way upstairs and out of earshot she said, 'Now, Mick, isn't that terrible what I've to put up with!'

Probably because I stayed in Madeleine's so often over so many years, she came to regard me as a confidante and a friend. At times, however, when she'd had enough of Myles, together with too many IRA visitors within a short period, she would vent her anger and exasperation on me. 'Mick, I'm tired of that brother of mine drinking all his money. He doesn't give me a penny. And I'm sick and tired of all them IRAs calling. I can't get a minute's peace. Now I don't mind you and Cathal, but some of the others! That Roger Byrne, I can't stand him. He's such a snob, just because he went to university. The cheek of him! My brother went to Clongowes, which is far better than any university, and he's not a snob. As for that Séamus Costello! He's so arrogant; I can't stand him. Martin Barrow is an upstart. And as for that, that so-and-so Maurice whatever his name is, I hate him. He's so shifty-eyed. He can't look at you straight. And you know, I caught him trying to kick Terry, just because Terry barked at him. He knows never to call to my house again. The cheek of him! No one treats my dog like that and gets away with it.' And so on.

Madeleine was a very good-natured and kind woman, despite how she may have appeared to the many casual 'visitors' to her home. She was very religious but she wasn't a prude and resented 'craw-thumpers', who paraded their sanctity in order to preach to others. She was a spinster and proud of it. When some new caller would address her with 'Hello, Mrs Heffernan' she'd respond with 'I'm *Miss* Heffernan.' Then, depending on her mood and whether she liked the visitor, she'd say, 'I'm Madeleine.'

Later, when I was no longer staying in Madeleine's, I called occasionally to say hello or to meet someone there. Madeleine would be at work, but I had my own key. I was now gainfully employed and I left £1 for her every week for about a year, by way of partial recompense for her kindness to me when I stayed there on the run and to help her out in her now financially difficult times. I did the same in another house. A £1 note doesn't sound like much now, but in 1967 that £2 a week was a sixth of my wages.

I regret the fact that I never asked any of those great people who fed us at great risk and cost to themselves why they supported us. What folk memory impelled them to participate in our vain struggle? But in those years we didn't question our own motives too much, let alone those of others. As in previous campaigns to free the country, the cause was almost sacred and beyond questioning. Doubting its validity or even its viability was tantamount to treason. Secretly the futility of the campaign had begun to dawn on some of us as far back as the summer of 1957 but one dared not voice the thought. One's doubts were smothered at birth. Our training led to the acceptance of orders without question and a belief in the inviolability of armed struggle as the only means to reach the end for which we were struggling – all the while without thinking very much about what that end was.

Of those of us who kept the campaign going until February 1962, it can be safely said that we did so more for the sake of 'the dead who died for Ireland' than from any belief or hope that we were going to succeed. One potent hope that remained was the provision of the bazookas that had been promised at the general army conventions in 1957 and again in 1959. It was on that promise that most of us younger ASU men voted overwhelmingly for the continuation of the campaign, as they would enable us to escalate our offensive to a credible level.

6

THE FINAL PHASE,
1959–60

When I arrived back on the Louth–Armagh border in autumn 1959, I set about organising operations for the south Armagh area. Given our limited resources my instructions were to target customs huts, transformers, bridges and so forth, although if the opportunity arose we could do so in combination with attacks on British forces.

I had been appointed to the seven-man Army Council at the 1959 general army convention. Theoretically this provided me with a new level of authority, but Dundalk was a town of personalities permanently at war with each other. The official OC was Billy Stewart, a veteran of the 1940s who had served eight years in Portlaoise Prison, two of them in solitary confinement, and been given thirteen strokes of the cat o' nine tails. However, as in many places, by the autumn of 1959 the local movement was unable to provide effective back-up service for a column. Billy Stewart did his best but he had few resources, apart from the nebulous one of being a long-standing republican with the myths deriving from that. He was unable to mobilise many republicans in and around the town behind the effort to reopen an effective campaign that autumn and winter because of the aforementioned personality clashes, a general disillusionment with the campaign and a consequent absence of hope in the chances of success.

My main means of transport remained my bike and Mark McLaughlin's car, a local publican and businessman but also a devoted member of the movement. By this time, those of us the police knew to be active and full-time were at constant risk of arrest anywhere in the South. Internment had ended in April, but after the Meath training camp raid there was an intensification of Special Branch surveillance and the Fianna Fáil government left us in no doubt that, while internment had ended, we could expect no respite from surveillance and arrest. This acted as a deterrent to many members who had been interned and didn't relish the idea of doing six months simply for refusing to account for their movements.

After two weeks trying to create some semblance of a back-up organisation, I moved to the border. I had two billets on the southern side and one on the north, but none of them were safe. I had the services of two excellent guides, one near Crossmaglen and the other just south of the border, who also billeted me. I now had with me an excellent full-time nor-thern volunteer, Tommy Smith. In the course of the next week I reconnoitred Crossmaglen RUC Barracks and a couple of less important targets, as well as assessing information on a regular combined British Army–RUC patrol that accompanied a post office van as it travelled on the Crossmaglen to Ballsmill road on Friday mornings, just a mile north of the border. Prospects for an ambush of this patrol began to look good.

I was still in the process of hardening up the intelligence on these targets when some high profile and damaging arrests were made. The arrest of Seán Garland took place in Belfast on 4 November as he was boarding a train. He told suspicious detectives he was a medical student, but couldn't name the bones in his body. The ambush and arrest of J. B. O'Hagan and Dáithí Ó Conaill occurred while 'walking a road' in Co. Tyrone on 10 November 1959. Ó Conaill was badly wounded when he made a dash for freedom.

Two or three days after hearing this bad news, I received a message from Billy Stewart, through his niece, that the adjutant-general, Ruairí Ó Brádaigh, had sent an extremely urgent message to me by courier. Having cycled all the way from Dundalk to the border and going from one likely billet to another to find me, his niece was an extremely tired young woman by the time she eventually did locate me. She was looking forward to a rest and a cup of tea, but didn't complain when I told her I'd have to leave immediately for Dundalk and that she'd have to take me there by the back roads to avoid patrols.

I borrowed a bicycle and about an hour later I arrived at the house where the courier was waiting for me. This was the home of Mrs O'Hagan, a veteran of the War of Independence and 1940s campaigns. The message was in a sealed envelope, which had Ruairí Ó Brádaigh's recognisable handwriting on it, and was indeed urgent. It said that already low morale had been worsened by the arrests in Tyrone and Belfast. We desperately needed an anti-personnel attack against the British Army or RUC, preferably the British Army, as soon as possible. The actual words were, 'Try to get someone to throw a grenade or two at a British Army patrol in Newry.'

I wrote a reply, confirming that I'd received and destroyed the letter, and stating that I hoped to carry out an operation within a fortnight and I'd need a few extra men and supplies. I handed my note to the courier and told her it was vital that she return to Dublin immediately and hand it personally to Ó Brádaigh. I then headed off again on my bike for my border billet. I decided to concentrate all our resources on planning an ambush against the Crossmaglen–Ballsmill patrol within two weeks. It had to be within two weeks, because although the patrol was every Friday about 8 a.m., there was insufficient intelligence and resources to carry out an operation on the coming Friday, a few days hence.

The patrol consisted of a five-man RUC armoured jeep, which followed the post office van at a distance of 50 to 100 yards, and a British Army armoured car with a heavy machine gun, which was usually a good distance, about a minute in time, behind the jeep. This was a serious snag, and it wasn't the only one. We would be hitting the jeep in broad daylight. There was a British Army helicopter stationed in Whitecross, only two minutes' flying distance away, and the terrain was flat, affording very little cover. So our withdrawal to the border would be extremely hazardous. But as this was the only available target, we had no option but to attempt it.

Given the fact that there was only Tommy Smith and myself with a Lee-Enfield rifle, a Thompson sub-machine gun and twenty-five pounds of gelignite available in the area – and that we were broke, as usual – I sent a request to HQ for at least three experienced volunteers, a minimum of fifty pounds of gelignite, some electric detonators, a Bren gun, another rifle and another Thompson. I also requested some ten or twenty pounds to buy essential supplies and some cigarettes. I suggested that the North Monaghan column could most speedily supply the men and materials I needed, which was only thirty miles west of my base.

Of course I could have used volunteers from the Dundalk unit, but none of them were physically fit enough to participate, nor had they any experience of this kind of ambush. Moreover, they were all known members or sympathisers whose homes or places of work would be visited by the Special Branch within half an hour or so of the job taking place. Anyone missing would be asked, as soon as they were apprehended, to account for their movements. As IRA volunteers were duty-bound to refuse, they faced jail for three to twelve months, depending on the whim of the judge. As there were too many people already in jail, I opted for the full-time active service volunteers already on the run.

The North Monaghan column comprised ten full-time volunteers, most of whom would welcome the opportunity. They had weapons for every man, including two Brens and three or four Thompsons with about two hundred pounds of gelignite. The OC of the column, Séamus Costello, was extremely selfish about sharing resources. But assuming he received an instruction from HQ to supply me with my quite modest needs, together with the fact that my proposed operation was certain to be carried out if I had the men and the gear required, I was reasonably certain that my request would be granted.

As I intended carrying out the job in ten days' time, I urged HQ to supply me with my needs at least two days beforehand. Unknown to me, despite the urgency of my request, the courier took an inordinate amount of time to deliver it to Ó Brádaigh. In the meantime, I made the usual preparations. Tommy and myself had everything ready for 'go' a few days before the job and awaited the imminent arrival of the men and the gear I had requested at our border jumping-off billet.

At about 8 p.m. on the Thursday before the job had been planned to take place, and just as I was about to postpone the operation, one man arrived on his bike. This was an excellent operator called Cathal McQuaid from Armagh, with a Thompson stashed in his carrier bag, along with his boots and operating clothes. He was nattily dressed, like someone on his way to a dance, a useful cover if he'd been stopped at a roadblock. He was casual and confident.

We were in the kitchen of the cottage home of the guide, a man called Lowry; the only other occupant was his widowed mother, who was ill and was lying in her bed. The kitchen was lit by an oil lamp and there was a good turf fire burning in the hearth.

'Will the others and the rest of the gear be arriving soon?'

'There's no one else coming, Mick. There's just me and the Thompson.'

Thinking he was joking, I said, 'Come on, Cathal, when will the others and the rest of the gear arrive, the Bren and the extra gelignite?'

He just grinned and said, 'Mick, there's no one else. No other gear is coming. This is it.'

I was surprised, disappointed and very angry. Of course it wasn't Cathal's fault and I couldn't direct my anger at him. I was for postponing the operation until the following Friday, on the assumption that I would get the necessary reinforcements by then. Given the target and the nature of the terrain, I needed the Bren for heavy, accurate long-distance attacking and covering fire, supplemented by two riflemen. Myself and one other volunteer would be only twenty yards from the target, in the only position that afforded a clear view of it with cover, when I exploded the mine. I needed the extra gelignite for an additional mine as it would increase our chances of hitting a target travelling at forty to fifty miles an hour.

I outlined in graphic detail my reasons for postponing the operation until the following Friday to Cathal, Tommy and Lowry. Cathal, fearless operator that he was said, 'Mick, I see what you mean, but it looks like you're not going to get what you're looking for. Costello has about eight men and plenty of weapons and gel over there, but you know him! He only let me come provided I'd get back with the Thompson by Saturday night at the latest, because he's a job planned for this Sunday … And he told me that if I didn't get back then, and with the Thompson, I'd be dismissed from the army.' He concluded by saying that he was prepared to operate the next morning, even as things were.

I then asked Tommy Smith what he thought. He said, 'I'm okay. I'll go ahead with it, but I'll leave it to you.'

Then I turned to Lowry, who was a first-class guide, had an excellent knowledge of the area and, moreover, had accompanied me on my reconnaissance trips back and forward to the ambush site. I asked him for his opinion. He was very shy and reluctant to offer an opinion. After a lot of encouragement, he eventually said: 'Well, lads, I don't know as much about these things as ye do, but I feel it's very chancy to go ahead with the operation. So I'll leave it up to you … But if you want to go ahead with it, I'll take ye in to the ambush site, stay with ye till the job is over and take ye back out. If you give me a gun then I'll be able to help out in the job, and then there'll be four of us.'

I wished with all my heart that I was in a position to accept his offer, but not alone had I no spare weapon to give him but he had no weapons training whatsoever; moreover, he was the sole supporter of his ageing mother. So, while I needed Lowry to guide us to the ambush site, there was no question of allowing him to remain with us for the operation.

Having weighed all the pros and cons, I decided to go ahead the next morning, Friday 20 November 1959. I briefed Tommy and Cathal on the plan of operation and the withdrawal. Then I went into the shed that adjoined the cottage, where the gelignite, detonators and bucket were, to assemble the mine, a simple enough procedure, which took half an hour. It was now about 11 p.m.

Having checked and re-checked the wiring of the mine in the dim light of the candlelit shed, I blew out the candle and went outside. It was a starry, moonless, windless night. I stood there for a few moments pondering our not-too-happy situation, before re-entering the cottage, which was now illuminated only by the turf fire, the oil lamp having been extinguished for security. I joined Tommy, Lowry and Cathal, who were sitting chatting around the fire. We swapped yarns and drank numerous cups of tea over the next three or four hours, until about 3 a.m., when it was time to go. Lowry shovelled ashes on top of the fire to douse the flame and ensure the fire would be alive in the morning. We checked our weapons, tied our bootlaces and generally readied ourselves to go.

We left the cottage, I picked up the bucket containing the gelignite from the shed and we set off silently on this dry, starlit night for our destination. We were only about one-and-a-half miles from the site, but what with the need to keep a safe distance from houses along our route and having to negotiate myriad ditches and hedges, it took perhaps two hours. We reached the site without incident at about 5 a.m., thanks to Lowry's excellent guiding.

We dug the mine into place in the clay bank about twenty feet to the right of a gateway where I would position myself, as it would enable me to identify the jeep as it passed. Having gone through the usual procedure, connecting the flex to the detonator wires, I trailed the flex back to our fire position, a three-foot clay bank twenty yards away.

Then, having briefly checked our weapons, the four of us hunkered down behind the bank to have a final surreptitious smoke. Afterwards I told Lowry that he'd better head home. He was very reluctant to leave us. 'Won't ye need me to take ye back across the border?' he asked.

'No,' I said. 'We'll be okay. I've got a compass … We'll just head straight south to the border ... so we'll be okay.' I'd prefer a good guide to a compass any day, but I'd no option. I didn't at all feel as confident as I hoped I sounded. We had no guide and no billet when, or if, we reached the border. We would just have to get in somewhere at the end of the day.

Lowry shook hands with us and with a whispered, 'Good luck, lads,' headed for home.

We settled behind the bank for our three-hour wait. And, simple as the plan of operation was, I went over it one last time. Immediately after I blew the mine and hopefully hit the jeep, the two of us with Thompsons would fire off a twenty-round magazine at the jeep, holding a spare magazine for defensive purposes on the withdrawal. The third man would fire off as many shots as he could from his Lee-Enfield rifle. As we would spend twenty to thirty seconds firing on the jeep, this would leave only half a minute before the arrival of the armoured car. In that time, we would run to the first ditch – which was about a hundred yards south and had a hedge – to gain at least some lateral cover before it arrived. The success of the operation depended on a direct hit with the mine and safe withdrawal.

We waited for the hours to pass. I glanced frequently at the luminous face of my watch. It was a twenty-first-birthday present from my godmother. How I envied her in her cosy home, just a few doors away from my own, and only fifty miles away! The day's first light slowly dissipated the darkness so that we were able to see each other's pale and somewhat wan faces and, of course, the increasing detail of the countryside around us. It was a pleasant sight but a disturbing reminder that we were going to be operating in daylight. I'd never fully appreciated the friendly cover night provided until that moment. So we met the dawn with somewhat mixed feelings.

From about 7 a.m. we ended all chat and concentrated on listening for the sound of the post office van and the jeep, just in case they arrived early. As there were so few privately owned cars at that time, virtually the only traffic at that hour of the morning was the van with its police and military escort. As we had no scouts or walkie-talkies and were positioned on flat ground, our only means of detecting the approach of the target was to listen for it. And because of the flat ground, I'd have only a second or two to visually identify the jeep as it passed the gateway and explode the mine, and as the mine was only twenty-five pounds it would need to hit the jeep broadside. So we concentrated on listening, saying nothing to each other, not even in a whisper.

I kept looking at my watch, first at five-minute intervals, then with growing impatience at one-minute intervals, until eventually I stopped looking at it altogether. The obsession with time was causing too much anxiety and there were more important things to think about. Would we succeed in hitting the jeep and escaping? What if we missed and were killed or captured? And in either event, how would the operation advance the cause of freedom, particularly as the campaign looked as if it was failing anyway?

So I went back to listening and fixing firmly in my vision the exact spot that was my marker for exploding the mine the instant the jeep's nose reached it. There was no room for error; blowing the mine a second too soon or too late would result in missing the jeep. A miss at any time is bad, but given our situation that morning it would be a disaster for us. And of course we didn't have the technology for exploding a mine by remote control. If it existed at that time, we didn't know about it.

Some minutes before 8 a.m. we heard what we'd been waiting for: the faint but unmistakable sound of the post office van and the jeep approaching from the west, to our left. I turned to look at Tommy and Cathal, who nodded their heads in agreement that 'this was it'. They took up their firing positions, their weapons pointing at the marker, while I stripped the insulating tape off the second terminal of the battery and, holding the battery in one hand and the exposed end of the flex connecting it to the mine in the other hand, fixed my eyes on my marker. And waited.

Half a minute or so later the van passed our position, followed a couple of seconds later by the jeep. As it reached my marker I touched the open end of the flex to the battery; I did this by touch, as I had to keep my eyes glued on my marker. The mine exploded. I prayed that I was on target.

The jeep was hit all right, because I could see some parts of it fly into the air and land a few yards away. We were showered with clay and debris. The three of us immediately opened fire on the jeep, or where we thought it was lying. The two of us with Thompsons each fired off our twenty-round magazine in a few bursts, while the rifleman got off a couple of rounds.

The entire operation only took about thirty seconds. But, as the armoured car was now half a minute away, we couldn't afford to move in on the jeep to finish off the survivors. I thought, even as we were firing, that our bullets were wasted, because it seemed that none of the occupants of the jeep could have survived the blast.

We made a hasty withdrawal, running southwards to the ditch a hundred yards away. This ditch and its hedge at least provided cover from the armoured-car observer, whose position was about eight feet above the ground. We reached it in record time. In that life-and-death situation, I wasn't aware of being tired. The racing of my heart, the gasping for air didn't seem to matter. There was a feeling of euphoria, as if I were in a dream sequence, and I was insensitive to the pain of extreme physical effort. For those few euphoric minutes, all that mattered was getting away.

We scrambled through a gap in the hedge, moved fast over the few yards to the next hedge on our right that ran north to south, and, staying close to it for direction and cover, we jogged on southwards to the next ditch, and so on.

About five minutes into the withdrawal, and while we were still about half a mile from the border, we heard the helicopter approaching. At that precise moment, and luckily for us, we reached a bushy mound (a 'fairy fort' or ring-fort), which was the only real cover from above for miles around. It was only about fifty feet in diameter but covered with gorse and bushes. We dashed the twenty yards or so to scramble under them and wait.

It was no more than thirty seconds before the helicopter arrived and hovered only a hundred feet or so directly above us. Obviously the pilot, or those directing him, knew it was the only real cover between the ambush site and the border. It stayed overhead for a minute at least – though it seemed like an eternity. The fact that it hovered there for so long almost convinced us that the pilot or spotter had seen us. So convinced were we that we began discussing firing the remainder of our ammunition at it, not that we'd have had much chance of downing it.

Our discussion was cut short when, apparently satisfied that we weren't in the ring-fort, the helicopter suddenly headed off making wide sweeps. As soon as it was out of sight we resumed our retreat, running alongside the hedges as fast as we could towards the border. We heard the helicopter from time to time but didn't see it again. Taking cover under a ditch when necessary for short rests, it took us half an hour to reach the border – or what I estimated was the border based on time and the compass – from the ring-fort. I was so convinced we were south of the border, and also hungry enough to believe it, that we stopped to pull a turnip from a field, peel it and chew a few slices while we sheltered under the cover of a high, leafy hedge. But even if we were in the South we were still within visual range of the helicopter and, moreover, the gardaí would now be looking for us as well.

It was imperative that we found shelter as soon as possible. I decided to try the next house that lay across our path. As ill-luck would have it, the next house was too prosperous-looking to be that of an IRA supporter; on the other hand, it would be a perfectly safe shelter if the owners agreed to put us up for the remaining hours of daylight. Of course we could have stayed in the barn, but the barns of even non-supporters were subject to search by the gardaí.

As we didn't want to be observed by the occupants of the house until we knocked on their door, we first made our way to the barn to have a smoke, gather our wits and decide how we were going to go gain access to the house. It was an unwritten rule that we didn't coerce anyone into giving us shelter, except in extreme circumstances, which were never defined.

We decided we had a better chance of shelter if only one of us went to the door. Tommy was my obvious choice. He was baby-faced and innocent-looking, and remarkably clean compared with myself and Cathal.

Tommy, however, wasn't too enamoured. 'Aw, Mick, come on!' he said. 'You always give me these jobs!'

'But, Tommy,' I said, 'you look the best for the job ...'

Tommy, however, was adamant. He refused to go to the door unless Cathal or I accompanied him. So not wanting to force him to do it, and as he had performed so well on the job and, indeed, other jobs too, I conceded. Leaving the weapons with Cathal in the barn, we walked across the yard to the two-storey house, knocked with a kind of gentle 'undemanding' rap on the door and waited anxiously for a response.

In rural Ireland in 1959 only total strangers knocked on a door. Friends, neighbours and relatives would just push it open and call out, 'It's me!'

The door was opened by a not-too-friendly-looking man in his middle fifties, who, having scrutinised us from head to toe, and evidently having a good idea we were IRA men – he may even have heard news of the ambush on the radio – gruffly said, 'Who're ye looking for? What do ye want?' Just at that moment his wife appeared and stood behind him. 'Eh, we're – eh ... we're the IRA,' I said. 'We're on the run, and we'd like to stay in your barn ... or in your house, for a few hours, until it gets dark ...'

His expression went from sour to hate. Almost frothing at the mouth, he said, 'You – you bloody murderers! Yiz aren't getting in here!' And he made to close the door. But just as he did so his wife said, 'Oh, John, don't turn them away; they're some mothers' sons.' At which point 'John' looked at us as though we were the scum of the earth, then looked at his wife with an expression that said, 'Be it on your head,' and, without saying another word, turned on his heel and went back into the kitchen.

I wanted to hug this woman, this answer to our prayers. I thanked her and then told her that there was another one of us, waiting in the barn. 'Oh, go and bring him in!' she said. Tommy and I returned to the barn and told Cathal the good news. Then we hid the weapons. Having warned him not to gloat if we heard that the news about the operation was good, we went back to the house. The woman, who had remained at the door, ushered us into the kitchen. John and his daughter were sitting at the table, having their breakfast. The daughter said hello and didn't seem at all disturbed by our presence. The woman, pulling a few chairs to the cooker, told us to sit in to the fire and that she'd make us a bit of breakfast.

'Oh,' she said then, 'I'm sure ye'd like to have a wash,' and, without waiting for our reply, directed us to the bathroom upstairs. A bathroom! This was indeed a prosperous Catholic house!

We made the most of the bathroom facilities, had a whispered chat about our situation and went back down to the kitchen, where the woman had prepared a great breakfast for us: sausages, rashers, eggs and pudding, plenty of brown bread and butter and strong tea.

Ravenous as we were, we tried to eat with a bit of decorum. There was an uneasy silence, the kind where you imagine you can be heard chewing. The daughter and the mother may have wanted to chat but, in deference to the father's unfriendly attitude, refrained except for saying, 'Have some more tea', or bread. And, of course, we couldn't chat to each other.

The radio was tuned to Radio Éireann. As it approached 9 a.m., or maybe it was 10 a.m., I began to grow uneasy at the prospect of the response of John – and perhaps even the mother – to news of the ambush. More importantly, though, we were hoping that the news was good, that we'd killed some or all of the patrol.

The news came on just as we finished breakfast. An RUC jeep had been ambushed at Ballsmill ... there were casualties, but it wasn't known if anyone had been killed. In view of the attitude of our reluctant host, we suppressed our sense of elation, merely glancing at each other with a kind of mute congratulation.

Our host, however, was incensed at the news. He looked from one to the other of us, and then, with a look of amazement on his face, turned to Tommy, the youngest and most innocent-looking of us and said, 'Well, ya little fucker ya!' Then, turning to us, he said, 'Aren't ye the right fuckers!'

What could we say? We said nothing.

Just at that moment, we were relieved of the need for a comment when the daughter announced that she was leaving for work. At the same time the mother, seeing that we'd finished eating, and apparently anxious to defuse the situation, said, 'Maybe you'd like to move into the parlour, lads. There's a nice fire going there.'

That was all the encouragement we needed. We stood up from the table fast, thanked them for the breakfast and headed for the parlour. Right enough, it was comfortable and there was a good fire going. We sank gratefully into the armchairs to speculate about the news and congratulate ourselves on making our escape thus far. We were awakened from a doze about 2 p.m. when the woman brought our dinner in to us. At dusk, we had our tea. We were fed royally in that Hibernian house!

As soon as it fell dark, we prepared to leave. We consulted the map, got a rough compass bearing for a billet near Dundalk, tied our bootlaces and buttoned our jackets. We thanked our hosts, genuinely and profusely, and, with the woman showering us with holy water, went to the barn, picked up our weapons and began the trek towards Dundalk, seven or so miles away. It was about 7 p.m. It was dry and dark, but not too dark, when, with our weapons tied with string and slung over our shoulders, we began trekking to the home of a supporter on the outskirts of the town.

A seven-mile trek on a road or over the high, clear slopes of a mountain is nothing to fit men or women, and we were fit. But despite this, and our eagerness to reach our billet, we made slow progress. The fields were small and hedged, so we spent a lot of time searching for gaps. We were further slowed by having to find suitable crossings of the numerous streams and dykes we encountered. (No compass or map, no matter how good, can compensate for a good guide.) Anyway, about four hours later, around 11 p.m., we reached our billet, where we were welcomed with open arms. Despite their poor circumstances and barely managing to provide enough food for their immediate family, our hosts said, 'Ye must be famished,' and immediately set about providing us with a slap-up supper with plenty of porridge, tea, bread and cheese.

Our hosts were avid IRA supporters and guessed that we had done the Ballsmill ambush that morning. Of course, adhering to IRA protocol, they didn't ask us anything about the job. Instead, and in a kind of backhanded congratulation, they talked glowingly about it and the details they'd heard on the radio, being too far out of town to see an evening paper.

After much questioning of our hosts about the news reports, I was disappointed to discover that the operation wasn't as successful as I'd hoped. Two RUC constables had been seriously injured but there were no fatalities.[1] In the meantime, the woman of the house removed their two children from their beds to make room for us. Before going to bed, I ar-

---

1   The two RUC constables were William Johnston and Trevor Boyle. The latter was a B Special.

ranged with our host to contact the local OC, Billy Stewart, next morning and ask him to arrange a lift to north Monaghan for Cathal.

Mark McLaughlin's car arrived at our billet the next afternoon and took Cathal back to his column. The driver also had a message for me from Stewart. I was to head back to Dublin for a meeting with the chief of staff. So I arranged for the driver to collect Tommy and myself and take us to a safe billet near Drogheda. We reached Drogheda without incident, spent the night there, and the following morning took a bus to Dublin.

The other four full-time OCs who were operating along the border had received the same message. On meeting the chief of staff, Seán Cronin, I learned, with a sense almost of euphoria that the bazookas and rockets had at last arrived from America. At that moment they were lying in a warehouse on the Dublin docks and a couple of days later the quartermaster-general, Cathal Goulding, and myself smuggled them out with the help of some docker friends.

Cronin went on to tell me, as he did the other OCs, that each of us, together with a second man from each column (my column being myself and Tommy), would be trained on the bazooka over the Christmas period – which was about four weeks away – in Co. Wicklow. We were to return to our areas, the next day if possible, to begin acquiring intelligence on suitable RUC and British Army targets, with a view to launching an attack with the bazookas in the first week of January. For maximum effect, and for other obvious reasons, it was desirable that we all strike on the same night. It was imperative, therefore, that the OCs acquired the necessary intelligence for presentation to the chief of staff when we reassembled for the training session.

Just before our meeting ended, Cronin told me that he was now appointing me assistant chief of staff and, in the event of his arrest, I was to take over as chief of staff as he believed I was the most experienced and capable of the volunteers still at liberty. This announcement should have pleased me – and it did, but only for a moment. While I was confident of my abilities 'in the field', and felt that HQ had been very inefficient up to that time, I still believed that somewhere there must be a reserve of highly qualified men waiting in the wings to take up positions in HQ.

Tommy and myself returned to our area the next day with a confidence that we hadn't felt since the early days of the campaign. The arrival of the bazookas and the rockets was the answer to a long-standing prayer. Even at this late stage I felt we had a good chance of salvaging an otherwise lost campaign. Moreover, the two new active service volunteers in my area, who had been assigned to it in my absence and whose morale hadn't been too good, went through a metamorphosis when I told them the news. When I met the other OCs at the bazooka training session four weeks later, they reported a similar rise in morale among their volunteers on hearing of the arrival of the bazookas.

I think we had all completed our various intelligence-gathering operations by the time we returned to Wicklow for training, a week or so before Christmas 1959. We all arrived at the training house at the designated time, an indication, perhaps, of the new enthusiasm. Cronin formally fell us in and gave us a short lecture on how important the weapon was and its potential tactical uses, before bringing us into another room where a launcher and some rockets were waiting for the training to begin.

The theory, handling, safety precautions, loading and firing procedures only took a few days. It was now almost Christmas. Cronin gave us a final wrap-up lecture and left to make arrangements for some of us to travel to an area where we could test fire a rocket. I was left in charge and Séamus Costello was my number 2.

The transport arrived on the evening of St Stephen's Day. There was a tremendous sense of excitement as we set off at dusk for the firing site. The target was a derelict stone building. I was the holder and Costello was the loader for the first rocket. The rest of the lads were lying to the rear of the rocket, to the left and right of the launcher, to be clear of the back blast. It was dark, dry, windless and quiet as I put the launcher on my shoulder and Costello, doing everything according to the drill, loaded the rocket. I braced myself for the pull when it left the launcher. I sighted the bazooka as best I could in the dark and squeezed the trigger. Nothing happened. There was just the sound of the magneto whirring.[2]

We weren't unduly surprised, as the training included a drill for misfires caused by incorrect wiring of the rocket to the launcher or a poor connection. So Costello disconnected the wire, rotated the rocket, rewired it, and indicated to me that it was ready for firing again. I squeezed the trigger, but once again there was nothing, just the sound of the magneto and one of the lads in the darkness saying, 'Oh, fuck!'

We were beginning to get uneasy, but Séamus and myself removed the first rocket – again according to the drill – and placed it carefully to one side. Taking extreme care to do exactly as instructed, we loaded the second rocket. With a silent prayer, I squeezed the trigger.

Nothing happened. At this stage, I was beginning to experience a certain amount of frustration. But, as this was our first time to fire the weapon, and I was hoping that we were somehow not following correct procedures, we decided to go through the drill for a misfire again. Hoping against hope that this one was going to fire, I squeezed the trigger. The magneto whirred, but the rocket stayed in the launcher.

Disappointed and angry beyond words, I laid the launcher, with the rocket still in it, carefully on the ground. Telling

---

2   A magneto is an electrical generator that produces short pulses of electricity.

everyone to remain clear of the rear of the launcher, just in case, I moved over to where Séamus was lying to discuss the situation. He, of course, was furious. However, after much cursing and swearing, and going against all the rules, we decided to attempt another firing of the second rocket. We walked back to where the launcher was lying. I lifted it carefully onto my shoulder and positioned myself for firing. Séamus carefully disconnected the rocket, rotated it very slowly and reconnected the wire to the launcher terminal. He was so careful about the wiring, and took so much time to do it, that I began to tire holding the launcher.

Eventually, he tapped me on the shoulder and said, without much enthusiasm, 'It's okay.'

I aimed at the target and, not very hopefully, squeezed the trigger. The magneto whirred for several seconds, but the rocket remained in the launcher.

There was a deadly silence. No one moved. I squeezed the trigger again in desperation, but in vain. I was almost speechless with anger and disappointment.

Again telling the lads to stay where they were, I laid the launcher on the ground, unwired the rocket and removed it. Once more following the drill to be carried out in the event of a misfire, Séamus and I took both rockets over to a gully about a hundred yards away to dispose of them, because they were too dangerous to take back to Dublin and so had to be blown up. We taped them together and I made up a charge, about four ounces of gelignite with a half-minute length of fuse and a detonator, which we'd brought along in case we had to deal with the 'unlikely' event of a misfire. I attached the charge to the rockets while the rest of the lads took cover in the adjoining field. I lit a match and ignited the fuse.

We raced back across the field to the gate that led into the next field. However, as we scrambled across the gate (and for some inexplicable reason we were giggling as we did), the gate collapsed. Fortunately, we fell on the right side, as the charge exploded a few seconds later. The explosion, however, wasn't what I'd expected from two high-explosive charges and four ounces of gelignite, but I didn't give much thought to it right then. I was still thinking along the lines of a wiring fault in the launcher being the problem.

A few seconds later I called the lads together and we headed across the fields to the road where our transport was waiting. None of us spoke; we were all too disappointed, or embarrassed, by the debacle. But as none of us had any prior experience of the weapon, there was still a hope that the problem was a mechanical or wiring one.

During the hour it took to get back to our billet in Bray none of us spoke about what had happened. However, a few hours later we did discuss it and I told the lads to wait until I made my report to the chief of staff the next day. I hoped we might get an explanation not covered in the manual, but I think we were all expecting the worst.

Cronin arrived with a look of expectation as he called us together and asked me, 'Well, how did it go?'

'The rockets didn't fire,' I said.

He looked at me as though I was joking, though I wasn't in the habit of joking about such serious matters, particularly to the chief of staff.

I repeated, 'The rockets didn't fire.'

'What do you mean they didn't fire?' he asked, almost angrily and certainly disbelievingly.

I went over everything we had done: the loading, wiring, all according to the training programme. While he could find no fault with my outline of the firing and loading procedures, he still found it hard to believe that the rockets didn't work. Like us, he had accepted as a fact the serviceability of the bazookas.

It was only after the most minute debriefing that he accepted that we had indeed carried out the drill correctly. He then said that we should go through the drill again, to see if we could discover the reason for the misfires. We all adjourned to the room where the launcher and some rockets were. Using the practice rocket, Costello and I went through the loading and firing procedure. Cronin was satisfied that what we'd done was in accordance with the drill.

Like us, he was perplexed.

Then we began examining the rockets, more or less checking that the wires weren't broken. I was tugging gently on the wires of one rocket to make sure they were firmly connected, when the wires and the black tar-like propellant in which the wires were embedded came completely out of the propellant housing. Even with our relative ignorance of the structure of the weapon, we realised there was something terribly wrong. The propellant shouldn't have fallen out like that. We stared disbelievingly at this black plastic or tar-like cone dangling at the end of the wires and looked at each other. It was now obvious that there was something radically wrong. We knelt on the floor to examine it. A minute or so later we discovered the awful truth. The so-called propellant was merely a lump of pitch or plastic. The rocket was a dud.

We examine the rest of the rockets. They were all duds, made for training purposes only. Worse was to come. On examining the launchers, we discovered that they too had been converted for purely training and drill purposes. The magnetos didn't work properly and the sights were defective. These weapons – which had come through Clan na Gael contacts in the USA – were supposed to be our saviours, but a consignment of bows and arrows would have been of greater value.

In money terms, the cost was enormous. The launchers were $1,000 each and the rockets $100 each. At this time most active service volunteers were almost totally dependent on those who billeted us for cigarettes, food and travel. For example, I hadn't enough money to buy a pair of socks. The shirt I was wearing came from a consignment of second-hand clothes American supporters had sent over some months previously. The cost of the dud launchers and rockets was devastating in financial terms, but also in terms of morale, confidence in HQ and for our prospects to revive the campaign.

Most of us who'd been active in the campaign from the start had seen the need for the bazooka about two months after it began; as soon, that is, as the RUC and British Army had devised effective counter-measures to our typical mode of attack on their strongpoints. I have to assume that HQ was equally aware of the need for bazookas at that time and had been striving to acquire them from that time on. Now it was Christmas 1959, *three years* into the campaign. We had no money, no reserves of weapons or ammunition, no more than a couple of dozen full-time volunteers on active duty, with another couple of dozen inexperienced men willing to volunteer. It was becoming increasingly difficult to buy or steal gelignite and now the bazookas had finally arrived, only for us to discover they were duds. Of the many low points in the campaign thus far, this was the lowest.

Cronin was, of course, also affected by this disaster, though he didn't articulate his feelings to us. Instead he instructed us to return to our areas and to carry out whatever operations we could. In the meantime, HQ would try to make the rockets and launchers serviceable, or get a new consignment from the United States.

It was an extremely disconsolate and demoralised group that parted a day or so later to head back to their areas.

A few days later, in January 1960, Tommy and myself arrived at the house in Dundalk where the other full-time volunteers were billeted. I told them about the failed bazookas and rockets. While they were disappointed with the news, they didn't register much surprise: they'd become sceptical as a result of too many unfulfilled promises. But they were still game to operate, at least for the few months it would take to either render the bazookas and rockets serviceable, or to obtain a serviceable consignment from America.

By way of compensating for this latest disaster, I decided there and then to try to hit two or more targets on the same night as soon as possible. I began updating our intelligence and three weeks later we were in a position to attack the following four targets:

(1) The sentries at the gate of Crossmaglen Barracks, when they emerged from the sandbagged pillbox to examine the credentials of any patrol leaving or entering the barracks.

(2) The customs hut at Drumbilla, two miles south of Crossmaglen.[3]

---

3   A customs hut was where customs officers checked documentation for imports and exports coming across the border that may attract excise, VAT or other charges, or violate various restrictions on the movement of goods and livestock.

(3) The customs hut at Killeen, eight miles east, which was the main checkpoint on the Dublin–Belfast road.

(4) The electricity transformer serving Crossmaglen.

The bombing of the transformer was an essential ancillary part to our attack on the sentries at Crossmaglen Barracks, the idea being to cut the power supply to the barracks, thereby cutting communications with its patrols and plunging the area, including the village, into darkness. This would also facilitate our withdrawal after we'd fired on the sentries from behind a three-foot wall, thirty feet away, and begun retreating over flat, coverless terrain. The only 'prestige' targets were the sentries. Blowing the transformer wouldn't make us popular, but was essential to our operation. Blowing the customs huts at Drumbilla and Killeen would be more popular with the locals. If all four operations were carried out successfully on the same night it would help underpin HQ's strategy and its propaganda claims that there was still a fair degree of resistance to British rule – at least in one area.

The situation in south Armagh at that time was reasonably good for operations. There had been no IRA activity for a couple of months and a relaxation of security on civil installations had resulted. Given the vagaries of patrols it was not possible to hit the targets at a set time; moreover, we had no radio or walkie-talkies with which to communicate. The problem of co-ordination was further complicated by the fact that the attacks on the transformer and the customs huts could not be carried out until after we opened fire on the sentries at the gate of the barracks. If any other target was hit before we had taken up position in front of the barracks, the security there, and elsewhere in the area, would be thrown into high gear.

Therefore, the sound of firing at Crossmaglen Barracks would be the signal for the volunteer at the transformer, which was only half a mile away, to blow it. On hearing that explosion our man at the Drumbilla customs hut, a mile from the transformer, would blow it and, on hearing the sound of either explosion our man at the Killeen customs hut, which was four miles further east, would blow that.

All operators would be in position by 10 p.m. We would have taken up our position opposite the barracks by then and the other three operatives would have their mines placed and ready to blow well before that. The critical element was that no one struck until after we had opened fire on the sentries. However, as I'd no idea how long I'd have to wait after 10 p.m. for an opportunity to hit the sentries, I warned the other volunteers that they would have to be prepared for a wait of anything from minutes to hours before they could strike.

The night of the operation arrived. Having made sure that the saboteurs were on their way to their different targets, the rest of us set out for Crossmaglen Barracks with plenty of time in hand. We were accompanied by a guide who knew the area like the back of his hand. The weather was good for operations:

cloudy and dark. We made good time, despite having to take a circuitous route out of sight and sound of dwellings in this thickly populated area. If a dog heard us and began barking, the odds were that the occupants of the house would investigate. Even if they didn't, that dog's barking would set others barking in front of us and behind us. Moreover, there was always the possibility that B Specials or RUC men lived along our route.

Though we maintained the usual silence, I knew from the odd giggle from the rest when someone fell into a patch of muck, and by the fact that there was no 'dragging of feet', that morale was good, even with the numerous ditches and banks to be crossed in this area of small farms. We knew we had more than enough time to take up our position.

Everything was going well right up to the time we were climbing across virtually the last ditch, which was no more than a quarter of a mile from the barracks. Just as I had clambered to the top of the last bank and was about to jump down to the next field we heard the unmistakable thud of an explosion coming from somewhere behind us.

I stood, transfixed, for a second or two, wondering what the hell had happened. I jumped down into the next field, where we huddled together with the guide to begin a whispered discussion about who or what caused the explosion. Just as we did so we heard the sound of a second explosion just behind us and, a few seconds later, the lights went out in Crossmaglen. The transformer had been blown, despite all my warnings. I was angry almost beyond words that all my planning and briefings were virtually for naught.

We immediately hunkered down in a rough semi-circle close to the ditch. 'Fuck it!' I whispered. 'Someone's jumped the gun ...'

One of the lads added another expletive or two. Then there was an uneasy silence as the lads looked at me for a decision about what to do next. Just at that moment we heard the sound, the somewhat fainter sound, of a third explosion, probably the blowing of Killeen customs hut several miles east. We were in an unenviable situation. We were only a quarter of a mile from our target, but that quarter of a mile was open and without cover. Moreover, given the blowing up of the transformer, Drumbilla customs hut and probably Killeen, Crossmaglen Barracks would now be on full alert, making it impossible to take up our firing position. I felt that we'd no alternative but to abort the operation and withdraw as fast as we could. However, I still wanted to get the feeling of the lads on the question. We had a huddled whispered exchange and all felt as I did. We immediately began a hasty but careful withdrawal to the border.

We were all extremely disappointed and frustrated. Moreover, even if all the saboteurs got safely home, the RUC and gardaí would assume that there was now an IRA active service unit in the area, which would result in heightened security and raids on safe houses. This would make it extremely difficult for us to survive, let alone operate.

Our guide brought us safely to the border in a couple of hours and I told him to return home as quickly as possible, hoping he'd get there before it was raided. Using the compass, and with the lights of Dundalk and the river as guides, we finally reached our billet just an hour before dawn. We were wet and muddy from the waist down, an extremely tired and demoralised group.

The billet was a house beside a bridge, at the junction of a river and a road. Tommy Smith had stayed there before and was able to identify it. However, while it was safe because the woman who owned it was not a known sympathiser, someone had neglected to tell me that following any border operation the gardaí always set up a roadblock at that bridge, which was only fifty yards away from the billet!

We approached the house extremely quietly as a result. It was a bungalow and we entered by the back door, which the owner had left unlocked for us. We locked the door and groped our way into the sitting-room, where we immediately sat down on chairs or lay on the floor. The rooms were in darkness, thanks to the good sense of the owner, who had closed the curtains and the blinds. But soon the room began to lighten up with the approach of the dawn.

I thought about how this house had better be what was promised, 100 per cent safe, because there was no escape route. I introduced a restrictive regimen, given the absence of the owner and the closeness of the gardaí, who might decide to investigate the house or merely call seeking a kettle of boiling water to make tea. There would be no switching on of lights or even lighting of candles. No one was to go outside (there was an indoor toilet, luckily), there would be no horseplay, conversations were to be carried out in whispers and any movement within the house would be as silent as possible. These instructions were normal under the circumstances and superfluous, because the lads were all experienced enough to know what to do in this kind of situation. But I was no longer prepared to take anything for granted.

The smokers lit up a welcome fag. I went into the kitchen to see what there was to eat. There was plenty of tea and sugar, some milk and a few slices of bread. But that was it. Someone had neglected to tell the owner to lay in food for us. We had some tea and ate the bread ravenously, then settled down to wait the ten hours until nightfall. Some were able to sleep for a few hours, but we were awake for most of the time. There was too much tension, too much disappointment and frustration.

Afterwards I had to decide what to do. It was a case of choosing the best of a few poor options. My primary concern was the survival of the unit and avoiding arrest. Two members had spent six months in jail recently and I was concerned about their morale.

While the billet was safe, the owner was away and we didn't know when she would be back. We had no food, no money, and within a matter of hours, would have no cigarettes.

For a couple of the lads at least, a smoke was more important than food. So my immediate task was to get a message to the local OC asking him to find new billets. Fortunately the garda road block was gone but, with the exception of Tommy, we were all dressed in military-style clothes and bound to attract attention. He was also the only one, besides myself, who was familiar with the geography of Dundalk. Naturally, he was not too happy to be nominated for the task. By way of a bonus, I told him that once he got my message to the OC he could head for the billet of his choice in the town. I would be relying on the OC's niece to cycle out with word about when we could expect either transport or a guide.

We waited impatiently, as usual, for the approach of darkness. Tommy made his own preparations, washing his face and hands, brushing the dried mud out of his clothes and boots, and generally making himself respectable. As soon as it was dark he headed off, amid whispered 'Good luck's and one, 'You'd better get some cigarettes out here fast, or else!' Tommy succeeded in his errand and next day the OC's niece arrived with cigarettes and the word that we'd be picked up that night. About twenty years old, she was a vision of the type of girlfriend most of us imagined in our dreams, so there was much flirting in the hour or so that she was with us.

We were picked up that night and dispersed to various billets.

I discovered a few days later what had gone wrong. One

of the saboteurs 'thought' he had heard the sound of shots or an explosion and decided to blow his target. Being the least experienced volunteer, he had thought he had been in position for several hours more than he had. The key factor was that he just didn't have sufficient experience to operate independently. He was so contrite that it took me a long time to convince him that he was forgiven and that we still needed his services in the future.

***

A while later I received a message from HQ to return to Dublin for a meeting. I was in Paddy 'the Gadgem' Duffy's when I got the message, so naturally I asked him if he knew of any lifts going to Dublin the following morning. From past experience I hadn't much faith in the Gadgem, but he'd already seen the HQ summons.

'No problem,' he said. 'Sure I'm driving Julia [his wife] up to Dún Laoghaire in the morning, and I can drop you off wherever you want. We'll be going in the van, so you'll be safe enough in the back. You won't be seen.'

I initially declined his offer, for the very good reason that he was a well-known sympathiser and there was a high probability of his van being stopped.

He discounted my worries with, 'Look, sure I'm on the road at that time at least a couple of times a week going to the Dublin market; and anyway Julia will be in the front with me, you'll be in the back where you won't be seen, so there's no reason for them to stop us.'

I had no viable alternative. I'd no money for the fare to Dublin and Mark McLaughlin's car was even more well known, so travelling in it was out of the question.

At 6 a.m. the next morning we set off for Dublin in the Gadgem's Morris Minor van. I was hunkered down in the back, just inside the rear doors. The four or five feet between us were filled with flowers and plants. I could still see out through both the front windscreen and the rear windows without being visible to any casual observer, and, of course, we were able to talk to each other.

We were a couple of miles south of Dundalk, not far from the Blackrock Road junction, when a Special Branch car appeared heading north towards us. It slowed as it approached. As it passed us the Gadgem said, 'Ah, Donovan is in it, but they're going on, they're not going to stop us.'

However, I was convinced that Donovan would come after us. So, peeking out the rear window, I watched the car as it proceeded ever so slowly down the road, as if Donovan was debating whether to turn around. As soon as it disappeared, I called on Gadgem to stop and let me out, into the fields, 'just in case'.

'Not at all,' he said. 'They're not going to come after us.'

But a few seconds later I saw the unmistakable outline of

Donovan's car coming up fast. I shouted, 'Stop the van and let me out into the fields! Stop, quick! Gadgem!'

But to my amazement Paddy said, 'There's no need for that. They're not going to stop us.'

I was apoplectic but I was physically out of reach of Paddy and could do nothing to make him stop the van.

The car passed us, braking hard to block us. I leaped out of the van before it had come to a stop. High, thick hedges blocked my way to the fields, so I ran back up the Dundalk road and crossed the first gate I came to, which was no more than fifty yards away. With Donovan now in close pursuit, I raced to the furthest end of the field, which was a two-acre, high-hedged, gapless enclosure, forcing my way through the hedge and, with Donovan no more than ten or fifteen yards behind me, emerged into a huge, short-grassed field, which offered no cover but was great for running.

I sprinted for the first hundred yards or so, to put a safe distance between myself and Donovan. Glancing around I saw he was finding the going a bit heavy; he wasn't as fit as he boasted, so I settled into a fast jog for the next quarter of a mile or so, by which time I was beginning to tire. I was so tired in fact that I had difficulty in crossing a mere three-foot wire fence and, once across it, and seeing that Donovan was at least two hundred yards behind, stood for several seconds to catch my breath. He was now walking. He shouted to me to halt and fired a warning shot in the air. I jogged on for another few hundred yards until I reached the yard of a farm-house.

I was surprised because I thought I was heading in a line that would keep me well away from houses and roads. (In hindsight, the explanation was simple. I hadn't compensated enough for the long bend in the Dundalk to Castlebelling-ham road at the point where I left the van, and had veered left and north instead of east, away from the Dundalk road.) Having glanced back to assure myself that Donovan was too far behind to see what direction I might take, I ran the few yards through the farmyard.

As it was only 7 a.m. there was no sign of life until I reached the roadway. Not realising at the time that this was the Dundalk–Castlebellingham road, I ran across to the other side, where, as luck would have it, there was a small wood. I scrambled across the ditch, ran the few yards to the edge of the wood, and then, because of exhaustion and the dense growth, I virtually crawled the first twenty yards or so into the welcoming covering arms of the wood and lay down.

I rested for a minute or two and then, fairly certain that I had lost Donovan, made my way slowly and quietly through the hundred yards of woodland. Then, using whatever cover there was to walk quickly over the fields for perhaps another half a mile, I reached a copse. There was a tiny path through it, so I crawled into cover so I could see anyone who might pass by.

As I lay down to rest and gather my wits, I retched and began to feel very sorry for myself. I cursed the Gadgem, and myself for giving in to his advice. I couldn't help thinking this was the fourth time I had been chased and had to escape capture in this area because I had been needlessly put at risk by bad advisers, who blandly refused to accept my estimate of the situation. I swore that I would never again go against my better judgement.

I realised it would be twelve or thirteen hours before dark. I wasn't familiar with this patch of the country around Dromiskin, nor did I know a single supporter or billet in it. I had only a few shillings in my pocket, which I had cadged from local supporters. I hadn't a cigarette and I was dying for a smoke. I was lying there for perhaps half an hour when I heard the sound of someone whistling a pop tune entering the copse from the Dundalk side. Since the intruder was a lad of only fifteen or sixteen, dressed in farm-clothes – and feeling instinctively that he was all right – I approached him to find out what was happening on the Dundalk road. When I emerged onto the path a few yards in front of him, he stopped, surprised at finding this 'city-dressed' man emerge from the copse.

'Good morning,' I said.

'Eh, hello,' he said, somewhat shyly.

'Look, you've nothing to be afraid of,' I said. 'Did you come in from the Dundalk road? Are the guards on the road?'

'Aye, I did,' he said. 'There's loads of guards on the road, and they're searching the fields on the other side, you know, not this side. Are they looking for you?'

'They are,' I said. 'I'm an IRA man.'

'Well, you've nothing to fear from me. I'll not say a word to anyone about you being here.'

Having elicited from him where I was, he told me he worked for a big farmer, 'who wouldn't be your way of thinking', and that they'd be hay-making up to about 6 p.m. He also said there was a post office, with a public phone outside it, in the village of Dromiskin, which was only a couple of hundred yards from the farmer's house, where he'd be having his lunch.

I asked him if, during his lunch hour, he could get to the phone and call the Eimear Bar in Dundalk, talk to the owner and tell him he was phoning for me. He might explain my predicament and ask him to try to get a safe car to pick me up near the phone box any time after dark, say about 9 p.m. I asked him to buy me a packet of Sweet Afton for which I gave him two shillings. Lastly, I asked if he could manage to get back during his lunch break to let me know what was happening.

The lad agreed to do what I asked. Just as he was about to go on his way, he asked me if I wanted a cigarette. 'By God, I'd love one!' I said. With that, he pulled a cigarette packet from his pocket and gave me the last two he had. The friendliness and the generosity of this young lad almost brought me to tears. He renewed my faith in human nature. I shook his hand and said, 'Now you'll do your best to do what I asked you? And if you can't, that's all right, but for God's sake don't mention a word to anyone about me being here. Get back to me during your lunch hour to let me know how you got on and what's happening.'

'I'll do my best,' he said, 'and I'll not breathe a word to a soul.'

He went on his way, and I went back to my secluded nook in the copse, where I lay down, smoked half a cigarette, tapped it and put it safely aside with the full fag. Then I settled down to doze my way through the waiting hours, until, hopefully, the lad returned at 1 p.m. or so.

Fortunately the day was warm and dry, good lying-out weather. Aside from a few scratches, and the deadness – a kind of ennui – that settles in after a chase, I was all right. But I experienced an awful sense of loneliness. Apart from the occasional sound of a bird and the low, sporadic sound of a mowing-machine in the distance, there was no sign of a human presence to disturb me. The hours to 1 p.m. passed pleasantly enough and I refused to dwell on the possibility that the lad might not be able to contact the owner of the Eimear, that he might not come back, or that he might, inadvertently, mention my presence to someone.

About 1.30 p.m. I heard the soft sound of someone

entering the copse and then the sound of a low whistle and 'Mick, it's me!'

I thanked him for getting back to me and then asked: 'How did you get on?'

He reached into his pocket and, producing a couple of slices of buttered bread and a packet of Sweet Afton, he said, 'Here, Mick, I got you these.'

Grateful as I was to get the bread and the cigs, at that moment I was more anxious to know how he'd got on regarding the phone call to the Eimear. 'Yeah,' he said, 'I phoned the Eimear and got talking to your man. He said he'd try to get someone to pick you up at the phone box sometime after dark.'

Having thanked him for this good news, I asked him if he had mentioned my presence to anyone and what news there was regarding the garda search. 'I never said a word to anyone, not a word, but the people in the house were talking about you, or talking about the search for you. The guards are still searching the other side of the Dundalk road, so you're all right.' And with that he said he'd better be getting back to the hayfield. Having obtained explicit directions from him about how I would get to the phone box, I shook his hand and thanked him for his help.

I devoured the bread and chain-smoked two or three cigarettes, then settled down to await darkness. I wish I'd asked the lad his name, for I'd dearly like to meet him now, almost sixty years later, both to thank him and get his account of our encounter that morning so long ago.

As soon as it grew dark, I left my nook and made my way over the fields to Dromiskin. Thanks to his directions, it only took me fifteen minutes. The post office was in darkness and there was no sign of life, but I settled behind the hedge on the opposite side of the road to await my lift. Given the poor record for promised lifts, I was none too confidant one would arrive, never mind on time.

Thankfully, this proved to be an exception to the rule. Only five minutes or so into my vigil, and while I was contemplating risking lighting a cigarette, I heard the sound of a car approaching from the Dundalk direction. A Volkswagen Beetle slowed to a stop at the phone box. The driver put out the lights and sat there for a minute or so. It was odds-on that this was indeed my lift. However, not being able to make out his features or recognise the car, I stayed where I was.

However, as soon as the driver stepped out of the car I recognised him as the Eimear's owner. I couldn't believe my luck. I immediately climbed over the ditch and ran across the road. 'How're ya doing, Mick?' he said. 'Let's get into the car.' I thanked him from the bottom of my heart. As we shook hands, he said, 'Mick, ya did it again. You've the luck of the divil. Where do ya want to go, or what?'

I asked him what, if any, garda activity there was on the Dundalk–Castlebellingham road. I told him that I'd no safe billet in the immediate area and needed to get to Dublin the next day. If I got to Drogheda that night, I'd find a safe billet and be able to arrange a lift to Dublin the next morning.

'Well,' he said, 'the guards have called off the search in the fields, but they have roadblocks at Bellingham and back at the Blackrock road junction. But you can stay in my place. It's only a mile from here, and it's this side of Bellingham. Or if you want, I can get you to Drogheda by the back roads. But I need to call to my house first.'

'Okay,' I said, 'that's great. We'll call to your house and then head for Drogheda.'

We reached his house five minutes later. While he did whatever he had to do, I gorged myself on tea, cheese and homemade brown bread with deliciously salty homemade butter. About fifteen minutes later, still savouring the taste of the food and enjoying the comfort of a totally safe billet, I was tempted to ask if I could stay there for a day or so, when my host came back into the kitchen and said, 'All right, Mick, are you ready to go?'

'Yes, I'm ready,' I said. And we set out for Drogheda by the back roads.

'I'm a Hib, you know,' he said, 'but I've great respect for Billy Stewart [the Dundalk OC], and most of the local lads are decent men too. And I remember meeting you when you came into the bar with Billy one day, way back, so I didn't mind helping you out. Anyway, I heard from one of our members on the border that he'd put you and another couple of lads up after the Ballsmill job, and he thought ye were decent lads.' Obviously the Ancient Order of Hibernians edict against contact with the IRA was not widely observed in the area.

We reached the Drogheda billet about an hour later. I asked him in for a cup of tea, but he refused. 'No, thanks,' he said. 'I don't want anyone else to know about this, you know what I mean? But if ever you're stuck again, I'll help you out any way I can.'

I thanked him profusely. We shook hands and parted. He headed for home, with a certain degree of relief I imagine. I was also relieved to have reached my billet safely, but I have to admit that I watched him go with a degree of envy. I walked up the short, steep path to the back door of the 'billet on the hill' and got the usual great welcome that the good people here extended to any IRA man on the run. My morale restored, we chatted for several hours before going to bed. I had a great sleep.

The following morning, after a hearty breakfast, the man of the house drove me to a bus stop on the Dublin road a couple of miles south of Drogheda. He headed off to his job and a few minutes later I boarded a bus to Dublin. I arrived about an hour later and took another bus to the meeting-place, where I discovered that the chief of staff, Seán Cronin, had been arrested for refusing to account for his movements. It was 7 June 1960.

There was a general army convention just after Cronin's arrest. The main issue was, of course, the campaign. A proposal to halt it was advocated by a few delegates, who pointed to the movement's weakness, but they stopped short of an outright proposal to end it, mainly because they did not want to be associated with what would be a very unpopular decision as far as the vast majority of members of the movement were concerned.

While those of us who supported the continuation of the campaign were all too well aware of the problems that confronted us, we still felt that, given the right weapons, such as bazookas, we had a fighting chance of at least raising the level of resistance in the North. We felt we owed it to those who had died thus far to continue the fight for freedom. It was a purely emotional argument, but an important one. Lastly, we had been taught by our leaders, especially Seán Cronin, to believe that the reunification of Ireland could only be achieved by armed force. There was also a feeling that the country was on its knees and the very concept of a distinct, united Irish nation would be lost for ever if the campaign was abandoned.

I had the feeling that the adjutant-general, Ruairí Ó Brádaigh, was really in favour of ending the campaign, but was one of those who wanted to avoid the opprobrium of saying so. Instead he pointed out the problems we faced and said that these should be kept in mind when delegates came to vote. I spoke in favour of continuing, as did every other active service volunteer, because for us stopping was unthinkable. The convention decided to continue the campaign and I was elected to the Army Executive. We met briefly after the convention, but before the delegates dispersed, to elect a chief of staff. Ó Brádaigh was elected once more to replace Cronin and he proceeded to appoint his staff.[4] Martin Shannon was his adjutant-general, Cathal Goulding was quartermaster-general and I was appointed director of operations. No director of intelligence or publicity was appointed. Ó Brádaigh instructed me to attend an HQ meeting in Longford the following day.

That meeting, in his mother's house, was attended by Ó Brádaigh, Shannon and myself. From the outset, the atmosphere was strained. I didn't know Ó Brádaigh or Shannon well, but felt I was being treated more as an enemy than a comrade. On Ó Brádaigh's part this may have been because I had criticised the decision not to carry out an inquiry into Dáithí Ó Conaill's mismanagement of the Athboy camp – Ó Conaill and Ó Brádaigh were close friends. I suspect Ó Brádaigh would have preferred to appoint a director of operations of his own choice, but as Seán Cronin – whose opinion carried a lot of weight – had nominated me, my appointment to the Executive had been ratified by the Army Council. Moreover, I was the most experienced of the can-

---

4   Ruairí Ó Brádaigh was first made chief of staff when Seán Cronin was arrested in autumn 1958. Cronin resumed as COS after his release in February 1959.

didates for the position, which may say more about the rate of attrition in the organisation than my own ability. On the other hand, Shannon's ratification as adjutant-general was surprising given his inexperience. Many felt that he was Ó Brádaigh's stooge.

Ó Brádaigh opened the meeting with a brief résumé of the convention's decision to continue the campaign and then turned to me and said: 'Well, Mick, you're director of operations, what do you see yourself doing? What's your plan of campaign?'

Although I had had no experience of being a member of HQ staff, as opposed to the Army Council, I did have some ideas about how the operational end of things could be improved. I said that as we had few resources and morale was low because of the failure of the long-awaited bazookas and the arrest of Seán Cronin, I needed time to devise a plan of campaign. It was now about 8 p.m. Ó Brádaigh said that was all right and, as we were staying overnight, we could meet the following morning and I could present my ideas then.

We headed down to the kitchen for our supper, which was served by Ó Brádaigh's mother. The conversation was strained: there was no badinage, no swapping of jokes or anecdotes. As soon as it was timely, I excused myself and headed up to my room to begin working out my ideas. I spent several hours thinking about the situation and eventually arrived at a few obvious conclusions.

I put my plan, such as it was, to Ó Brádaigh the next morning. I began with an overall review of the situation as follows:

1. There was little or no consultation by HQ with volunteers in ASUs about their ideas regarding operations and the conduct of the campaign in general. As I knew from my own experience this could lead to the frustration and disillusionment of individual volunteers, as well as the estrangement of units from HQ, and to HQ not having a realistic view of the problems confronting the ASUs. These included the increasing difficulty of obtaining gelignite, and fewer and fewer people willing to provide safe billets or transport. Virtually all ASU volunteers felt that HQ hadn't a clue about the problems they confronted, including the constant shortage of money or ability to contribute financially towards their keep.

2. Given the enemy's strength and the success of their countermeasures, as well as a continuing decline in our prospects of raising the level of operations – or even maintaining the current low level of activity – ASUs were, naturally, growing more and more reluctant to risk their lives or their liberty.

3. We were now without even the hope of the bazookas alleviating the military situation.

I went on to say that, as we were committed to keeping the campaign going, in accordance with the convention's decision, we should adopt the following course:

1. HQ to hold regular meetings with the ASUs, or at least their OCs, to receive feedback and generally improve the system of communications, as well as supplies of money and materials. I pointed out that HQ was not aware of how much the operational environment had changed on the border since the early days of the campaign.

2. Suspend operations for a month to six weeks, while (a) the OCs of the ASUs rebuilt the local organisations, including identification of good guides, sources of intelligence, safe dumps and safe billets; (b) volunteers were given a break from their areas for a month, or until such time as they were required to operate, thus easing the strain on their nerves and the financial burden on those billeting them; and (c) intelligence on targets, prior to reopening operations, was gathered. I also felt that the preparation of safe dumps for gelignite was particularly important so that ASUs would have enough material to last them through the first phase of operations and into the second phase. This would reduce the risk of running the gauntlet of police roadblocks once operations resumed.

3. Immediately call a meeting of the ASUs, either collectively or separately, whichever was most feasible, to give them a report on the convention, its decisions and our new operational plan, and to seek their opinions and ideas on how best to implement the plan.

4. Instruct the OCs to report back to HQ in a month with the results of their search for safe billets, dumps and suitable targets. At those meetings HQ would decide which targets would be hit.

After some discussion about logistics, Ó Brádaigh accepted this plan and allocated tasks to the three of us, as well as to the quartermaster-general, Cathal Goulding, who wasn't present.

The ASUs were pleased that HQ was at last consulting them, and following the six-week pause there was a greater volume of operations than at any time since 1957; albeit they were the low-level sabotage jobs, which were all that was possible given our resources.

But success was short-lived. We soon ran out of suitable targets within range of our ASUs' operational bases. Furthermore, with increased security measures, constant raids on billets, heavier security on likely targets, and, above all, the absence of new weaponry, the ASUs once again had to devote their energies and ingenuity to survival. Operating in the North more than five miles from the border was out of the question because of the absence of any kind of back-up organisation. Soon morale sank to such an extent that some volunteers sought a leave of absence.

Towards the end of 1960, about a month before Seán Cronin's release from his six-month sentence in Mountjoy, Clan na Gael in America sent a letter about him to the Army Council. The letter was delivered to Ó Brádaigh by Paddy McLogan, who was president of Sinn Féin and the Clan's man in Ireland, or perhaps more correctly, the Clan was the organisation by which he often transmitted his own views to

HQ and the Army Council. The letter said that Clan na Gael had been supplied with the following information:

(1) Seán Cronin, while he was a member of the Free State army, participated in a firing squad that executed a member of the IRA in the 1940s.

(2) Seán Cronin was a member of the Communist Party for a number of years.

In view of these revelations, the Clan said it had no option but to demand that he be removed from any position of leadership within the IRA and that he never be reappointed to any such position in the future. Failure to comply with the Clan's wishes would leave it with no option but to end all support for the IRA.

The letter left no room for inquiring into the sources of these allegations or for an investigation, not that anyone on the Army Council believed them or suggested they required an investigation. Most of us on the Army Council felt that McLogan, who virtually controlled the Clan and was hostile to Cronin and to anyone who dared oppose his views, inspired the letter. The letter was in effect an ultimatum: get rid of Cronin or else.

Ó Brádaigh, as chief of staff and chairman of the Army Council, read the letter at the next meeting, about two weeks after it was received. The reaction was a mixture of astonishment and anger. No one gave any credence to the allegations, particularly the one about the firing squad. The second allegation was not considered very serious, although it has to be said that no member of the Army Council was an avid supporter of communism at the time.

The discussion ended with a unanimous decision to reject the allegations, reprimand Clan na Gael for making them, reappoint Cronin to HQ and co-opt him to the Army Council on his release, and, if necessary, accept the consequences of that decision, namely the end of all future support from Clan na Gael. It was also decided that the chief of staff would write to notify Clan na Gael of our decision.

However, Ó Brádaigh then proposed 'to suspend our decisions for two weeks, till the next Army Council meeting, to allow members time to consider the full implications of the Clan letter'. The council agreed to defer its decision. I believe Ó Brádaigh, cautious man that he was, was anxious to ensure that the Army Council should be cool and unemotional in reaching its decision and that members should be fully cognisant of the consequences of their decision. And there is no doubt that emotions did run high at that first meeting.

Ó Brádaigh had been McLogan's protégé and was McLogan's nominee to escape from the Curragh in 1958 so that he could take over as chief of staff, and so there was a view that he was in McLogan's pocket. I think, though, that Ó Brádaigh was acting independently, as he certainly took a stand against McLogan at meetings of the 'co-ordinating committee', the joint committee of the IRA and Sinn Féin, right up to the end of the campaign.

Meanwhile, almost everyone on the Army Council, and the twenty or so remaining active volunteers, were anticipating Cronin's release and the boost to morale that would follow his return. In retrospect, it's clear that there wasn't much more he could have done to save the situation than we were already doing. Nevertheless, we were in dire need of experienced leaders.

The next meeting of the Army Council, two weeks later, voted unanimously to reject Clan na Gael's allegations and its demands. It decided that the Clan be informed, in writing, of our decision and of our abhorrence at its allegations. It was to be further informed that Seán Cronin's future role in the army was a matter to be decided solely by the Army Council and HQ. The letter made it clear, without spelling it out, in case it fell into the wrong hands, that Cronin would be reappointed to the HQ and co-opted onto the Army Council, and that the Army Council would not be intimidated by Clan na Gael. This was duly communicated via McLogan.

I met Cronin on the morning he was released in early December and brought him to see Cathal Goulding, although I don't know why the meeting was with the quartermaster-general, rather than Ó Brádaigh. It was held in Brendan Behan's house and I met Goulding again minutes afterwards.

What he told me, and repeated at the next Army Council meeting, was that Cronin had heard of the letter while in Mountjoy and had also been told that the Army Council had inquired into the allegations. Cronin was angry, not alone at the reported investigation, but at the fact that the letter had even been read out and discussed at an Army Council meeting. Goulding said he assured Cronin that there had been no investigation of any kind into the allegations and that the letter was read to the Army Council as a matter of form. He also told Cronin that he had been defended to the hilt by the council, even to the point of cutting off its last remaining source of support. He then offered Cronin an opportunity to defend himself, if he wished, but Cronin was unmoved. He said that the mere reading of the letter lent it credence. He concluded his meeting with Goulding by saying that because of the Army Council's handling of the affair he had decided not to accept any leadership position in the army. He also refused to meet the Army Council to discuss his views or hear its side of things.

I was bitterly disappointed with Cronin's attitude and I know that almost everyone else felt as I did.

7

MORE DISAPPOINTMENT AND CAPTURE, 1960–61

The adjutant-general, Martin Shannon, who maintained contact by letter with the few IRA support groups in England, came to me at a billet in Rathgar one Saturday with a request. He had arranged a meeting with an English contact the next morning, Sunday, at the Central Hotel in Exchequer Street, but now had to meet an important unnamed individual instead. He wanted me to go in his place, bring his English contact to my safe billet in Rathgar and keep him there for a few hours until Shannon was free to meet him.

As the Central Hotel and its bar were frequented by members of the Special Branch, who then worked out of detective headquarters in Dublin Castle a couple of minutes' walk away, it was the last place in Dublin that I would have chosen to meet anyone. There was no point in my refusing to go, however, because Shannon worked hand in glove with Ó Brádaigh, who, I believed, was looking for the least excuse to remove me as director of operations.

As I had never met Shannon's contact, I asked how we were going to recognise each other and whether his contact would know in advance that he was meeting me. I also asked if the cover addresses he was using to contact this man were safe. Shannon assured me they were 'absolutely safe'. He said our visitor had been told to sit in the lobby, gave me a description and concluded our brief meeting with a peremptory, 'I don't see what you're worried about: you'll have no problem recognising him, and it's perfectly safe.'

Without being paranoid about it, I ranked security high on my list of priorities, and the more I thought about the meeting, the more my instincts and common sense convinced me that it was too risky. I decided to ask the shrewd, twenty-one-year-old son of my host if he would meet the English visitor at the Central Hotel and bring him to me at the house of Myles and Madeleine Heffernan, making sure that they were not followed. I explained why I was reluctant to go to the hotel myself and explained that while he would risk being arrested, there was no possibility that he would be charged and jailed for simply delivering a message. I told him that in the unlikely event of arrest he should give his name and address, deny he was a member of either the IRA or Sinn Féin, which was a fact, and ask for a solicitor.

As soon as he left for the Central Hotel I walked the quarter of a mile to Madeleine's to wait. Given the vagaries of Dublin's Sunday bus service, I wasn't too worried when neither man arrived at the appointed time. Anyway, the IRA was notorious for its lack of punctuality. But after two hours I was convinced that something had gone wrong, particularly as I had asked my courier to wait no longer than half an hour for the man from England and the fact that the bus journey would only take half an hour at the most.

About four hours after the appointed time a sister of my courier arrived and told me that he had been arrested and was being held in the bridewell. She said that the Special Branch had raided their house, had spent a couple of hours searching it from top to bottom, and that they were looking for me. 'They left about an hour ago,' she added. She was certain she hadn't been followed. I told her to go back home and to tell her mother to go to the bridewell and plead for her son's release, to point out that he had no involvement with the IRA and to tell him to sign the form denying membership.

Meanwhile, feeling somewhat guilty for having placed him and his mother in this situation, I decided to risk a visit to their home as soon as it got dark. I entered the house by the back door, having climbed numerous back-garden walls, just in case there was a watch on the house. The family, including the mother, was gathered in the kitchen when I entered. They looked at me with a shocked expression, which I mistook for anger, and then one of them said, 'Mick! What are you doing here? They've just left; they raided the house again only half an hour ago looking for you, and they've just gone out the door!'

None of them blamed me for their son's arrest but told me, 'Don't, for God's sake, stay too long in case the Special Branch come back.' Nevertheless, I wanted to hear from the mother what the branch had asked her, as well as to reassure her that her son would be released. We went upstairs to have the chat, but beforehand I asked the family to lock the back door and delay answering any callers for a few seconds to allow me to escape through the skylight.

The mother, a solid republican like the rest of the family, didn't require my assurances or apologies. Instead she was anxious to tell me how much the Special Branch knew of some of my habits. When I was about to take my leave the front doorbell rang. I headed up to the roof and waited, looking down through the skylight to see if it was the Special Branch again. After a couple of minutes, however, the man of the house, a small, friendly, generous individual and one of the few honest clerks at work in Ireland, came up and indicated that it was all right to come back in.

'Who called?' I asked him.

'A branch man, of course. They must think we're terrible eejits, thinking we wouldn't know them. He asked, "Is Mick here? I've an important message for him."

'"No," I said, "there's no Mick here. Have you got the right house?"

'And then he just looked at me and said, "Ah, yeah, I must have the wrong house."'

I left the same way I came in a few minutes later and a further five minutes later was safely ensconced in Madeleine's. The son was released that night.

Anxious to get my go-between's account of his arrest, I arranged to meet him at a safe venue the night after he was released. He told me that he recognised my contact from the description he'd been given and introduced himself as a messenger from Shannon. When they stood up to leave Special Branch men arrested them under Section 21 of the Offences Against the State Act.

When my contact explained that he was 'not Mick Ryan' as the branch thought, he was told they were taking him in anyway. Clearly, they had been expecting me.

Despite all their threats to have him jailed for at least three months, my young friend continued to assert his innocence and insisted he was only delivering a message for a friend. I subsequently discovered that the man from England was let out the following morning. I never did get to meet him.

When I met Shannon a couple of days later he apologised and congratulated me on my narrow escape. I decided not to trust his judgement again.

***

Since the failure of the bazookas at Christmas 1959, an electrical engineer, who was a friend of the quartermaster-general, Cathal Goulding, had been working on the trigger mechanism of the launchers and on manufacturing a propellant for the rockets. Eventually, by September 1960, Goulding reported at a meeting at HQ that the engineer had developed both and was reasonably confident these would work and that the weapons were now ready for testing. He couldn't proceed with further experiments until they were test-fired. As I was the only member of HQ who had been trained on the bazooka, I was the obvious choice to carry out the test.

A few days later, in the pre-dawn gloom of a stormy September morning, Paddy Murphy, a farmer from Kilkenny who had attended the summer training camp in the Slieve Blooms, and myself left the city with a launcher and two rockets. He drove in the 'HQ car', a really old Ford Prefect that had been bought for £100, and headed for our old training ground near McGrath's shooting lodge at the Sally Gap in the Dublin Mountains. About an hour later, thanks to Murphy's coaxing of the Prefect's old engine, we reached our destination.

It was about 8 a.m. The rain had stopped, but the sky was filled with grey-black clouds that were so close to the ground I felt I could touch them. It was more like twilight than an hour after dawn and the wind was blowing at gale force. Though there wasn't a soul in sight – even the birds weren't flying that morning – we were taking no chances. We parked the car in a secluded spot, unloaded the gear and walked a couple of hundred yards away from the road until we reached a suitable target, which was a huge mound of rocks. As the sights on the launcher didn't seem too reliable, I decided to set up the fire position about fifty yards from the target.

The engineer had replaced the magneto with a 4½-volt battery, strapped to the side of the launcher, which would – theoretically – provide the power to ignite the propellant. He'd also replaced the magneto trigger with a simple switch, which meant that simply throwing the switch to 'on' would instantaneously fire the propellant. It all looked fine to me. Paddy and I were the best of friends, but we weren't saying too much to each other. I think we were too conscious of the fact that we were engaged in an experiment that might just save the campaign. At the same time, having seen too many unfulfilled promises, we were reluctant to celebrate too soon.

Having an open breech, the bazooka was described in the manual as a 'recoilless rifle'. The only thing the firer had to compensate for when firing was a slight pull forward as the rocket left the launch tube. And just to make sure we hadn't forgotten the loading and firing drill, it being almost a year since we were trained on the weapon, we spent a few minutes going over it verbally. Confident to continue, I placed the launcher on my shoulder and Paddy loaded a rocket. I lined up the sights as best I could and, not really expecting much of a result in view of the poor history of homemade devices, I threw the switch.

There was a result all right, but it wasn't quite the one I expected. The propellant exploded rather than burned and drove the rocket out of the launcher with such force and with such a powerful back-blast that the muzzle guard, which was welded to the launcher, was blown back against the trigger guard, which sliced it like butter. The uncovered sight struck me right between the eyes, and some small pieces of debris embedded themselves in my face.

I was momentarily blinded, stunned by the blow and badly cut about the face. Semi-conscious, I laid down the launcher and sank to the ground. Then, according to Paddy, I blacked out for a minute or two, until he revived me. He thought I was dead, he told me afterwards. I thought I was dead too.

Paddy tended to my cuts as best he could. We'd no first-aid kit, just a couple of none-too-clean handkerchiefs. Three or four minutes after the 'launch' I was fine, particularly when I discovered that my right eye – while it was in bad shape – was still there and that I could see out of it, although with blurred vision, which took a few hours to disappear.

We broke the launcher down into its two halves, packed it into its container (a sack) and stowed it and the second rocket in the boot of the car. As the rocket we'd launched had no explosives in the warhead and we were anxious to see what condition it was in, we decided to try to retrieve it from where it was supposed to have hit the rocky mound. However, having searched for five minutes or so, we could find no trace of it. It had either embedded itself deep into a clay section of the mound, shattered into small pieces on hitting rock, or had overshot the mound, in which case it would take dozens of people hours to find it.

A few minutes later, with Paddy driving, we headed back along the mist-covered roads to Dublin. Other than Paddy's periodic enquiries about the state of my health, we didn't say much. Each of us knew what the other was thinking: we were still a long way from having serviceable rockets.

Paddy dropped me off at my billet, Myles and Madeleine Heffernan's house in Rathgar. We arranged to meet Goulding later that night to report on the launch and Paddy went off to dump the gear. It being a Friday morning, Myles and Madeleine were at work, so I had the house to myself. I had a look in a mirror to see how my eye was. It didn't look too bad; however, there were dozens of tiny black particles of something embedded in my forehead and face, as if I had chicken-pox, only a black chickenpox. The gash between my eyes didn't look too good, though it had stopped bleeding. But overall I felt all right. I washed and disinfected the gash and plucked out as many of the particles as I could. Then, overcome with a kind of lethargy, I went to bed and slept for a few hours.

We met Goulding that night. He was shocked at our report and, assured that I was all right, said he'd contact the engineer immediately, tell him what had happened and get him to begin work on a modified version of the propellant.

Of course, even if the engineer succeeded in coming up with a suitably modified propellant we still had a long way to go. There were the equally difficult problems of arming the warhead with the right type and quantity of explosive, the method of detonation and getting the right sights for the launchers. But if, as seemed likely, we weren't going to get a replacement consignment of serviceable launchers and rockets from America, we'd no alternative but to keep experimenting. The engineer was not a member of the IRA and was only helping as a favour to Goulding. The absence of a competent director of engineering was one of the biggest weaknesses of the IRA at the time.

About a month later Goulding reported that the engineer had gone as far as he could with the modified propellant, and that it was ready for another testing. Paddy and myself volunteered to carry out the test again. This time, however, we'd take the precaution of firing the rocket by remote control, so to speak. We would mount the launcher on a tripod, 'barrel-sight' it on the target, then secure it to the tripod with a rope before loading the rocket. We would then attach a string to the switch and arrange to fire it from a covered position twenty feet or so behind the launcher.

Once more we headed for the Dublin Mountains before dawn in the Ford Prefect to reduce the risk of being spotted by the Special Branch. We set up the tripod and the rest as planned, took cover and pulled the string. There was a slight bang and not much of a flash, but the rocket did leave the gun.

We walked over to the launcher to examine it and discovered it was intact. Nor did it appear to have been dragged out of position. However, as we had taken great care to anchor the tripod to the ground and had lashed the launcher to the tripod more securely than it could be held in human hands, we had no way of knowing the extent of drag on the launcher as the rocket left it.

So far so good. It was at least an improvement on the previous test, although we still had a long way to go. And time was running out.

When I told the active service volunteers, the dozen or so who remained in counties Louth and Monaghan, of the success of the propellant, they greeted the news with barely concealed scepticism. They had been given too many broken promises about bazookas. The bazookas weren't the only problem, of course. The lack of public support, the shortage of money and the absence of even the most rudimentary intelligence network or safe billets in the North meant mounting the simplest operation required immense effort and risk.

I've no idea what could have revived morale at that stage. Yet, despite all the problems, volunteers were still prepared to stick it out. No man resigned, sought a leave of absence or went sick.

The campaign drifted on.

***

In the spring of 1961 Cathal Goulding and myself were arrested in two separate places. To our surprise we were each sentenced to just three months' imprisonment, relatively short terms, for not accounting for our movements. Goulding was arrested near Brendan Behan's house in Ballsbridge, which had been his main billet for almost two years, and where I stayed occasionally. I was arrested in my parents' house in Caledon Road, which I hadn't visited in almost two years before the day of my arrest.

In visiting my parents' house that morning, I was breaking my own golden rule of never visiting home while I was on the run. The main reason for my visit was to collect a letter that might have arrived from a cover address nearby. It was that of a woman who lived a few doors away in East Wall. She was not a member of the movement and had no other connection with it, but was very trustworthy. As soon as she received a letter for me, she would deliver it to my home, only a minute's walk away. The letter would then be passed on to a courier, who also lived close by and he usually delivered it to my billet at the Heffernans' house on the same night, by bus or bike. However, because I travelled a lot, I often would not get to read the letter for several days.

Some of the letters that came for me to this address con-
tained references that concerned Martin Shannon's department. Following an HQ meeting the previous night, he had
told me he was expecting an important and urgent letter at
my cover address. It was so urgent that he didn't want to wait
the normal day or two for it to be delivered. He wanted me to
check if it had arrived and to bring it to his 'drop' immediately
afterwards. He concluded by saying that a delay in delivering
another letter had 'caused some problems', although he didn't
elaborate.

I pointed out to him what he already knew, that this
meant calling to my home, which I'd scrupulously avoided
for almost two years. 'I know, Mick,' he said, 'but it has to
be done. There's no other way. This is a very important letter.
And anyway, since you haven't been home for so long, the
branch aren't going to be watching for you.' I felt this was the
equivalent of a direct order and I reluctantly acceded, despite
my previous experience.

When I was in Dublin, where the bicycle was my main
means of transport, I seldom moved about in daylight. But
about 10 a.m. the following morning I arrived at my home in
East Wall. Only my father, a semi-invalid now on crutches,
and my sister, Monica, who had come home on a holiday
from England, were there. My mother was at work. Both of
them were amazed to see me.

About two or three minutes later – I hadn't even sat down

but was standing at the kitchen table – there was a knock on the front door. Monica went to answer, and the next instant the kitchen was full of branch men, headed, I think, by Johnny Walker, a senior Special Branch officer.

In a matter of seconds, I was being hustled out the front door under Section 21 of the Offences Against the State Act. Parked outside were three branch cars, with another one blocking the junction with Boolavogue Road fifty yards away. I heard afterwards that a car was blocking the other end of Caledon Road at the East Road junction as well, while other branch men had entered houses to the right and left of mine and were at the back to cut off any escape at the rear. It was the kind of operation that could not have been mounted at short notice and I'm certain that no more than three minutes had elapsed since I entered the house.

My father hobbled out to the door after me, shouting abuse at the branch men. By now a couple of housewives living opposite, who had been sweeping the footpath outside their homes, were standing with brushes in hand watching. When they heard my father shouting abuse at my 'abductors' they joined in and began to shout, 'You leave him alone! What are you doing to him?'

My father and Monica began pulling and dragging at Walker and the other branch men who had a hold of my arms. My father had let go of his crutch and was gripping the garden railing with one hand and Walker with the other.

Walker, who was accustomed to a more surreptitious kind of arrest, said to me, 'Look, Mick, will you go quietly?'

I said I would if they let my arms go and let me get into the car. So Walker and the other man let go of my arms and started pushing me towards the open car door, only a few feet away. I immediately made a dash for it, but, being surrounded, it proved a futile gesture and with that the two women began swinging their sweeping-brushes at the branch men and shouting abuse at them. My father and Monica, whom I could hear but not see, were also abusing the branch men, who apparently were now restraining them.

It was a real melee for a few seconds. Without the use of violence, it is no easy matter to get an unwilling person into a car. Eventually, one branch man opened the other rear door, grabbed hold of my legs and dragged me in. He then lay on top of me and another one, entering from the other side of the car, piled in on top of me as well.

And that was that.

We sped off and two or three minutes later I was in the bridewell situated behind the Four Courts. Less than an hour afterwards I was starting my three-month sentence. As I was taken down from the dock one of the Special Branch men said, in a real pally voice, 'Jeez, Mick, you were in luck, you got off very light.' When he handed me over to the jailer, he added, 'No hard feelings!'

I arrived at Mountjoy Prison at 7 p.m. that evening to the

usual ribbing from my comrades. It was an easy three months
up to my release on 31 July 1961.

8

THE END OF
THE CAMPAIGN,
1961–62

From 1960 to February or March 1962 a co-ordinating committee, comprising three members of the Army Council and
HQ and three members of the Ard Chomhairle of Sinn
Féin, met monthly – or more frequently, if necessary – to co-
ordinate the activities and policies of Sinn Féin and the IRA.
Those who most frequently attended on the Sinn Féin side
were Paddy McLogan, Jack Guiney, Seán O'Mahoney and
Micky Traynor. Those who most regularly attended from the
army side were Ó Brádaigh, Goulding, Shannon and myself.

My contribution in the course of the first year of these
meetings was minimal, because of a lack of experience. By
October 1961, however, I had gained more confidence and
began to see that there were serious differences between the
Sinn Féin representatives and ourselves. They could hardly
conceal their resentment of us, the younger element, and
no opportunity was lost in pointing out the futility of the

campaign. Traynor made some particularly cynical suggestions for improving the state of affairs. For instance, he suggested at one meeting that the only hope lay in seeking volunteers for suicide missions deep within the North against British Army personnel. The suggestion never got a hearing from our side, nor did other mad-hat schemes that don't deserve a mention. That said, Jack Guiney, to my mind, was one of the most dedicated and genuine men of that era and was generous to a fault. His house was always open to those on the run. His car, his money and any other resource he had were available, and he continued to help us even after the rift became serious.

Even before the reintroduction of special military courts on 22 November 1961, HQ and the Army Council had finally agreed that the campaign was lost and were considering how to end it with minimum loss of prestige, men and armaments.[1] This was important if we were to maximise our prospects for a future campaign to 'free the North'.

We had first discussed ending the campaign in September 1961, and from that time on serious thought was given to the question. Ironically the introduction of the military courts interrupted those discussions, as did increased police surveillance. The prospect of savage sentences for possession of arms and for harbouring members further reduced the number of

---

1   These military courts were composed of army officers and met *in camera*. They could impose a range of sentences, including the death sentence, but that had to be approved by the government.

safe houses, even in Dublin. Travelling to meetings became increasingly hazardous, particularly in the border areas.

In November Ruairí Ó Brádaigh concluded a meeting with a warning that there would be a round-up in a matter of days. He told Shannon and me to get the word out to the men on the run. Turning to Goulding he said, somewhat apologetically, 'I think, Cathal, you should stay away from home, at least for the next couple of weeks.'

To which Goulding replied, 'Yeah, I know, I know, but you see, I use the bike any time I go home, and, you see, when I'm cycling through Rathfarnham, through the village, I'll notice if there's any branch activity, and if there is I won't go home.'

Ó Brádaigh was obviously sceptical, but, realising that there was no point in labouring the issue, and in a characteristic signal of resignation – pursing his lips – he nodded his head. Three days later Goulding was arrested while cycling through Rathfarnham.

Ó Brádaigh, Shannon and myself met about a month after the introduction of the military courts. We had been holding mini staff meetings to discuss the situation and in the course of that meeting we discussed the need for the Army Council to convene and give serious consideration to ending the campaign. Police activity was intense, our billets had almost dried up, and the few that were still open to us were under regular surveillance. Free State intelligence had an almost complete breakdown of our structure, or what was left of it.

Ó Brádaigh, Shannon and myself were the only members of GHQ still at liberty. Our main objective was survival so as to prevent the annihilation of the movement and that of the ten or so full-time active volunteers on the border. We had about twenty weapons and 200lbs of gelignite left, no money and little transport beyond our bikes to get around Dublin. The campaign was over in all but name and, by formally ending it, we argued, we would at least give the impression that we still held the initiative.

We notified the other members of the Army Council that there was to be a meeting in early December. Ó Brádaigh and myself travelled together from Dublin to attend it. But having waited two hours at the venue near Portlaoise and realising that no one else was coming, we called another meeting for the following week. The weather during those weeks was particularly bad, with prolonged periods of fog, ice and frost, so that meeting was aborted too.

By this point it was apparent that there was something radically wrong. The non-attenders said that the weather, together with the difficulty in getting someone to drive or lend them a car, was the problem. With the need for a meeting becoming more urgent by the day, I suggested to Ó Brádaigh that the only way to get them to a meeting was for us to set a venue in the west of Ireland that would be convenient to everyone, except Ó Brádaigh and myself, and that I would call to the member in Co. Tipperary, then the member in Co. Limerick, thence to Clare, on to Kerry, and then to Galway, telling each of them of the meeting and that I would return to pick them up. Ó Brádaigh would make his own way there. This was agreed and I made the trip in a borrowed car, calling to every member and leaving nothing to chance. That's how we finally got an Army Council meeting.

At the meeting we discussed ending the campaign, and other things, but it was decided that only the Army Executive could end it. So we fixed an Executive meeting for a fortnight later in Bray. The Executive agreed that the campaign should be ended, after some serious questioning of the manner in which a halt would be called. The Army Council then met again and ratified the decision, leaving the date and the issuing of the statement to HQ – which meant in effect Ó Brádaigh, who was the only one capable of framing and writing such an important document.

We agreed that we would first have to inform all those still on active service (of which there would have been about fifteen at this stage), as well as some of the more important people around the country, so that they would be psychologically prepared for the shock. None of us were in any doubt that many would be shocked, disillusioned, angry and disappointed with the decision. But only the blind and the ignorant could have seen any point in continuing. The campaign was long over, to all intents and purposes; it just hadn't been formally ended.

On the first weekend in February 1962, as we were on our way to attend the second Army Council meeting, the Minister for Justice, Charlie Haughey, announced an amnesty for anyone handing up weapons and abandoning the campaign. The timing couldn't have been worse, as there would be those who would see a connection between it and our own decision to end the campaign. But it was agreed to press ahead as the only course possible.

Along with the danger of serious misunderstandings and differences of opinion within the army, there was the danger of misinterpretation by the press. Already, at the end of January, the Sinn Féin members of the co-ordinating committee had claimed the right to issue a statement from the Ard Chomhairle expressing its position on the ceasefire and on the campaign generally. At the meeting there was McLogan (I think), Jack Guiney and Micky Traynor, with Ó Brádaigh, Shannon and myself representing HQ. Despite our lack of political experience, we immediately saw the significance of their suggestion and objected to it. The decision to start or end the campaign was solely the business and responsibility of the IRA. We argued that, as Sinn Féin had made a statement supporting the campaign in the opening weeks of 1956, and had been banned in the six counties as a result, it should not risk such a ban in the South.

The other side, with Traynor as the main spokesman, said they had a right to comment on the conduct of the campaign and its calling off if they wished. It was obvious that their real aim was to regain control of the army by blaming the failure of the campaign on the present HQ leadership and calling for a special general army convention as soon as possible after the declaration on 26 February.

But we refused to budge. In the end, we invoked the constitutional pillar, 'that the Army Council is the supreme body within the entire organisation and that the Ard Chomhairle was subordinate to it'. We won that round; but it was quickly followed by a demand to call a special Ard Chomhairle meeting to discuss the issue. However, that meeting accepted our position and decided not to issue a statement.

Shortly afterwards McLogan, Traynor and some others refused to participate further in Sinn Féin and quietly eased themselves out. It then became the turn of younger members to take control of the movement.

The statement, and an excellent statement of our position it was, was written by Ó Brádaigh and cleared by the Army Council before being issued to the media on the night of 26 February 1962. The thrust of it was to condemn the Free State government for its 'stab in the back', to make clear that the IRA was not surrendering its arms or taking advantage of the arms amnesty, that this was only a halt to 'this phase' of the struggle for 'Irish unity and freedom', and that we were only dumping arms until such time as the IRA could strike another blow for freedom.

Óglaigh na hÉireann – (Irish Republican Army)

Ard-oifig – Dept of A/G. General Headquarters

26th February 1962.

TO THE PEOPLE OF IRELAND

The Army Council of the Irish Republican Army has ordered the termination of the Campaign of Resistance to British Occupation launched on December 12th 1956. Instructions issued to Volunteers of the Active Service Units and of local Units in the occupied area have now been carried out. All arms and other material have been dumped and all full-time active service Volunteers have been withdrawn.

The decision to end the Resistance Campaign has been taken in view of the general situation. Foremost among the factors motivating this course of action has been the attitude of the general public whose minds have been deliberately distracted from the supreme issue facing the Irish people – the unity and freedom of Ireland. Other and lesser issues have been urged successfully upon them and the sacrifices which could win freedom in the political, cultural, social and economic spheres are now stated to be necessary to bolster up the partition system forced on the Irish people by Britain forty years ago. This calculated emphasis on secondary issues by those whose political future is bound up in the status quo and who control all the mass media of propaganda is now leading the people of the 26 Counties towards possible commitment in future wars.

The Irish Republican Army stands firmly against any such course of action while Ireland is unfree and will use all its resources towards restoring in full to the Irish people their sense of national values.

For over five years our Volunteers have fought against foreign occupation, native collaboration and the overwhelming weight of hostile propaganda. Supported loyally by the Republican people of the Six Occupied Counties they have faced fantastic odds. 5,000 British regular troops, 5,000 Territorials, 12,500 B Specials, 3,000 RUC, 1,500 specially trained commandos and sundry security guard forces totalling close on 30,000 armed men bar the road to freedom. Their considerable resources have included armoured vehicles liberally supplied by the British Government, heavily fortified strong-points and the most modern war-equipment. Terrorist tactics against the civilian population, draconian laws, imprisonment without charge or trial, torture-mills to force 'confessions' from prisoners, long and savage penal servitude sentences, the shooting down of unarmed people at road-blocks and threats of even sterner measures including flogging and hanging have all been employed to maintain British rule in the Six Counties.

The collaborationist role of successive 26 County Governments – acting under British pressure – from December 1956 has contributed material aid and comfort to the enemy. Border patrols by 26 County military and police working in collaboration with the British Occupation Forces were instituted 48 hours after the opening of the Campaign. The press was muzzled and the radio controlled in the interests of British rule. The methods and eventually the aims and objectives of the Irish Republican Army were misrepresented to the Irish people and to the world by the professional politicians of the 26 County state. Top-level conferences with the Crown Forces and the continuous supplying of information to the enemy – secretly at first but later quite openly – were other and lesser known features of collaboration.

Unarmed active service Volunteers found within the 26 Counties were arrested and jailed while armed patrols of the British Forces could cross the Border at will. Jailing of Resistance supporters and even moral sympathisers throughout the 26 Counties followed while quisling Irishmen from the same area were permitted to join the enemy forces. Homes were raided and people followed about by the Special political police. The Curragh Concentration Camp was opened and maintained for close on two years with 200 uncharged and untried prisoners. When public opinion forced its closing down, the Prisoners' Dependants' Fund was attacked and hundreds of collectors jailed.

When this tactic too was defeated proceedings against I.R.A. Volunteers and their supporters at 26 County District Courts were superseded by the introduction of a Military Tribunal in November last. The savage sentences since imposed for technical offences culminated in the imprisonment of a young I.R.A. soldier from County Derry for eight years. In the teeth of such provocative action by those whose aim appears to be civil strife in the 26 Counties the discipline of Republican Volunteers in adhering to their instructions over the entire five-year period has been magnificent.

When repeated warnings by the Resistance to cease bearing arms against their own people were disregarded, the R.U.C. and B Special Constabulary were listed as legitimate military targets. The international provisions governing belligerent status including the wearing of means of identification, the carrying of arms openly and being under the control of responsible officers have been observed by the Irish Republican Army but in no case has the enemy recognised the status of the men fighting for their country other than as criminals.

During the five-year Campaign over 600 operations against enemy patrols, strong-points, communications, transport and civil administration have been carried out at enormous cost to the enemy. Casualties inflicted total six killed and 28 wounded. (This includes British soldiers, B Specials, R.U.C. and Commandos.) In addition, four members of the Crown Forces – apart from British military, naval and air force personnel for whom figures are not readily available – were killed other than by Resistance action. In the same period the Republican Forces suffered two killed in action and seven killed accidentally. Also a Sinn Féin organiser was murdered by British Crown Forces near Swanlinbar, County Cavan.[2] A small number of active service Volunteers were wounded. Forty-three prisoners of war are serving sentences of from four to 15 years in Crumlin Road, Belfast, and three are jailed in England while Mountjoy Prison, Dublin, holds 42 Irish Republicans.

No aid from any foreign source has been received by the Irish Republican Army. Irish exiles in many countries have been more than generous in their support of the Campaign while some returned to participate actively in the fight. The Army Council wishes to pay a long overdue public tribute to all the loyal Irish people of every class and creed who gave support – whether in the form of billets, transport, intelligence, funds, munitions or even encouragement – and to all who had the moral courage to speak out in private or in public in defence of the men fighting for Ireland. In future, an even greater volume of support will be needed so that the Cause dear to the hearts and minds of all who have actively contributed to the Resistance Campaign of 1956–62 will ultimately triumph.

The Irish Republican Army remains intact and is in a position to continue its Campaign in the occupied area indefinitely.

---

2   James Crossan.

It realises, however, that the situation obtaining in the earlier stages of the Campaign has altered radically and is convinced that the time has come to conserve its resources, to augment them, and to prepare a more favourable situation. The policy of not taking aggressive military action within the 26 County state remains unaltered and the Army takes its stand against any attempt to foment sectarian strife which is alien to the spirit of Irish Republicanism.

The Irish Republican Army renews its pledge of eternal hostility to the British Forces of Occupation in Ireland. It calls on the Irish people for increased support and looks forward with confidence – in co-operation with the other branches of the Republican Movement – to a period of consolidation, expansion and preparation for the final and victorious phase of the struggle for the full freedom of Ireland.

Issued by the Army Council

Óglaigh na hÉireann

February 26th 1962.

Some elements of the media chose to distort the statement and implied that the IRA had 'at last surrendered and given up its fight'. Not surprisingly, this created difficulties with some hard-line supporters and friendly houses. We had half a dozen billets in Dublin at the time and when I returned to one of them a few hours after the radio announcement of the campaign's end my then girlfriend greeted me with open hostility. 'Mick Ryan,' she said, 'I'm ashamed of you ... I never thought that you, above all people, would do this.' Not having heard the distorted account of the statement, I was amazed at her outburst and asked what she was talking about. 'You know what I'm talking about!' she said. 'I'm talking about this complete ending of the fight, for ever!'

A more serious instance occurred a week or so later. Ó Brádaigh, Shannon and myself met after the announcement to discuss how best to withdraw the remaining full-time volunteers, a dozen in all, from the border. We wanted to move them to relatively safe billets further south and find safe dumps for the few weapons and gelignite that remained. I had purchased 200 pounds of gelignite a month or so before the end of the campaign from a sympathetic quarry owner, and had already dumped it in Co. Louth. We had no money left and I was going to try to sell it back to the supplier. I picked up the gelignite in north Louth and, after a careful and circuitous journey, reached the house in north Co. Dublin where I was going to dump it pending the hoped-for resale. Throughout the campaign this house had been one of our main transit dumps. Now it was virtually the only one left.

I heaved a sigh of relief as I drove into the yard. Moreover, I always had a great welcome whenever I called. As was customary when calling to such billets, I gave the usual token rap on the back door before lifting the latch and walking in. Just as I was opening the door the woman of the house, a grand, friendly and hospitable woman reached the door, smiled and said hello. She was in the act of ushering me in when her husband walked up behind her and said, 'Who's that?'

While she was in the act of saying, 'It's Mick,' he edged her to one side and, instead of ushering me in with his usual welcome, stood in front of me on the doorstep and said with barely concealed hostility, 'Well, Mick … what do you think of this, eh, this ending of the campaign, this surrender?'

I said, politely, 'It isn't a surrender, Pat. I agreed with the calling off of it, but we'd no other option. It was finished; we had to call it off.'

With that a look of hatred spread across his face. He looked as if he was going to spit on me. 'You're a fuckin' traitor, you and the rest of them. You, you're another de Valera! You're not gettin' in here, ever again, ya, ya fuckin' traitor!'

I was speechless and almost paralysed in the face of such viciousness. He began to close the door on me. But as he did, his wife, who'd been standing behind him, said, 'Pat, for God's sake, let him in. Don't turn him away. He's some mother's son!'

But he was beyond reasoning. He turned angrily to her and said in a dictatorial manner: 'Go in, woman! This is none of your business!' The woman, intimidated into submission, released her grip on the door and, with a look that said, 'I don't want to turn you away, but I've no say', slowly and tearfully retreated to the kitchen.

Pat then pulled the door towards him and said, 'Get outa here, you traitor!' But as he went to close the door on me, I made one last plea. 'Pat,' I said, 'look, if you don't want to keep me, that's all right, but will you dump the gelignite for me? I've a couple of hundred pounds with me and I've no other dump for it.'

'I'll do nothing for yous bunch of traitors,' he said, as he slammed the door shut.

That was one of the worst moments of my life. I was saddened beyond description as I slowly walked to the car and sat into the driver's seat, dismayed at this perception of me as a traitor.

After a minute or so, when I got over the trauma of this awful reception, and having thought over the problem of where to dump the gelignite, I decided to head for another billet some forty miles to the west. It was the nearest one I could think of that was both safe and likely to take me and the gelignite. Having driven for a couple of hours over back roads to avoid roadblocks, I reached the billet at about 1 a.m. Here, at least, there was no problem. I woke the occupants and told them of my predicament. They accepted me, and the gelignite, with open arms.

I also had to contact members on active service in north Louth and north Monaghan, get them safely billeted further south and get their few weapons dumped. A day or so later I headed for Co. Donegal to pick up Tommy Nixon, the only active service volunteer left. I found him near Rossnowlagh. As it was too late to head back to Dublin, our hospitable hosts insisted that I spend the night. I didn't need much encouragement. We spent a most pleasant, if somewhat sad evening. One of the girls played the piano and entertained us with songs, finishing the night with a beautiful and haunting rendering of 'Róisín Dubh'. It was her way of acknowledging the sacrifices that had been made by the IRA men and mourning the end of an era.

We rose very early but, early as we were, the family were up to make us breakfast and to say farewell. Fifteen minutes later we were safely across the bridge at Ballyshannon. There had been a permanent garda roadblock on the bridge throughout the five years of the campaign, but that morning there wasn't a garda in sight. The rest of our journey was pleasant and uneventful.

***

A couple of days later there was a meeting of HQ in Dublin. After I reported on the safe transfer of the men and the weapons from the border, Ó Brádaigh suggested that in view of the media's distortion of our statement about the end of the campaign, there was an immediate need to visit our supporters, explain the statement and thank them for their magnificent sacrifices during the campaign. We decided to supplement these visits with a printed 'thank you' leaflet from HQ.

I was assigned to cover the area from north Louth to Ballinamore in Co. Leitrim, excluding north Monaghan, along with an odd billet elsewhere. I got a lift to north Louth, where, having split the task with another full-time volunteer, I trekked from billet to billet that March explaining the situation and leaving our 'thank you' leaflet with each supporter. It was a thankless and extremely difficult task, but there was no other means by which we could hope to preserve the skeleton – and it was only a skeleton – of a once vital organisation.

Having covered the north Louth and south Armagh area, I got a lift to Cavan, where I linked up with another full-time volunteer, Peadar Murray from Mayo. He had operated along the border from Cavan to Ballinamore and accompanied me as my guide for these 'visitations'. It was a cold, wet Sunday morning in March when I was dropped off at the home of the Cavan OC. I was with him for only an hour or so. All too well aware of the justification for formally ending the campaign, he had only to take his own area as an example of how close to total extinction we were and, appreciating the urgency of my task, he organised transport.

My partner and guide, Peadar, was an extremely quiet man, but he knew the billets we needed to call to and was familiar with that mountainous stretch of border country.

Our allocated driver was 'Fuck-fuck', so named because of his propensity to use that word to describe any and every situation. 'It's a fuckin' great fuckin' day ... Hurry fuckin' up, yous'll be fuckin' late ... Do yous fuckin' want fuckin' cigarettes or a fuckin' few fuckin' quid?' But he was a decent and generous man to us.

It was a depressingly wet day when we started out on the half-hour drive to our first Co. Cavan border call. Cavan, like Monaghan and Leitrim, is a beautiful little county, with its hundreds of small lakes, its unpretentious and gentle hills and little old woods dotted across the length and breadth of it. But on this rainy Sunday in March 1962 its beauty was lost on me because of the depressed state of the area, the deserted homes of those who had had to emigrate to make a living and the widespread poverty of those small farmers and workers who remained. It was a brutal reminder of the failure of our campaign for unity, freedom and a prosperous Ireland. Otherwise the rain was a blessing in disguise. The windows of the Volkswagen were nicely fogged up, making it virtually impossible for an observer to identify the passengers as strangers. The driver was widely known as an IRA supporter and it would be assumed that any young male strangers in his car would be IRA men. In addition, the curious-minded, who spent every free moment standing outside their houses watching whoever passed by, would remain indoors.

After a thirty-minute drive, we turned off the main road

onto a narrow, roughly surfaced mountain track. Five or so minutes later, we arrived at the billet. It was about 2 p.m. As we were getting out of the car, the man of the house, Jack McGuire, a widower, came and stood at the front door. As soon as he saw Peadar and the driver, he immediately invited us to 'come in out of the rain'.

I was also made welcome as soon as I was introduced as a comrade of Peadar's and a member of HQ. As soon as we entered the kitchen the whole family, who were sitting down to their dinner, shouted a hello to Peadar, welcoming him like a long-lost brother. They went on with a bit of bantering directed at him. Shy man that he was, he responded with a smile and shrug of his shoulders. Our driver left a few minutes later to return home to Cavan. From here, Peadar and myself would be on foot.

Having convinced Jack that we didn't need any dinner, he sat us down at the fire with, 'It's great to see you, Peadar, and you too, Mick. Yiz are welcome. That's a terrible cold day! Yiz'll have a drop to warm yiz up.' Before we had time to say yes, aye or no, he got up from the fire and returned with a bottle of his own poitín. Jack, it turned out, supplemented his meagre income from the farm with distilling and selling it, as well as a bit of smuggling. He held the bottle up to the light and said, 'Look at that! That's the best of stuff. It's as clear as well water, but better!' Peadar nodded an 'aye', while I, not knowing anything about poitín, and for politeness' sake, agreed, whereupon Jack handed each of us a cup and poured a liberal amount into each. He then replaced the cork in the bottle and set it down on the hearth 'to keep it warm'. Raising his cup, he said, 'Well, here's the best of luck, lads.'

Each of us took a swallow. I wasn't really a drinker at that time and luckily took only a sip, a sip that burned its way right down to my toes. 'What do you think of that? Isn't that the best of stuff?' We agreed that it was. Then, having gone through the ritual welcome, Jack said, 'Well, boys, how're things? They're bad, I take it. But sure what could ye do.'

I explained the reasons for the ending of the campaign, which Jack, practical man that he was, fully understood, and he agreed with our plans for the future, such as they were. That led to an inevitable swapping of anecdotes about volunteers who had passed through his house, and of smuggling and so forth. At one point Peadar left us for about half an hour to chat to Mary, Jack's eldest daughter, who had virtually mothered the rest of the younger children and who was sitting quietly at the other end of the kitchen.

With the great chat and the friendly atmosphere, the three or four hours until dusk flew. As soon as it was dusk, I began the process of taking our leave. I looked at my watch and said, 'Jack, we'll have to be going soon. Can I go into the parlour to change into my walking gear?'

Jack looked at me, then to Peadar, then back to me, and suggested that we stay the night. 'What's your hurry?'

Peadar said nothing. But the children, particularly Mary, chimed in, urging us to stay the night. I insisted pleasantly, but firmly, that we'd have to be on our way. But Jack wasn't a man to give up easily. 'Aw, come on, Mick, stay the night. Sure what difference can another night make?' Looking at Peadar, he said, 'Peadar'd like to stay the night, wouldn't ya, Peadar?'

Peadar just smiled shyly and shrugged his shoulders non-committedly, indicating that it wasn't up to him to stay or go. It was a kind of non-verbal deferring of the decision to me. I took the cue and, repeating the urgency of our task, insisted that we really had to be on our way.

The family, not realising that I was ignorant of Peadar's relationship with Mary, looked at me as though I was a cold-hearted bastard. We took our leave a few minutes later.

So at about 8 p.m. on that wet and windy Sunday night, we left the warmth of that hospitable home to walk to our next billet, which was about twenty miles west. Jack, good man that he was, guided us through myriad small fields and on up the mountain until we reached a point on a path through a forest that was familiar to Peadar and from which he would be able to find his way to the next billet. On reaching this point the three of us sat down to rest. Jack pulled a packet of cigarettes from his pocket, handed one each to me and Peadar, stuck one in his mouth and lit our cigarettes. No sooner had we the cigarettes going and taken our first drag than he produced a naggin of poitín, pulled the cork out with his teeth and handed the bottle to me. 'Here, Mick, take a swallow of this. It'll do you good. It'll keep the cold and the damp out of your bones.'

I took a swig and passed the bottle to Peadar who, having taken a token swig, passed it back to Jack, who in turn took his token swallow. Jack then offered a second round, which I declined with, 'We've a long way to go, and we want to have our wits about us.'

He didn't press us. 'True for ya, I know what you mean; but I'll have another drop meself.'

In the few minutes it took us to smoke our cigarettes Jack and I made small talk about the weather and such things. Peadar, however, took no part in the conversation but sat in sullen silence. (And no wonder, in hindsight!)

As soon as we finished our smokes, I said, 'We'd better be on our way, Jack,' and I thanked him once again for his support and for his help that day.

'It was nothing, Mick; sure it was the least I could do, and you're always welcome at my place, any time,' he said. We shook hands with Jack, who then, with a final whispered 'Good luck, lads,' turned to walk back down the mountain to his home. We set off through the forest to our destination. It rained throughout the march. Nevertheless, we made good time, thanks to Peadar's intimate knowledge of that stretch of country. But it was an extremely silent four or five hours' march. I couldn't get Peadar to engage in chat at all.

Between 1 and 2 a.m., we finally reached our destination. It was an ancient cottage, 'Tom's place', that sat at the edge of a forest on Ballyconnell Mountain, miles from the nearest house or village. Peadar lifted the latch of the door, which was unlocked, and we entered the kitchen. He closed the door silently and we quietly padded across the floor to the dim glow of the barely smouldering turf fire. We'd just hunkered down by the fire and were kneading our hands over it when Tom, who had been sleeping in the room behind the fire, shouted, 'Who's there?'

'It's me, Peadar.'

'Hould on, I'll be out in a minute,' said Tom enthusiastically.

Tom was a fiftyish bachelor who lived alone in this lonely, isolated cottage. He welcomed almost any visitor, but particularly Peadar. This poor man was living in conditions that were virtually unchanged from what they would have been a century previously. He had no electricity, as the rural electrification scheme hadn't reached that part of Ireland yet, and even if it had, Tom couldn't have afforded it. Water for drinking, cooking or washing had to be brought by bucket from the nearest well. Candles and an ancient oil lamp were his sources of light, and turf his source of heat and means of cooking, such as it was. His source of spiritual or mental sustenance was the company of an occasional friendly caller and the sharing of a bottle of poitín, which he always had stashed away for 'emergencies'.

Within a minute or so, dressed in a heavy woollen vest and trousers, which he was still buttoning, Tom was standing barefoot in the kitchen. 'Jasus, Peadar, what's up? ... You're welcome, and your comrade too. I don't think I know this man, but you're welcome too.'

'No, there's nothing wrong. This is Mick Ryan. He's from HQ and he's calling on ya, eh, to have a chat with ya, ya know!'

We shook hands and Tom said, 'You're welcome. Sit down, sit down, and don't pay any mind to the cut of the place. Peadar, rake the fire there and get it going; ye must be famished.'

Peadar raked the fire and carefully and expertly set some fresh dry turf on top and around the red embers. Tom reached in to the crook, the iron bar suspended above the fire, pulled a pair of socks off it, and, after vigorously rubbing them together to get the stiffness out of them, as they were as dry and stiff as tinder, put them on. He then pulled up a chair and sat down by the fire.

I was just about to give my wee talk to Tom when he said, 'It's as cold as the divil, and I haven't a drop of water in the house to make a cup of tea for yiz ...' I interrupted him to say that we were all right, we didn't need any tea, and anyway we'd only be staying for an hour or so because we had to walk to Ballinamore before daybreak.

'Well, if ye're in a hurry that's all right, but ye're welcome to stay as long as ye want. I've a drop of the stuff and ye'll surely have a drop to warm yourselves up.' With that, he went over to the settle bed and rooted around until he found the bottle he'd hidden there. 'Here we are,' he said, coming back to the fire. 'This is good stuff. This'll warm ye up! Peadar, get the cups down.' And while Peadar was getting the cups he pulled the cork and, holding the bottle in front of the now brightly glowing fire, said, 'Look at that! It's as clear as day … This'll do ye no harm.' One thing all the makers and buyers of poitín had in common was an unshakeable belief in the purity and superiority of their 'drop'.

Tom poured liberal amounts into the cups, placed the bottle down in front of the fire, and, with his cup held out in front of him, said, 'Here's the best of good luck to ye.'

'The best of luck to you too,' Peadar and I both said as we all three raised our cups and drank a toast. It was so strong – it tasted like turpentine – that I nearly choked on it. I wondered how I was going to avoid drinking what remained in my cup while not insulting my host. Moreover, drink was taboo when one was on IRA business.

Only then did I get a chance to explain to Tom why the campaign had ended and to thank him for his help, concluding with the hope that he would give us the same support in the next campaign, which I innocently thought would begin 'in a few years'.

Tom listened without interrupting – except for an odd 'aye, aye, I know, I know' – to what I had to say, which took only five minutes anyway. I handed him the small 'thank you' leaflet and said, 'This is from HQ, and we're giving it out to the people, like yourself, who supported us in the campaign.'

He took it from me, looked at it almost reverentially, and said, 'I can't read it in this light but I'll read it tomorrow.' He folded it carefully and placed in on the mantelpiece. He offered us another drink, which we firmly declined. Taking a drink himself, he said, 'Well, Peadar, and you, Mick, you and all the other lads were brave men, but sure what could ye do with all them whores of B men, the fuckin' RUC and the whoorin' guards chasing ye from morning until night.' He paused to take another sip from his cup. 'Ye tried, and I'll not hear a word said against ye.' Then he made a fist of his right hand and, slapping it into the palm of his other hand, said, 'By God, lads, ye're welcome to come here whenever ye want. No IRA man'll ever be turned away from that door. God knows I haven't much, and you know that, but the door'll always be open and there'll always be a bed and cup of tea and a bit o' heat, and that's the truth.'

I couldn't help wondering what motivated this man, this extremely poor man, to share what little he had with us, risking jail to support us, even in defeat. But I didn't ask because that kind of question wasn't asked in those times and because he would have been insulted had I asked. Now, as I struggle to describe those people and those times, I regret not having asked, regardless. But Tom is long dead, as are most of his kind.

We chatted for a while more, perhaps half an hour or

so, until it was time for us to be on our way. When we said our final goodbyes Tom stood at the door until we were out of sight. It was now about 2.30 a.m., which meant that we'd only five or so hours of darkness to walk the ten miles to McLaughlins' house, near Ballinamore, Co. Leitrim. Fortunately, the rain had stopped and being on the clear, high slopes of the mountain for almost the entire journey with no hedges, ditches, fences or bogs to slow us down, we were able to maintain a fast pace. Even so it was daylight when, with McLaughlins' still half a mile away, we emerged from a forest path half a mile or so above the house.

We stood for perhaps a minute at the edge of the forest, deciding whether to head on down over clear, coverless ground to the house and risk being observed, or hide out in the woods for the twelve hours till dusk. However, we were tired, cold, damp and hungry, and McLaughlins' house was tantalisingly close, so, as there was no smoke issuing from the chimneys of the nearby houses or anyone in sight, we decided to risk it. We trotted the half-mile down to the house, which was set about fifty yards in from a narrow road. With Peadar leading, we entered the house by the unlocked back door and quietly made our way to the kitchen, where we pulled a couple of chairs to the still-smouldering fire and sat down, exhausted but relieved, to await the rising of our hosts.

We hadn't long to wait. Within half an hour, we heard the sound of someone moving about overhead. A few minutes later Mrs McLaughlin entered the kitchen and stopped short with the surprise at seeing us. On recognising Peadar, however, she heaved a sigh of relief and said, 'Oh, good God! It's yourself, Peadar. I got a shock. I never heard ye come in. But you're welcome.'

Peadar introduced me, and as we shook hands I apologised for surprising her. She waved her hands dismissively and said, 'Och, that's all right, you're welcome here. Ye must be hungry. Is everything all right with ye?' she asked. But without waiting for or hearing our reply she began to stoke the fire and said, 'I'll make ye something to eat as soon as I have the fire going. John'll be down in minute, he'll be glad to see ye.'

Sure enough, John came down a few minutes later. Having heard his wife talking to someone in the kitchen, he wasn't surprised to see us sitting there. 'Ah, it's yourself, Peadar. I was wondering who it was here,' he said. 'How're ya doing? I was beginning to think we'd never see you again!'

Peadar smiled and said, 'Eh, this is Mick Ryan from HQ, and he wanted to have a chat with ye.' I shook hands with John, who said, 'You're welcome.' Just then his wife, Mary, called for us to sit over to the table and we sat down to a delicious breakfast of fried bacon and eggs and loads of well-brewed tea. I delivered the same talk I'd given to the other supporters along the way. As with the others we'd talked to, Mary and John's reaction was, 'Sure what could ye do? Ye did your best. And sure there'll be another day.'

Mary, who was busy getting the children ready for school, turned to John and said, 'John, maybe the lads would like a bit of a sleep. They can sleep in our bed. I've made it up.' With that, and having asked Mary to call us at 5 or 6 p.m., we went up to their bedroom and crawled gratefully into the still-warm bed. We fell asleep in a matter of minutes. But we were asleep for only an hour or so when we were shocked into wakefulness with the sound of Ellen, the eldest girl, bursting into our room and shouting, 'Peadar, Mick, get up quick! There's a car pulling up at the gate. Get up, get up!'

We leaped out of bed, scrambled into our trousers, and, still buttoning them, raced down the stairs. Mary, who was standing at the bottom of the stairs, said, 'Quick, quick, get out the back window here,' as she directed us towards a small pantry at the rear of the house. The back door was really on the side of the house, so anyone emerging from it could be seen from the front gate. I raised the lower portion of the tiny window and scrambled through head first, with Peadar close behind.

We raced barefoot over mud, cow shit and thorny twigs to a low bank. We scrambled over and lay behind it to get our breath and await developments. There was no other cover for a quarter of a mile. Of course if we heard the gardaí approaching we'd have been off and running. And as we were fitter than the gardaí, the odds were in our favour in any cross-country chase. However, I didn't relish the prospect of running barefoot and in only a shirt and trousers on a cold and damp March day.

While we awaited developments, we plucked the thorns out of our feet and rubbed them to get the circulation going. Even after lying for five minutes behind the bank we began to grow stiff with the cold and were tempted to either make a run for it or to return to the house. In a few more minutes, that seemed like an hour, we heard Ellen calling, but not too loudly, 'Peadar, Peadar! Mick! Are ye there? It's all right, the guards have gone.'

I peeped over the bank and called Ellen over. I asked what had happened. 'The guards,' she said, 'just pulled up at our gate, but they didn't get out of the car. They just sat there for a few minutes and then drove off. And Mammy says they were just stopping for a rest, they often do it at our gate, and that they don't know ye're here.'

We followed Ellen back to the house, entering by the side door. Mary, who was waiting just inside the door, said, 'Ye must be famished! Sit in to the fire there and warm yourselves up while I make a cup of tea for ye.'

We didn't need any more encouragement. We sat in close to the fire and, what with the heat of the turf and roasting-hot tea, we were soon warmed up and ready for bed again. We slept soundly until we were called at 6 p.m. As we dressed, I asked Peadar what he wanted to do. I was now aware that he was engaged to the McGuire girl back in Co. Cavan and he was obviously anxious to head back to her. Moreover, I was now in familiar country and therefore in a position to call to our other supporters under my own steam.

'I'll hold on here for a while,' said Peadar, 'and then, then I'll maybe head home.' Home was in Co. Mayo.

'Will you be able to make it all right? Have you money to get there? Because I've none,' I said.

'I'm all right, I'll make it okay,' he said. I suspect he made a call back to Co. Cavan first.

We shook hands, wished each other good luck, and went downstairs where the whole family was having their tea. 'Move up there and make room for the boys,' said Mary as we entered the kitchen. There was a shuffling of chairs and some little but quiet argument among the youngsters as they made room for the visitors. We had our dinner. Mary had kept it hot for us and chatted for a while afterwards. By 7 p.m. I was ready to take my leave and head on to John Joe McGirl's in Ballinamore, from where I'd make a few more calls before heading back to Dublin.

'How're ya getting to Ballinamore?' said John.

'Well, I was thinking I'd borrow your bike, if that's all right,' I said.

'Of course you can, and sure Ellen'll go in with you. You'd never find your way on these roads. Won't you go in with Mick to John Joe's, Ellen?'

'Aye, surely,' said Ellen.

'That's great,' I said.

'Now, Ellen,' said John, 'be sure and stay on the back roads right until you get to X's house. Leave the bikes there and take Mick over the fields the rest of the way to John Joe's back door, and be sure to bring him into the kitchen and not the bar. The crowd that go into John Joe's are sound, but you never know who's going to gossip afterwards, you know what I mean?'

'Of course I do,' said Ellen, somewhat impatiently: she was a highly intelligent and shrewd sixteen-year-old.

'That's great, that's fine. I'd better be going now,' I said. And with that, Ellen and I moved to the back door, where I said goodbye to John, Mary and Peadar.

It was only a two-mile journey, but what with having to take a very circuitous route to avoid the main road, and having to dismount and walk the many steep inclines, it took us half an hour or so to get to X's house. On reaching it we parked the bikes by the hedge and, with Ellen guiding, walked through the fields the rest of the way to John Joe's back yard. We climbed over the back fence and ran to the kitchen door. Mrs McGirl was inside, as unflappable as ever. She looked up as we entered and said, 'Hello, Ellen. Mick, you're welcome. Is everything all right? Are you all right?'

I told her everything was okay, that I was calling to a few supporters and I wanted to stay the night. I asked her if she could get word to the Mulvihills that I wanted to see them that night and discuss how best to go about contacting the rest of our supporters, the two or three main ones, that is. I also needed a lift organised to Carrick-on-Shannon, from where I could get a bus or train to Dublin a couple of days hence.

'I'll do that, to be sure,' she said in that slow and ever so soft way she had of speaking. 'Now, ye'll have a cup of tea, won't ye?' We both declined, as we'd only just had dinner. At that point Ellen, who was anxious to return home to let her parents know that I was safely deposited in John Joe's, said that she'd better go.

Being virtually the local IRA headquarters, John Joe's was subject to constant surveillance and periodic raids during the campaign. Now that it was over, however, surveillance was at a minimum, and houses like John Joe's were only raided when there was a strong suspicion that weapons, explosives or IRA men on the run were there. As I hadn't been observed entering, I felt reasonably safe.

The Mulvihills arrived at John Joe's about 9 p.m. We discussed what I needed to do over the next couple of days. My needs being fairly simple and straightforward, our meeting ended within the hour with the promise of a lift to Carrick a couple of days hence, a promise that was fulfilled to the letter. Shortly after they left, I borrowed John Joe's bicycle to call on Mrs McKenna and the Rooneys, who had provided great service during the campaign and were only two miles south on the Dromod road.

Tom Rooney was a veteran of the War of Independence. He was the lone survivor of an ambush in 1920 that had gone wrong. He and other members of the local IRA column were lying in ambush for a British patrol by the side of a road on Sidhe Mór hill. The British had learned of the proposed ambush from a local informer – a woman who lived nearby, legend has it – and the column was surrounded. They tried to fight their way out, but after a short battle against vastly superior firepower, the entire column, with the sole exception of Tom Rooney, lay dead. The British commander, having been assured that the entire column was dead, withdrew his forces. However, the soldier whose job it was to examine the dead either didn't see Tom, who was seriously wounded and lying prone in a marsh, or assumed he was dead. Shortly after the British withdrew, Tom crawled out of the marsh and somehow made his way to the nearest friendly house, where, after a rough cleaning of his wounds, he was moved to a safe house. A friendly doctor treated his wounds and Tom survived.

Tom was ill when I visited, however, so I spent only fifteen minutes with him before moving on to Mrs McKenna. I arrived at Mrs McKenna's about fifteen minutes after leaving Tom Rooney's and parked my borrowed bike at the back of the house. I quietly entered the kitchen and, putting a finger to my lips, indicated to Pat, her young son, not to say anything. I didn't want either of the two customers in the tiny bar that adjoined the kitchen to know that someone had arrived, a visitor they'd probably assume was an IRA man because of the hour.

Pat, who was only a lad but well-tutored, nodded his head. We chatted in whispers for the half hour or so until closing time. Eventually Mrs McKenna said good night to the customers, locked the front door to the bar and came into the kitchen. On seeing me she stopped and said, 'Good God! It's yourself. I never heard a bit of ya! It's just as well that that pair didn't hear you come in … You're welcome.'

We shook hands and, having exchanged the usual pleasantries, I explained the purpose of my visit. When I'd finished she said, 'Ah, sure, Mick, there was no need to go to this trouble on my account. Don't I know well that there was nothing more ye could do? Ye did your best. And do you know, I couldn't find fault with any of the lads that passed through here: they were all fine, well-mannered young men. And let me tell you, Mick, that any one of ye are welcome to a bed here any time, and God knows that's little enough.'

In the face of such generosity, a mere verbal thank you and the leaflet felt very inadequate, but that was all I had to offer by way of acknowledgement of her efforts and sacrifices on our behalf. Moreover, to offer money, which we didn't have, or any other material gift was out of the question, because she, like other sympathisers, would have been insulted at the mere idea. In a good week the wee bar would have made only enough profit to cover the cost of heat and light for the home, and her main source of income came from whatever she could produce on her thirty or so acres of poor land.

I thanked her once more and, declining her offer to let me stay the night, headed off on my lampless and gearless but otherwise reliable Raleigh bike. It was only 11 p.m. and I'd still to make one other call that night, to the Gillespies, who lived about half an hour's ride away. Time was of the essence, and as I couldn't risk moving about in daylight, I had to make as many calls as I could between dusk and midnight.

The light was still on in the Gillespies' kitchen when I arrived. In case some unknown visitor was there, I peeped in through the kitchen window before knocking. I needn't have worried, for there were no visitors, just themselves kneeling around the kitchen saying the rosary. I remained outside until they finished. The nightly recitation of the rosary was still observed in the great majority of rural Ireland's homes in 1962. The family, as well as any visitors, would kneel on the floor and, with elbows resting on the seats of chairs, would recite it, which, even without the 'trimmings' of additional prayers, would take anything from five to ten minutes.

As soon as I saw them rising from the floor I knocked on the door, which was opened a few seconds later by one of the girls, who said, 'It's yourself! Come in,' and she turned to call to the rest of the family, 'It's Mick Ryan.'

I went in, and there was the usual general welcome

accorded any IRA man. 'What were you doing knocking on the door! Don't you know you and the other lads can lift the latch any time? Sit down there by the fire.'

Soon we were all gathered around the now replenished fire and I was once again explaining the reasons for my visit. The response was exactly the same as with other supporters. We chatted on for another hour or so before we all adjourned to bed.

After a great sleep (who wouldn't sleep like a top in a feather bed?), I got up at 10 a.m., had breakfast and spent the next few hours chatting and reminiscing with the Gillespies until 2 p.m. when my lift arrived. After the usual goodbyes and receiving a Miraculous Medal, I was driven to Carrick-on-Shannon, where I got the bus to Dublin.

I had mixed emotions as I boarded that bus, a strange mixture of sadness and relief. For me this was the real end of the campaign. It was no shock, because it had been a failed campaign for several years, but it was still a dreadful anti-climax. I found it difficult to hold back the tears. It was a lonely experience too. I had no one to talk to on that bus journey, no one to lean on who might say, 'Ah, you tried, you tried, but there was too much ranged against you', as others, such as the old man in the forest hut on Ballyconnell Mountain had said a few nights before.

I was still on the run and was going to go to one of only half a dozen safe billets left in Dublin and meet the chief of staff, Ó Brádaigh, to decide – or rather, to hear his decision – about where we would go from here.

We had lost virtually everything: arms, ammunition, men; hundreds were in jail, North and South. Eight more were dead, mostly in accidental explosions. We had no popular support and even our hard-core supporters, who numbered no more than a few hundred in the whole country, were demoralised and depressed. It was a bad time.

And we had no money. I borrowed, or rather was given, a few pounds from each supporter I called on, got cigarettes and this and that and was fed by them. We lived off the people, those poor but magnificent few supporters on the border and scattered throughout Ireland who, though they knew better than we did that we had lost – and we were badly beaten – still never uttered a word of condemnation or a depressing word, only 'Lads, ye did your best. There was too much against ye.'

It was all a far cry from my early dreams of a victorious homecoming that were so romantic that I was embarrassed to even think about them now.

I didn't feel personally defeated, however, and I was sustained by the IRA's final statement that this 'was only the end of this phase of the campaign for unity and freedom … We would reorganise and train, and a new generation would continue what we had started …'

As I looked out the window of the bus at the little fields

of Leitrim on a wet March day, I thought of all the times in those six years of risk and hardship when my resolve was shaken, and I was thankful for whatever had sustained me and helped me stick it out to the end. And I was proud that I had taken part in a campaign for a united Ireland. I was somewhat sustained by Terence MacSwiney's dictum that 'it is not to those who can inflict the most, but to those who can endure the most, that ultimate victory is finally assured'.

But we still lost.

AFTERWORD

With regard to the claim by J. Bowyer Bell in *The Secret Army* that there was an improved intelligence system in the North in the summer of 1957, I can only say that this is inaccurate. For one thing, after the northern government introduced internment practically none of our active members escaped the net. Secondly, the few who did were very restricted in their movements, for lack of safe houses. And thirdly, there was practically no spontaneous active resistance by the ordinary people: what little resistance there was took enormous organisational effort and required the participation of active service volunteers who were mainly from the South. There was no district in the North after December 1956 that could raise a column of men native to the area. Even in the beginning, every column in the field had a ratio of almost five southern volunteers to every northerner. Our own north Antrim column had only two Antrim men to ten from Cork and Dublin. The only exceptions were Lurgan and Newry.

What did happen was that the British forces, RUC and B men organised themselves, and, like all big organisations at that time, worked to a fixed system. With the regular patrols and a uniform type of defence system for barracks and strongpoints, gathering operational intelligence was easier. It wasn't until much later that they introduced staggered patrolling, with no fixed times, as well as light aircraft and helicopters.

The operating environment became harder as the euphoria of the nationalist population in the opening weeks of the campaign evaporated. I think the nationalist population, like the people of the South, saw the IRA as just a group of dedicated young Irishmen who would continue to carry out spectacular and successful stunts, such as the arms raids at Felsted in Essex, Ebringham in Devon, Armagh and Omagh. I feel too that they thought the opening of the border campaign on 12 December 1956 was a continuation of the raids idea on a more ambitious scale and that it would be halted after a couple of weeks. Most of the lads I talked to in the opening phase saw it as a one-month, or perhaps at most, a three-month stint. In fact, during that first week, when the remnants of our original north Antrim column were marching for their lives over the Glens, we had plenty of time to talk, and a couple were so naïve as to suggest that we would have the conflict 'won' by March.

But most of us had no real idea what the campaign was about, of the overall strategy, or the history of struggle in Ireland, let alone the history and conditions of the people, Protestant or Catholic, in the North. Though I wasn't the least intelligent of the young men then on active service, my knowledge of the republican tradition itself was minimal, and my knowledge of the peculiar northern tradition was even worse. I was not alone in this. Both leaders and the led were focused on purely military operations in the belief that once we achieved a measure of success, the majority of people in the North would rally to our support. We were imbued with an almost fanatical belief in the righteousness of our cause and our methods, and believed the people of Ireland couldn't but support us. We were convinced that we were the true inheritors of the republican tradition and followers of the men of 1916. Paradoxically, our ignorance of the complexity of Ireland's past reinforced our confidence that even a limited degree of success would be sufficient almost to guarantee us victory.

For most of us that meant clearing the British Army out of the North and uniting the country under an Irish government. What form of government, or what social or economic system would be introduced, were not matters for us to decide. We just felt that a government of decent, patriotic Irishmen would bring an end to emigration, as well as unemployment and other problems. Anyway, the people would surely be happier and better off if the country was united under an all-Ireland government, perhaps even a Sinn Féin government.

The only signs of radical politics were the mass marches of the unemployed through Dublin, and the election of their spokesman, Jack Murphy, to the Dáil.[1] But the great majority of the people stood back from all that. Radical ideas were certainly not a part of our thinking, and most of us would have been antipathetic to anything smacking of communism. Our leaders were politically conservative and almost all republicans jailed during the 1957–62 period were avid mass-goers, participated in community rosary recitals and did the 'Nine Fridays'.

My parents had inculcated a commitment to equality and a crude form of socialism in me years before I ever joined the movement in 1955. My mother, especially, was a great respecter of the truth and of having the moral courage to pursue it. She had a strong ethical code and insisted on respecting women; part of showing this respect involved me sharing household tasks with my sisters. My ethics, my sense of honour and respect for the truth were an integral part of my character before ever I joined the movement and were probably the prime movers for my joining in the first place. I only began to read more widely after the campaign ended and I was searching for reasons for our failure.

---

1   Jack Murphy was elected in March 1957 as an Independent TD. He was nominated for the position by the Unemployed Protest Committee, which had mobilised thousands on the unemployment issue. He had been a member of the IRA but left before the start of the border campaign. He resigned his seat in May 1958 because of the 'appalling indifference' of the main political parties to the unemployment problem.

The split in the Curragh between Charlie Murphy's group, intent on escape, and the camp leadership left a bitter legacy and generally weakened the movement. Some of us didn't participate in the escape for the sake of preserving unity and because a split couldn't achieve anything inside the camp anyway. We were torn between supporting Charlie Murphy, who was held in high regard, and giving our continued allegiance to Tomás Mac Curtáin, one of the most charismatic, likeable, courageous and impressive men I ever met. Speaking for myself, and I think many others, the split came as a shock and engendered serious disillusionment. Where before there was camaraderie, now there was suspicion and hostility. This was very different from the mutual respect and friendship that I had come to expect from comrades, and from the high-mindedness of the 1916 leaders.

I have no doubt that the split led many younger volunteers to take no further part in the movement, but I was so committed to the cause that I couldn't even think of quitting. I supported the view that our differences should await settlement at the army convention that would be held as soon as we were all released. However, by now I had come to realise that idealism alone would not guarantee success. I still believe that if the quality of our leadership and organisation had been equal to the soundness of the great people who billeted us, things might have gone differently.

Looking back, it was clear that the plan for the campaign

was based on a simplistic view of what a guerrilla campaign entailed in the mid-1950s, not to mention naïveté regarding the mindset of the unionist population and, for that matter, the extent to which nationalists were prepared to support a guerrilla campaign. The leadership mistook the relatively safe protest against the status quo that was casting a vote for IRA prisoners as candidates in elections as a willingness to support a military campaign. It was as if they were in a time warp and equated everything with the War of Independence era. They ignored the historical fact that the IRA, strong as it was in the 1920s, was only effective in about twenty per cent of the South and a few enclaves in the North.

Moreover, our weaponry in 1956 was virtually the same as the IRA weaponry of the 1920s. The bolt-action Lee-Enfield Mark IV rifle was only a minor improvement on those used by the IRA in the 1920s; likewise the Bren light machine gun was not much better than the Lewis gun of the 1920s. The Thompson and Sten sub-machine guns were the only more modern weapons we had. The operating environment had also changed. Roads were now paved or tarred, making rapid movement possible by the enemy, who had spotter planes, helicopters, radio communications and fast armoured cars and armoured jeeps. Attacks could only be mounted for minutes in darkness, not hours of daylight. The dawn ambush on the Ballsmill road succeeded because the border was only a few hundred yards away. Even then we had to take cover before we could reach it to avoid the helicopter. Such opportunities were rare.

Our manual of operations was HQ's thirty-page handbook, *Guerrilla Warfare*, and was totally inappropriate for our operational environment, aside from the maxim that 'the guerrilla should be resourceful at all times'.

EPILOGUE

Pádraig Yeates

After the campaign ended, and the Irish government was no longer prosecuting IRA members, unless they were blatantly breaking the law, Mick Ryan managed to obtain a job as an agent with New Ireland Assurance, due in large part to Myles Heffernan, who, with his sister, Madeleine, had provided a safe Dublin billet in the last years of the campaign. Mick soon found he could do the job and earn a good commission selling new policies by working three-and-a-half days a week, leaving him free to spend the rest of his time helping to rebuild the IRA.

Cathal Goulding was appointed chief of staff in September 1962, following the resignation of Ruairí Ó Brádaigh, who returned to his native Roscommon to resume his career as a teacher. Goulding made Mick Ryan a full-time organiser and the latter assumed a number of roles in the organisation, including quartermaster-general, director of intelligence and director of operations. Over the next few years both men were part of a small group, including other veterans of the border campaign such as Seán Garland, Tom Mitchel, Séamus Costello, Billy McMillen and Malachy McGurran, who slowly rebuilt the IRA and took it into new areas of activity. This included an attempt to develop a popular base which would feed into and support another campaign, and was achieved through greater involvement with Sinn Féin and by participating in ground rent strikes, industrial disputes, fish-ins, emigrants' rights campaigns, housing protests and, most significantly, the Northern Ireland Civil Rights Association (NICRA), an organisation that was campaigning for equal rights for the Catholic minority.

Ironically, the political crisis that erupted as a result of the NICRA campaign in Northern Ireland saw the re-emergence of sectarian tensions, particularly in Belfast, where disagreements over how to respond to the Orange pogrom of 1969 led to a split in the republican movement.[1] Some veterans of the border campaign such as Mick Ryan, who were now in leadership positions, continued to advocate a strategy that gave priority to political action, while traditionalists, such as Ruairí Ó Brádaigh and Dáithí Ó Conaill, called for a purely military response. Although some of the latter figures had been relatively inactive during the intervening

---

1   A pogrom is a violent riot or series of riots aimed at persecuting a particular religious or ethnic group. The Orange Pogrom of 1969 refers to a period in August 1969 when loyalists/Protestants, assisted by the RUC, attacked nationalist/Catholic areas in Northern Ireland, centred on Belfast. Dozens of Catholic-owned houses, businesses and factories were burned out, while thousands of Catholics were driven from their homes.

years, their past record and links with an older generation of Belfast republicans saw a revival of the IRA along traditional lines in the city. The deployment of British troops in Derry and Belfast after the Stormont government had clearly lost control of the situation also provided opportunities for direct confrontation with the British government that had not been possible since the 1920s.

While relationships formed during the border campaign played a role in the split that now emerged, first in the IRA at a convention in December 1969 and then at the Sinn Féin Ard-Fheis in January 1970, the underlying dynamic was generated by the division between those who saw the crisis created by the civil rights movement as an opportunity to seek a radical political solution to Northern Ireland's problems and those who saw it as an opportunity to renew the armed struggle on a level that was inconceivable only a few years earlier. Official and Provisional wings of the IRA and Sinn Féin emerged from this split and the offensive campaign of the latter led to increased British repression, the mass mobilisation of loyalist militants and growing polarisation within Northern Ireland.

Mick Ryan was to play an important role during this period and for many years to come, but that is another story.

INDEX

H/RAISER

01924
671859

SLIPKNOT

07519
635397.